FROM
POLICY
TO
PRACTICE

FROM POLICY TO PRACTICE

By MARTIN REIN

M. E. SHARPE, INC.
Armonk, New York

To Lisa and Glen

Library of Congress Cataloging in Publication Data

Rein, Martin.
  From policy to practice.

  Includes bibliographical references and index.
    1. United States—Social policy—1980- 2. Social service—Government policy—United States. 3. Social service—United States—Evaluation.
I. Title.
HV95.R43 1983   361.6'1'0973   82-19672
ISBN 0-87332-194-4
ISBN 0-87332-219-3 (pbk.)

Contents

Acknowledgments

The author gratefully acknowledges permission from the following publishers and co-authors to reprint earlier versions of the essays in this volume:

1. "The Social Policy of the Firm," *Policy Sciences*, Volume 14, Number 2, April 1982, pp. 117-35.

2. "Claims, Claiming and Claim Structure." An unpublished essay written collaboratively with Lisa Peattie.

3. "Social Services: Purpose and Form," appeared as "Decentralization and Citizen Participation in Social Service," *Public Administration Review*, Special Issue, Volume 32, October 1972.

4. "The Plea for Coordination of Services to Young Children," by Janet A. Weiss, Martin Rein, and Sheldon White, in *Children and Society: Issues for Pre-School Reform*, CERI, OECD, 1981. This chapter was written by Janet A. Weiss, based on two papers prepared for the Early Childhood Project, CERI, OECD, Paris, 1978: Janet A. Weiss, "Coordination of human services in the face of obstacles," and a paper by Martin Rein and Sheldon White.

5. "Design of In-Kind Benefits." A somewhat different version was published under the title "Income Testing of In-Kind Transfers," in *Income Tested Transfer Programs*, edited by Irwin Garfinkle, New York: Academic Press, 1982.

6. "Value Tensions in Program Design." The model used in this paper was developed with the help of Burton Weisbrod, who applied it to the analysis of health issues. Hugh Heclo suggested how the model could be further specified. Tom Willemain, Don Schon, and Mike Miller offered critical comments on an early draft.

7. "Implementation: A Theoretical Perspective" (with Francine Rabinovitz), in *American Politics and Public Policy*, edited by Walter Dean Burnham and Martha W. Weinberg, Cambridge, Mass. and London, England: MIT Press, 1978.

8. "Practice Worries" (with Sheldon White), *Society*, Volume 19, Number 6, September/October 1982, pp. 67-98© 1982 by Transaction, Inc.

9. "Comprehensive Program Evaluation," in *Evaluation Research and Practice: Comparative and International Perspectives*, edited by R. A. Levine et. al, Beverly Hills and London: Sage Publications, 1981.

10. "Knowledge for Practice" (with Sheldon White), *Social Service Review*, Volume 55, Number 1. Reprinted by permission of the University of Chicago Press.

11. "Policy Research: Belief and Doubt" (with Sheldon White), *Policy Analysis*, 1977, Volume 3, Number 2, pp. 239-71. Reprinted by permission of John Wiley & Sons, Inc.

12. "Action Frames and Problem Setting." A rewritten version of this essay was published as "Knowledge for Policy" (with Lisa Peattie), *Social Service Review*, Volume 55, Number 4, December 1981, pp. 525-43. Reprinted by permission of the University of Chicago Press.

13. "The Interplay of Social Science and Social Policy" is a revised version of an article from the *International Social Science Journal*. Vol. 32, No. 2. © UNESCO 1980. Reprinted by permission of UNESCO.

Introduction

The chapters in this book were written as separate articles between 1975 and 1980; the final product, however, is more than a collection of independent essays. As I wrote, I began to realize I was developing an implicit framework, which I wish to make explicit in this introductory essay.

A common method, concern, and argument underlie all of the essays. The method is "value critical."[1] The concern is with a more institutionally grounded understanding of why governments do what they do. The argument is substantive, dealing with concrete issues such as the claim for economic resources, social protection, and the organization of social services. After discussing these themes, I review how I develop them in individual chapters.

The method is critical rather than analytic. The critical approach probes the assumptions that organize evidence and provides a way of identifying what is significant and what is problematic. The canonical (that is, the conventional and normative) view is thrown into question, on the implicit assumption that things do not work as expected, that there is inherently a difference between the text and the message. This skeptical approach becomes value critical because it assumes that values provide a framework for interpreting, and hence understanding, the actions we take, and that values are crucial in the formulation of what we accept as problematic and what we accept as given. The task of the critic is to ferret out the implicit rather than the expressed, i.e., the unnoticed normative or value assumptions that guide action and thought, and then to subject it to critical review. A value-critical approach looks beyond the canonical stories that frame understanding and action. The task of disengaging ourselves from our own faith is difficult when we challenge values we passionately hold.

By contrast, an analytic approach takes the problem as given and disaggregates it into its components. At its best, analysis separates wholes into parts as a way of understanding events and actions. A critical approach, on the other hand, starts with parts and tries to grasp the whole that integrates them. The outward expressions need not have logical relationships to each other, though they derive from a common origin. Thus, an illness may have a series of what appear to be logically unrelated manifestations that, in fact, derive from a common origin. I do not wish to push this part–whole analogy too far, but only to suggest that an analytic approach takes as its task dividing an accepted whole into logically consistent categories; the intellectual challenge is to identify common features that are congruent or consistent with each other. A critical approach takes the given whole as problematic.

Our next concern is the relationship between the critical and the conventional analytic approach. I take the view that the relationship between the two must be complementary. In the social sciences it is a mistake to view them as alternatives to each other. We are all positivists to some extent—in other words, we are all in search of objective, analytic understanding. But although there is common ground, there are also important differences.

In the United States most schools of public policy accept the analytic rather than the critical approach. The term *rational policy analysis* is used as if to imply that there are no other ways to think about policy questions. Most of these schools interpret the task of analysis as the application of the logic of microeconomics to problem solving. According to this logic, regression analysis and other similar technologies are the accepted mode of thinking about how the world is put together. Relationships are thought of largely in terms of a nonproblematic dependent variable. The important questions are: What are the determinants of the dependent variable, and what is the relative importance of a set of independent variables that can be manipulated to modify the dependent variable? Yet, paradoxically, this form of analysis can be quantitative without necessarily describing the world as it is, because the account depends on abstracted, nonobservable phenomena. Consider, for example, the study of housing benefits that makes use of concepts such as housing service units, price per unit of service, utility, and perfect competition.

Since so much of the modern literature on public policy is shaped by this mode of thought, I hope that this book will provide an alternative approach. A major task of this approach is understanding the problem-setting process and unraveling the implicit frameworks that lead to the selection of certain independent variables for attention, to the neglect of others. The value-critical approach looks at alternative ways of framing the problem. It tries to examine the links between the problem definition and interests, broadly interpreted, in order to subject tacit assumptions to reflection, review, and correction.

The value-critical method can also be contrasted with the value-committed approach favored by groups that have a primary commitment to action and need a theory to guide their action. Some Marxists, but definitely not all, fall into this category. Here one starts with a strongly held position about why things are as they are and how things ought to be, and then works out the implications of this commitment for action. In the analytic approach, "seeing is believing"; in the value-committed approach, "believing is seeing." The belief system is accepted and is itself not subjected to critical review. From an analytic approach, which strives to be value neutral, the value-committed approach seems too biased. The value-critical approach lies somewhere between the two.

I believe we need all three approaches: sometimes we require neutrality, at other times, commitment, and at still other times, criticism. The task of critical analysis is not only difficult but frustrating. When deeply held values are challenged, we run the risk of feeling that we have nothing left to hold on to firmly. Such a situation can be deeply unsettling to the analyst, and in this circumstance value-neutral or -committed research then seems attractive. I do not wish to develop an argument for the exclusive reliance upon one or another method, independent of our purposes.

Although it is important to take account of practice, i.e., to be grounded in the world as it is, rather than in an abstracted view of the world, our task is difficult because values and theory shape our understanding. In social science there are no important facts independent of the theories that organize them. Hence, we must take account of the conflicting "frames" that organize thought and action.

I believe it is a mistake to address questions of policy as abstract purposes, independent of questions of design and practice. I assume that the way in which practitioners set about transforming intention into action makes a difference for both purpose and practice. Thus, this book is essentially about how policy, design, and practice go together, and the legitimating role of social science at each stage.

Since publication of my book *Social Policy: Issues of Choice and Change* in 1970, I have reevaluated my emphasis on policy choices and become increasingly dissatisfied with the divorce of policy from design and practice. Once we accept that within the social sciences these dimensions must be interrelated, our task becomes more complicated. How do these elements fit together? An analytic approach to the subject treats purpose, design, and practice as logically and sequentially linked. Essentially, rational analysis starts with intent, which is determined by social values, and tries to design a program that is consistent with that intent in an efficient and effective way. Practice translates design into action in order to achieve the intent. Social science has little to say about purposes. Its major contribution is in the development of congruent designs and the evaluation of practice.

Is it helpful to map the terrain of policy, design, and practice in this way? Is the task simply that of disaggregation, in which design implements the purposes embedded in policy and practice becomes primarily a study of compliance? This book is based on the argument that there is more than a tidy, logical, unidirectional relationship among purpose, design, and practice. I have become convinced that the order linking thought and action does not proceed from thought to action: we more typically start with practice, and then design policies to justify what we do. The sequence is then from practice to design to purpose. Thus, policy rationalizes and legitimizes actions that arise from quite different processes.

At the same time, another process is also taking place. We often design programs that seem curiously out of touch with the problems that arise in practice. In this process, we seem unable to grasp the real nature of action, which remains hidden, tacit, and inaccessible. Clearly, there is more to understanding policy than the task of legitimizing action. At the least, we seek to discover meaning and purpose from our action.

Design seems awkwardly nestled between policy and practice. The concept of "translation" is inadequate because it implies a graceful transformation from one logical stage to another. Design is more than the translation of purpose into form, just as practice is more than the translation of form into action. Sometimes design itself becomes a kind of practice—for example, when academics think about social problems and actively try to create programs consistent with their disciplinary knowledge.

When we turn to policy, we discover that this world characterized by intentions is both highly abstract and inherently ambiguous. It is not surprising that this should be so, because agreement on policy requires a fair measure of ambiguity. As my colleague S. M. Miller has noted, "Behind every political agreement lies a misunderstanding." We are able to reach consensus only by papering over the differences that divide us. We thus create a false image of unity in the face of contention. The ambiguities enter the process at the point at which design or practice enters. Hence, we are likely to discover our intent through our actions and design rather than the other way around. Action and design are not merely constraints imposed upon the real world: they serve both as social purposes and as limiting conditions.

How, then, does social science enter this process of purpose, design, and practice? The dominant conception of social science accepts the problem-solving approach, which assumes a linear, orderly relationship in which thought leads to the choice of purpose. Design is interpreted as the rational selection of the best means to realize chosen aims; and practice is seen as the orderly implementation of design. Social science evaluates the outcome of practice and leads to the choice of new designs and new purposes. This view is incomplete, however; it does not take account of how we evaluate broad-aim programs whose purposes cannot be articulated or how we use social science to understand the circular and dialectical process I have outlined above.

Using this preliminary sketch of the method, the concern, and the argument in this book, I want to summarize how these themes are expressed in the sections and chapters that follow.

Section One examines the issues of policy.

Chapter 1 examines the social policy of the firm as a way of criticizing the traditional distinctions in social policy, such as public and private, or social and economic. Conventional wisdom holds that social protection is provided separately in the private and the public sectors, but I take the view that public and private benefits systems are not entities that can be analyzed individually; instead, the two sectors interact extensively, forming a single interlocking system. This chapter examines available evidence that demonstrates the increasingly complex interactions between the two sectors. Although its focus is on the co-mingling of the public and the private sectors in social welfare, the argument has broader implications for a reconceptualization of modern industrial societies.

Chapter 2, on claims, criticizes the view that the distribution of economic resources is best understood as a reward for contribution to productivity. The social welfare vocabulary of benefits and benefactors is misleading, because it provides an incomplete account of the processes that lead to the distribution of economic resources. The idea that resources are distributed through a direct and an indirect process of claiming is presented. The theory of claims leads to a different approach to policy research. This theme is further explored in the concluding chapters.

Section Two is concerned with program design. It is not surprising to discover that there is a discontinuity between policy and design. Policy questions may center on ideals, such as equality, productivity, control, etc. Yet, as we address the more specific question of design, other concerns emerge that have not been covered by these general ideals—which is not to suggest that abstract ideals are completely irrelevant in design, but that other matters seem equally or more urgent. This theme is explored with special reference to social services and cash transfers.

Chapter 3, which deals with social services, describes how the same design can serve many purposes. For example, social services seem concurrently to serve both the principle of individual rights and the principle of community prerogatives. It is only in action, however, that the weighting of these principles is clarified. The form we invent to explain our intent is not merely the abstract statement of principles but their realization in practice. Because the elements of social policy are so intertwined, implementation and practice are not just extensions of programmatic designs but subjects on their own terms.

Chapter 4 takes up one of the central design questions in social policy. How can social services be more effectively coordinated? Local, national, and international bodies spend a great deal of energy designing strategies of service coordination. But the problems coordination addresses are elusive. Our language is loose; we typically fail to specify the problem coordination is expected to relieve. The chapter seeks to illustrate how unrelated are proposals for coordination to the ongoing problems met in practice.

Chapter 5 deals with issues in the design of in-kind benefits. I discuss the paradoxical situation in which, despite philosophical commitments to unrestricted cash grants as a way of promoting individual choice, there has been a steady growth in earmarked cash grants. How do we account for this growth when we seem to be philosophically opposed to it? There are, of course, theories about public goods and collective consumption that provide a rationale for restricting choice by earmarking. But theory and practice diverge. When in-kind benefits are "cashed out," we find that the value of these benefits to individuals do not seem closely related to what they cost the government. An analysis that identifies the difference between cost and value and regards this difference as a "dead loss" when distributing benefits is not satisfactory because it does not resolve the question of who benefits from these services.

Chapter 6 concerns value conflicts in the design of income-support programs. It starts with the premise that any program should be so constructed as to be able to reach those for whom it was intended and to exclude those for whom it was not intended. This statement is a self-evident truth, but it leads to one of the most difficult problems in the design of systems of income support. I call this design problem the "inclusion-exclusion" dilemma. This dilemma arises because the more determined we are to exclude those who are not eligible for a program, the more we fail to reach those who are eligible.

The issue of design calls attention to the importance of implementation and practice. Design derives its meaning from its practice as much as it does from its broad statement of purpose. These themes are the focus of Section Three.

Chapter 7 develops a theoretical perspective for identifying stages of implementation, from the development of guidelines to what practitioners actually do. The basic argument developed here is that as we move from legislation to design to practice, we discover that the realms of design and practice are influenced by a social world outside the world of narrowly defined policy. These social realities intrude into the nature of practice and design, driving them back to any conflict of purposes unresolved in legislation. After the legislative stage there is a potential conflict among three imperatives. There is a legal imperative to follow the law as understood in the legislation, on the assumption that the law is clear about its meaning. There is a consensual imperative to do what is feasible, given both the consensus and the existing conflicts in the social world for which the legislation was designed. Finally, there is a bureaucratic imperative to protect oneself so as not to endanger one's position within the bureaucracy. Implementation is the study of how these conflicts of imperatives are resolved in practice.

Chapter 8 deals with the everyday practice worries of practitioners. A worry is defined as a diffuse, inchoate sense that something is wrong, a "something" one cannot precisely identify. At the stage of worry, practitioners find it difficult to articulate what is problematic in their practice. The move from worrying to setting a problem leads to a redefinition of both practice and policy.

Chapter 9, "Comprehensive Program Evaluation," explores how questions of implementation and practice enter the study of program evaluation. I argue that a comprehensive evaluation is needed, because mechanical attention to the relationship between outcomes and purposes misses what is most essential to an understanding of the outcomes of our practice.

In Section Four, three chapters are devoted to ways in which social science contributes to the value questions posed by design, policy, and practice.

Chapter 10 looks at what practitioners who have direct contact with clients actually do. But when we consider the skill exercised by the minor professions, such as planning, social work, and education, we discover frequent instances of what Peter Marris describes as the separation of meaning and action. Practitioners often find that they cannot act upon what is meaningful; on the other hand, what they are capable of responding to is often not regarded as meaningful in terms of what is problematic. The separation of meaning and action leads to doubt. This chapter examines how social science both creates doubt and tries to mitigate it.

Chapter 11, "Policy Research," develops the theme of doubt further and applies it to the practice of social science. Along with the growth of research, which is often mandated by legislation, there has grown a chronic sense of frustration among those who carry out the research and those who commission it. The feeling is that research does not really serve to guide policy, that it is misused, or lies on the shelf unused. The policy—research alliance is painful to all participants, giving rise to both faith and doubt in the enterprise. How these issues are managed is the subject of this chapter.

Chapter 12, on frames for action and setting problems, explores how knowledge and action are reciprocally interconnected. Both are shaped by interests: programmatic interests, arising out of existing institutions and programs in the world of action, and disciplinary interests, originating in the structure of research and teaching. Problem setting, which constrains thought and restricts action, takes place within a framework of interests and the ideas they generate of separate political, economic, and social realms. I describe an alternative way of thinking that draws on the claims perspective developed in Chapter 2.

Chapter 13 takes up the theme of the uses of social science and explains how the subject of "use" can fruitfully be studied. Various methods for exploring the use of social science are reviewed and criticized. Finally, the claims perspective serves to illustrate how an alternative approach to study of the utilization of social science knowledge for policy could be developed.

NOTE

1. For a fuller discussion of the "value-critical" approach, see Martin Rein, *Social Science and Public Policy*. New York: Penguin Press, 1976; and Martin Rein, "Value-Critical Policy Analysis." In Daniel Callahan and Bruce Jennings, eds., *Ethics, the Social Sciences, and Policy Analysis*. New York: Plenum Press. In press.

FROM
POLICY
TO
PRACTICE

Chapter 1

The Social Policy
of the Firm

Discussions of the welfare functions of the state mistake the nature of modern industrial societies. These discussions imply a distinction between the "public" and the "private," between the "social" and the "economic," and between an "original distribution" of incomes and the post-transfer distribution produced by government welfare policy. None of these distinctions fits reality.

Conventional analysis treats the economy as being composed of two subsystems: the private sector, in which the market and the voluntary sector operate, and the public sector, in which the economic activities of government are carried out. This view fails to take into account the substantial role of government as an employer, the role of government as a consumer of private products, or the role of government in mandating, stimulating, supporting, and regulating private enterprise.

Conventional conceptualizations treat wages as an economic return for labor and sharply distinguish such economic compensation from transfers in the welfare system. Fringe benefits overlap these categories, directing attention to the welfare components of wages and the economic functions of welfare.

Conventional economics treats the economy as generating "an original" distribution of income, brought about by the market principles of supply and demand and marginal productivity, and a redistribution of income, brought about by government's active intervention to realize social objectives. But this conceptualization fails to take account of government's role in shaping "original income." To suggest the magnitude of these influences, Lester Thurow points out that government in the United States directly and indirectly (through government purchase of goods and services produced by private industry) employs two-thirds of all female professional workers. In general, Thurow believes that government is basically a producer of middle-class and upper-middle-class jobs. Hence, the state's action sharply influences its "original" income distribution.[1]

This chapter proposes to explore these issues in the conceptualization of modern industrial societies through an inquiry into the phenomenon of fringe benefits. These benefits comprise the implicit social policy of the firm. Although we conventionally distinguish a "core" we call wages, and interpret as a return for productive labor, from "fringes," which do not directly, or over a short period, affect effort and production,[2] in practice the boundary between wages and fringes proves to be a fuzzy one.

Once we press the distinction between wages and salaries and occupational welfare, which is on "the fringe" of the basic return for wages, the distinction between the core and the fringe becomes very blurred.[3] Wages are set not only in terms of compensation for productivity but also in a welfare support context, in which wages are linked to family need. For example, the Australian Arbitration Commission in 1911 established a convention for thinking about wages as the income needed to support a family of four persons. Women needed only 54 percent of men's wages because they were treated as single persons who did not have to support a family. One implication to be drawn from this convention is that almost half of wages may be interpreted as a welfare fringe.[4]

It is not only a matter of wages' themselves including an element of fringe but of many fringes' being convertible back into cash wages. For example, in many countries sick pay is both cumulative over time and eventually (at the end of the year or tenure on the job) convertible into a lump-sum payment.

We also conventionally distinguish between "welfare," which is provided by government, and "fringes," which are provided by firms as a supplement to compensation for work. But this distinction also proves to be unsatisfactory, because government is both provider and employer, providing wages and fringe benefits. About one-fifth of the civilian labor force in the United States works for government (we shall return to this topic later). There is no good, direct, quantitative estimate of the extent of co-mingling of the public–private sectors. The degree of penetration of fringes into the core of wages and salaries for productive labor remains largely unknown. Governments have recently begun to be interested in the range of employment-related benefits that complement, duplicate, or obviate the necessity for public transfers or services. For example, federal employer wage rates are set by surveys that compare public and private compensations. The government has been evaluating the desirability of shifting from pay comparability to total compensation comparability (i.e., wages plus fringes) because it believes that such a change would reduce total costs.

By taking social benefits, whether provided by the public or the private sector, as the unit of our analysis, we redefine the role of "welfare" in industrial society. This more comprehensive definition of social protection calls attention to "those policy decisions whose implementation costs are carried by the private sector of the economy, and are not explicitly identified in national accounts."[5]

It is widely recognized that the societies of Western Europe and North America have changed over recent centuries from ones in which economic welfare (security and adequacy of income) is primarily a function of a market economy and money wages to ones in which an elaborate range of both public and private institutions serve as intermediaries between the economy and the family to ensure particular levels of economic welfare throughout the life cycle. The scope of this change can be grasped from National Income Accounts, which treat the whole economy as if it were a single household and explore where this ageless household (households across the life cycle are aggregated) acquires its income. The figures produced by this approach are fascinating because they provide a very different picture of the whole society's economic resources than we get when we examine just cash incomes of households in the active labor market. After taxes, wages and salaries account for no more than one-third (in many countries one-quarter) of the economic resources of the household sector; the rest is accounted for by public and private transfers and services plus money and services derived from household savings.[6]

Most analysts who have attempted to classify these intermediary institutions accept the distinction developed by Richard Titmuss in his famous essay "The Social Division of Welfare."[7] Titmuss distinguishes between the fiscal and social welfare activities of the state and the occupational welfare of the firm. His important insight is the recognition that the social policy implicit in the indirect system of tax forgiveness that encourages the firm to develop social welfare activities is very similar to the system of direct distribution of government goods, services, and transfers provided in the public sector. He insists that similar activities should be grouped together, because fiscal and occupational welfare serve the middle classes and thus undermine the redistributive effect of direct public welfare programs. In this framework, "occupational welfare" (i.e., fringe benefits) signifies those activities that arise from the initiative and interests of the private market.

This formulation of a social division of welfare among occupational, social, and fiscal welfare is helpful, but it fails to give sufficient attention to the extent to which occupational welfare is directly brought about through the action of the state. For example, some countries have developed a social contract among the state, the firm, and the workers in which the state trades off fringes for wages in the hope of reducing the rate of growth of inflation. State initiative is crucial in understanding the origin and development of a wide range of employee benefits, including paid vacation, sick pay, disability, retirement, maternity leave, etc. Management may turn to fringes as a way of augmenting the real value of employees' wages, because the fringe is a superdollar, worth more than a regular dollar, since it is exempt from taxation. So extensive is the active role of the state in shaping the welfare activities of the firm, and so extensive are the state's own employee benefits arising from the state's role as employer rather than provider, that the traditional distinction between the public and the private welfare sectors is obscured. The dichotomy between public and private forms of social protection needs to be reconceptualized.

We do not have adequate statistics to identify the full extent of the state's influence in the private sector. (Later in this chapter I shall present what evidence is available to show how the inclusion of the private sector dramatically alters our insight about the distribution of economic welfare in industrial society.) We do know, however, that enormous sums of money are involved. For example, in 1979 about $390 billion in fringe benefits were financed through the firm. We are not dealing with an interesting, but esoteric and trivial, aspect of modern economy. So vast is this role of the state as employer and as indirect and direct initiator of employee benefits that it is necessary to think in terms of a *welfare economy* to highlight the close integration of economic and social policy, on the one hand, and the activities of public and private sectors, on the other.

THE WELFARE STATE PERSPECTIVE

The focus we propose on the welfare economy should be contrasted with the more conventional interpretation that social policy is carried out by the welfare state. There is, of course, no universally accepted definition of the welfare state. A very broad framework is proposed by Bernard Cazes, who defines the welfare state as "the sum total of *civilian* governmental furnishings of services, of formulating norms of behavior, and of providing transfer payments in order to increase the level of well-being of the community as a whole, or to change its distribution."[8]

Cazes's emphasis on consumption, investment, subsidies, and transfers designed to modify behavior and alter the distribution of income makes his definition much broader than many definitions of welfare as the provision of entitlement to ensure minimum standards of health, housing, education, and income as a political right. Even so, it does not include the nonbudgetary operations of the state, such as regulation and tax expenditures,[9] and off-budget outlays for loan guarantees. These limitations are widely understood. A commission of the European Economic Community (EEC) is now in the process of measuring tax expenditures for all of its member countries. Although there is no comparable effort to measure the scope of governmental regulation, increasing interest in the size of the public debt has contributed to growing awareness of the importance of government loans.

At present there is no statistical series comprehensive enough to capture the broad meaning of "welfare" and the "state" implied in the concept of the welfare state.[10] Within the limits of existing measures, published statistics provide information on expenditures for social transfers and other welfare state functions.[11]

Table 1 presents the available evidence about welfare expenditures for a number of countries in the mid-1970s. When education, services, and transfers are added together, the size of the welfare state in Europe and in the United States accounts for

Table 1

Welfare State Expenditures in 1973–75*

Country	1 *Total nondefense as % of GNP*	2 *Social transfers as % of public budget*	3 *Ratio of social transfers to GNP*	4 *Welfare state % of GNP*	5 *Social protection accounts in EEC, % of GDP, 1977*
France	37.8	46.0	17.8	27.1	23.9
Italy	40.9	43.8	17.2	28.8	23.1
Belgium	40.4	40.6	16.0	28.7	25.1
Netherlands	50.9	46.5	23.5	37.7	28.8
Norway	43.5	34.9	15.5	28.7	——
Austria	38.8	33.2	12.8	27.5	——
Germany	40.9	34.5	14.2	31.1	27.4
Sweden	48.3	33.5	16.4	36.7	——
Denmark	44.0	30.0	13.2	33.8	25.3
United Kingdom	39.5	24.3	10.8	26.1	19.7
Switzerland	(31.3)	33.5	8.8	22.9	——
United States	(29.3)	33.4	11.9	21.0	21.3

Sources: For social protection accounts in EEC countries: *Les Comptes de la Protection Social: Methodes et Series 1959–1978.* Paris: Institut National de la Statistique et des Etudes Economiques (INSEE), 1979. For the United States: U.S. Office of Management and Budget, *The Budget of the United States Government, Fiscal Year 1980, Appendix.* Washington, D.C.: U.S. Government Printing Office, 1980. For all other countries: Organization for Economic Cooperation and Development (OECD), *Public Expenditure Trends.* Paris, June 1978.

*Three-year average, 1974–1976.

about one-fourth to over one-third of GNP (Table 1, column 4), and between 24 and 46 percent of the public budget (column 2). Transfers alone account for between one-tenth and one-fourth of GNP (column 3).

One of the persistent ambiguities in the analysis of welfare state expenditures is the treatment of transfers, services, and goods generated in the public sector as separate from government's role as employer.[12] When the government provides fringes for its employees, they are better interpreted as occupational pensions, and should be grouped together with other occupational fringe benefits. It is misleading to treat the fringe benefits of public employees as part of the expenditures of the welfare state.

How large is the occupational welfare generated by the government as employer rather than as provider? The data available for the United States are informative.

In 1975, about 13 percent of all public cash transfers were for public employee retirement. These figures exclude veterans' benefits, which amounted to some $14.5 billion in 1975, or 8 percent of public transfers. Disaggregating these figures by the level of government, we find that at the local level, more than one-third of total transfers are accounted for by public employment retirement programs.

Another way to look at the data is to compare the relative size of Social Security with private and occupational pensions available to public employees. In 1975, $79 billion was spent on Social Security and Railway Retirement programs. About half that amount was spent on occupational pensions ($11.2 billion for private pensions and annuities, $12.6 billion for federal government and military retirement, and $4.7 billion for state and local government employee retirement).

THE WELFARE ECONOMY PERSPECTIVE

As we shift our focus from measuring the amount of expenditures in the welfare state to an analysis of the various institutional means by which society carries out its welfare function, we gain an altogether different understanding of the pattern of welfare expenditures in Europe and the United States.

To highlight how the broader framework alters our understanding of the present structure of social protection, we present a typology of four different ways in which the state plays an active role in the welfare activities of the private sector. These include the following: mandating, stimulating, regulating, and supporting.

Mandating

Mandating is the procedure by which the state passes legislation requiring that private enterprise implement a particular social objective specified by the state. Obviously, the state can mandate with or without providing direct financial reimbursement. Naturally, the firm itself may try to pass on the additional costs of the mandating to the consumer in the form of higher prices. The public mandating of private initiative in the area of welfare thus sets in motion a complicated chain of events in which the firm tries to offset the costs of complying with the mandate by passing them on to the consumer. This makes it difficult to trace in detail who actually pays the cost of the mandate. Perhaps precisely for this reason, governments have in the past relied, and are likely to continue to rely, upon mandating as a device for "hiding" public expenditures. But without speculating on the many motives behind mandating, it seems clear that mandating is already very extensively used by governments in the realization of welfare objectives. In Europe, for example, it is very common for a government to require that firms provide paid vacations for employees. The government may mandate procedures for both hiring and firing workers, the former being an aspect of the government's affirmative action program and the latter, an attempt to reduce government unemployment benefits by preventing firms from firing or laying off workers during periods of economic fluctuation.

Governments may also actively mandate the payment of benefits. Two examples may help illustrate the point. In Sweden, national superannuation benefits are mandated by legislation that requires that the firm pay the total cost of wage-related pensions. Moreover, in the Swedish case not only does the state mandate pensions but it also controls the investments of the trust funds created by the legislation. In this situation mandating can be understood simply as a tax on the firm for resources administered and controlled by the state. In other words, pensions in Sweden are privately financed and publicly controlled. A more typical pattern prevails in the United States, where the government mandates that only a portion of the pension program be financed by employers. The principle of mandating is, however, similar in both situations.

Perhaps one of the most interesting areas in the development of mandating concerns sick pay. Most countries have a parallel system of sick benefits provided by the state and sick pay provided by the firm. Sick pay can be won through collective bargaining, but it can also be achieved by mandate. The latter situation arose in West Germany in the early 1970s, when there was a rather dramatic and fascinating shift from a public to a private benefit. In 1973 new legislation required that the first six weeks of sickness benefits be paid directly by the firm; for longer periods, the public sickness benefits system would assume responsibility for the payment of benefits. This new legislation sharply reduced, at least for a while, the expenditures of the public sickness fund.

There is no sharp line between benefits achieved through collective bargaining between workers and managers and those mandated by the state; the two processes interact. Unions may actively lobby governments to pass legislation requiring firms to provide certain benefits as well as bargain with individual firms or industries.

Regulating

Regulation involves the establishment of procedures for overseeing the activities of the firm so that they have a benign and beneficial effect on the workers' well-being. Occupational safety and health offers an illustration of the regulatory process: firms are required to provide a safe working environment for their employees. Governments may also be concerned about the health of employees and require that firms make medical service available for periodic medical checkups.[13] The government may send its own inspectors to determine whether there is compliance with these regulations or may empower unions to play the oversight role. (There is some controversy about the most effective procedure for implementing regulatory procedures by government, but this need not concern us here.)

Stimulating

Stimulating refers to the devices the government uses to provide incentives for firms to comply with the government's programs. The major incentive takes the form of tax reductions designed to encourage business to carry out some activity the government regards as worthwhile and desirable. (Of course, the government can use these tools to provide disincentives as well.) Thus, when government relies on stimulation, it pays part of the cost of the fringe in the form of forgone taxes. Manpower training is an interesting example of stimulation through tax incentives. In the United States and in many European countries, governments have tried, through a variety of incentives, to encourage enterprises to develop apprenticeship programs, manpower-training programs, and hiring procedures for special disadvantaged groups.

Supporting

A government can actively support a firm that is not economically viable to make sure that the workers do not lose their jobs. The state can act to promote job security through various devices, such as making loans to the firm so that it can continue to function or giving the firm a large contract to assure that it will have a market for its product. The state's role as support is particularly visible when it cannot politically afford to let a large firm go bankrupt and cause thousands of workers to lose their jobs. The state's financial rescue of the Chrysler Corporation arose out of the recognition that Chrysler's value to the economy had to be understood not in terms of the product it produced, because there was a glut of cars on the market, but in terms of the income, jobs, and security Chrysler provided for its workers. In a state support situation such as this, the productive system is converted into a distributional system, that is to say, the system of producing cars is maintained so that it can function as a system for the distribution of income.

The management of systems of production to realize distributional aims has recently become a political issue in Sweden. In 1969, through a Parliamentary act, Sweden established the Statsföretag, a holding company for the thirty-odd state-run firms. These companies can be divided into two types: those that operate under normal commercial conditions and, in fact, make a profit, and those that the government classifies under a "special program" and shores up with injections of large amounts of state capital to keep operating. The major political reasons for maintaining the latter firms is the state's policy of maintaining a certain level of employment. Both socialist governments and the current (since 1976) nonsocialist government have subsidized industries hit by competition from developing countries and by the recession of the mid-1970s.[14]

Welfare in the Welfare Economy

We have criticized two of the critical assumptions of democratic capitalism: first, that we can meaningfully separate the public and the private sectors and treat them as two independent entities; and second, that within the private sector of the economy, the systems of production and distribution are best understood as separate, but interdependent. These two themes are related because the politics and management of production are different when we find that the production system is driving the distributional system or the reverse, that the production system is used directly as a distributional system for maintaining jobs, security, and economic wellbeing. In this latter situation, the boundary separating the structure of wages, viewed as compensation for productive labor, cannot be sharply distinguished from fringe benefits directed toward the welfare of the worker and his family.

The "social protection accounts" of the European Economic Community provide data that integrate the actual and imputed social contibutions of employers and individuals.[15] These statistical series thus integrate private social benefits and state outlays. Data from the social protection accounts show that the welfare societies of Western Europe look much more similar when both private and public benefits are taken into account (Table 1, column 5). Even the United States does not look like an outlier.

Another way of approaching the level of expenditure in the welfare economy is to examine the structure of fringe benefits. Here we want to distinguish who initiates fringe benefits and why they are initiated. We can identify three patterns: First, they can be mandated by the state. Here the public sector requires that the enterprise sector provide fringes mandated by law. Second, fringes can arise as a result of collective bargaining. Here the union bargains for fringe benefits by negotiating in collective bargaining for their inclusion as a part of compensation. Third, the firm initiates the fringe on the assumption that it can improve its competitive position in the industry in which it operates, perhaps as a way of buying loyalty or as a resource for investing in the firm's human capital. In addition, the trust fund set aside from a pension or retirement scheme provides a source of capital the firm can use for purposes of investment.

An examination of all three types of fringe benefits, expressed as a proportion of total labor costs in the mid-1970s, reveals the following patterns: a high expenditure of 40 percent or more of labor costs in Austria, Belgium, France, Italy, the Netherlands, and West Germany; medium expenditure of about 25 percent of labor costs in Sweden and the United States; and low expenditures of 20 percent or less in Denmark, Great Britain, and Ireland (see Table 2).

A review of trends in expenditures for fringe benefits serves to highlight both the growing importance of fringes and the variability among countries. Consider trends in West Germany, Britain, and the United States.

In West Germany, from 1966 to 1977 legally required employee benefits as a proportion of wages increased by almost two-thirds, while other employee benefits increased by a little more than 40 percent, for an overall increase of 51 percent.

In Britain, there has been increased reliance on fringe benefits for both managers and manual workers; statistics prepared for the Royal Commission on the Distribution of Income and Wealth make this dramatically clear.[16] In 1960, wages accounted for 85–90 percent of total labor costs for manual workers; but by 1977, wages accounted for only 67 percent of total labor costs. Fringe benefits for the manual worker had grown dramatically during this period, from less than 10 percent to over a third of labor costs. For nonmanual workers, fringe benefits accounted for 40 percent of total labor costs. Although the British trends are not universal, they

Table 2

Average Other Labor Costs as Percent of Total Labor
Costs for Industrial Workers in Selected Countries

Country (year)	Total other labor costs	Time Vacations and other paid free time*	Shelter and consumption Other legally required personnel costs	Other contractual and voluntary costs
	(1)	(2)	(3)	(4)
Italy (1972)	46.6	9.9	25.7	10.8
Austria (1975)	44.2	7.4	16.6	20.2
France (1972)	39.8	8.4	19.3	12.0
Netherlands (1972)	39.6	11.8	14.1	13.7
Germany (1977)	39.6	12.9	16.2	10.5
Belgium (1972)	39.3	12.3	19.5	7.3
Sweden (1975)	28.5	7.9	17.4	3.1
United States (1975)†	26.5	10.1	6.5	9.9
Great Britain (1973)	19.2	9.1	5.6	4.5
Ireland (1975)	18.1	7.4	8.3	2.5
Denmark (1975)	16.9	10.4	3.7	2.9

Source: H. Sakowsky, "Personalzusatzkosten als Wettbewerbsfaktor." *Reht der Arbeit*, Mai/Juni 1979.

* Includes legally required minimum vacations in countries that have them (most European countries). Most of these costs are legally mandated.

†Large firms only. The total amount for all industrial workers is probably lower; the legally required proportion, higher; and the other two categories, lower.

must clearly alert us to the obvious importance of the development of fringe benefits in industrial society.

In the United States, the figures are equally dramatic. In 1966, wages, i.e., the pay for time worked, constituted 83 percent of total compensation for the private nonfarm economy. Fringe benefits accounted for 17 percent of total compensation. By 1979, pay for time worked had declined to 75 percent, and fringe benefits increased to 25 percent, of total compensation. We can furthur distinguish which types of fringe benefits grew during this period. Vacation and holidays increased by 32 percent; sick pay, bonuses, and severance pay, by 4 percent; legally required Social Security, unemployment, and workers' compensation, by 60 percent; payments for employer insurance contributions for health, disability, accidents, and life insurance, by 126 percent; and pensions, retirement, and savings plans, by 83 percent.[17]

Several facts emerge in our review of the welfare economy. First, fringe benefits as a percent of labor costs are impressively high and rising. Second, when these fringes are added to the transfer payment we conventionally identify as welfare state expenditure, the range of outlays among countries is much narrower. Third, the role of government as employer and the role of private fringes are critical in understanding the excluded fringes, and in some countries are the dominant factor.

What, precisely, is the "welfare" component in the welfare economy? The elaboration of nonwage components of economic resources through public and private enterprises in the form of directly provided cash benefits and indirectly provided transfer, goods, and services has two quite different side effects. It protects individuals from the uncertainties of the self-regulated market, producing a sheltered society for most of its members. But the increase in shelter may bring with it a sacrifice of freedom of action as the structure of consumption is restricted. By their very nature, earmarked fringe benefits are resources set aside for the consumption of specific goods and services such as medical care and education; they are not unrestricted cash, as are wages. Thus, the increase in sheltering can be combined with broadened control of the individual; and the more generous the fringe, the greater the risk of a reduction in the scope for personal autonomy and occupational mobility.

Although the search for shelter may be inspired by communitarian and protective ideals, such as job security and social protection against risk and uncertainty, it also appears to have the perverse effect of multiplying inequalities in the distribution of economic resources. Democratic industrial societies have certainly created a welfare economy, and this welfare economy is made visible when we use a broader definition that includes the range of private forms of welfare in addition to that of the welfare state.

However, the character of the welfare society created by the sheltered welfare economy may be one of widening social control and of growing social inequalities. The combination of economic sheltering and equality varies from country to country. In Sweden, they are tightly integrated, and we can think of an egalitarian welfare society. In other countries, they are more loosely put together, and the character of the society can be paternalistic and authoritarian, as was the Bismarckian welfare state, or it can take many other forms, as the Japanese reliance on the social policy of the firm illustrates.

These large questions about the character of industrial society are likely to become even more important in the future because of the further expansion of fringe benefits. We can identify three factors that will contribute to accelerated growth of these fringe benefits.

1. The rise in inflation affects the pressure for fringes in a number of ways. First, as incomes increase to match the rising cost of living, more and more mid- and upper-management personnel find that their income exceeds the level at which the effective tax rate reaches 50 percent. As a result, executives begin bargaining for, "and in many cases receiving, a variety of perquisites as inflation eats away at their salaries."[18] Since most fringe benefits are tax exempt, their value is worth

more than a dollar to the employee. As noted above, the fringe benefit becomes a "superdollar" because it is a tax-exempt dollar.

But the problem is more complicated because of the Internal Revenue Service rules specifying that if the benefits are to be tax deductible by a firm, they must apply to a "broad cross-section" of employees. This implies that fringes must not discriminate in favor of highly compensated employees. It seems plausible that firms will try to discover some legally acceptable way to reintroduce privilege and thus undermine the rule of broad coverage; attaching fringes to working conditions or Social Security benefits are examples of such devices.

We might also speculate that in an inflationary period, governments become concerned about the rise in wage levels, which can fuel inflation. An implicit standard emerges that leads to the conversion of wages into fringe benefits. Historically, fringe benefits developed during World War II when there was a freeze on wages; the fringe was a way of bypassing the system of wage controls.

2. Many economists believe that the growth in public expenditure inhibits investment and feeds inflation. High property taxes to support local welfare state activities further fuels the anxiety about the growth of welfare state expenditures. This attack on the growth of the welfare state should not lead to a cutback in the demand for protection and shelter. What seems most likely is that it will change the institutional arrangements through which social protection is secured. One pattern is suggested by the German experience, namely, the use of the state's power to mandate that private enterprise carry out the state's social policy objectives. Affirmative action and vacation time are other examples of government initiative in this area. Of course, private enterprise will, in turn, try to find ways of "passing on" to the consumer the increased costs associated with mandating. Perhaps the government will try to block the passing-on by informally exerting pressure on firms that increase the cost of their products. But whatever the final net distribution of costs and benefits may be, anxiety about the growth of the public sector will contribute to further expansion of enterprise-dominated social policy.

3. Since World War II there has been a dramatic change in the gender composition of the labor force, women now accounting for about 43 percent of the total labor force in the United States. The entry of women into the work force is likely to expand the demand for fringe benefits so that women can better accommodate family and work life. This will naturally give rise to demands for maternity leave and day-care services. But an even more important fringe benefit is likely to be the redefinition of time. The integration of work and family can best be served by redefining the time boundaries of the job, permitting part-time work, flexitime, time away from work to care for a sick child, time to give birth to a baby, etc. Of course, as many women enter work on a part-time basis, they may become exempt from these fringe benefits. Paradoxically, then, the use of time as a fringe benefit in one sector can displace other fringe benefits. As this trade-off becomes recognized, there will be mounting pressure to shelter and protect the part-time worker from exclusion from entitlement to fringe benefits.

MAPPING THE TERRAIN

To understand the kind of "welfare" that exists within the welfare economy we need to examine fringe benefits from several different perspectives: what they are substantively; their rationale and distributive effects; and who controls them and how this control changes over time. These questions are linked, each providing a different insight into the structure of fringes and the contribution they make to the welfare society. Although these questions form a research agenda for further inquiries, the broad shape of some of the answers can nevertheless be noted.

The Substance of Fringes

The task of classifying the types of fringes is made difficult because of lack of uniformity in their definition and absence of a single, summary, statistical series that describes them. Together the different sources of information provide the basis for a preliminary typology of fringes.

Shelter against insecurity. The Social Security Administration has, since 1950, prepared annual statistics on the coverage, contributions, and benefits under employee benefit plans that are not paid for directly by the government. This American definition has been restricted to the broad category that deals with shelter against two forms of insecurity: lost wages, and the high cost of medical care. More specifically, the series is organized to highlight the income maintenance provided by employers during periods when regular earnings are cut off because of death, accident, sickness, retirement, or unemployement.

But in addition to the maintenance of income, the series covers medical expenses associated with illness or injury, presumably under the assumption that no comprehensive public program for medical care exists. Consequently, Workmen's Compensation and other forms of statutory provision for employers' liability are not included. To a much lesser extent, employers provide actual health care rather than payment of medical bills. This type of fringe, however, has apparently not grown extensively, though one can find it in specific industries, such as higher education.

During the past quarter-century, the expansion of benefit plans has been impressive. "Almost every type of employee benefit plan registered coverage gains in the past quarter century that exceeded the growth in the paid labor force."[19]

Time away from productive work. The Chamber of Commerce in the United States commissions the Conference Board to carry out a periodic survey designed to assist executives in thinking about the "leading edge" practices that have been developed by industry in each benefit area. The survey was first begun in 1937 to track down personnel practices of large American firms.[20] The Chamber of Commerce in its definition of fringe benefits includes most forms of time away from productive work as a fringe benefit. The survey is limited to paid time away from the job; it does not include time-off allowances during paid hours of work for rest periods, coffee breaks, etc. However, data on vacations, including bonus salaries for vacations and public holidays, are included.

The report notes that since 1971 the federal government of the United States has attempted to make uniform the system of celebrating holidays on a Monday in order to provide for a long weekend. Four new holidays —Memorial Day, Veterans' Day, and Washington's and Columbus's birthdays—have been instituted. Paid vacations continue to be tied to years of employment. The two-week vacation is conventionally accepted; and a third and even fourth week of vacation are available to employees who have been with the company for ten or more years.

The cost of these holidays and vacations and other paid leave accounted in 1976 for over 7.4 percent of the wages and salaries of the private nonfarm economy.[21] Pay for time worked as a proportion of wages and salaries fell by about 2 percent between 1967 and 1979, largely because of the increased fraction of wages and salaries attributed to paid vacations and holidays.

With the changing gender composition of the labor force, time as a fringe benefit is likely to become increasingly more important in the future.[22] Consider two examples: First, many firms permit workers to accumulate and "cash out" sick leave at the end of the year or their tenure on the job. Some countries, like Sweden, permit workers to take sick leave when their children are sick. Second is the question of maternity leave; women have begun to win the security of a job while on maternity leave. Still unresolved is the question of whether they should get paid when away from their job bearing children. At issue is the question of who should bear the burden of responsibility: the parents, because they wanted the child; the firm, because it responds to the family needs of its employees; or the state, because it must resolve the enduring question of the social reproduction of labor.

Consumption subsidies. We can distinguish two types of consumption subsidies. One type is universally available to all workers. It includes free or subsidized meals, sports and recreation facilities, goods at discount prices, and other benefits in kind. There is no statistical series on the value of these consumption benefits in the United States. The study by the Royal Commission on the Distribution of Income and Wealth in Britain refers to them as welfare benefits and states that they "are generally available to all employees in a firm. Their structure was often the result of historical accident; their recent growth has been the result of negotiations between employers and unions."[23]

That these benefits have a long history can be illustrated by the "truck" system, which was introduced in the latter half of the eighteenth century in Britain. It was designed to reduce real wages by forcing employees to take part of their reimbursement in kind or requiring that they spend their income in the company store. The modern equivalent of the truck system is product discounting for employers/employees.

The motives for introducing subsidized canteens and playing fields and social clubs appears to be quite different from that of product subsidies. They seem designed more to build morale, improve nutrition, make workers more physically able to perform their jobs, and prevent workers from leaving the building at lunch hour. In more modern terminology, they have been designed as an investment in

human capital, i.e., a way of keeping the human machinery functioning smoothly.

The truck system and welfare benefits are interesting because they illustrate the fact that there is a dynamic operating in the area of fringe benefits that accommodates to the changing norms of society over time. What is particularly interesting is that these benefits are not abandoned completely when they become historical anachronisms, but are transformed into a modern equivalent.

The second type of consumption subsidy is much broader: it includes subsidized housing, assistance in purchasing housing, educational benefits for workers and their children, low-interest loans, bonuses, and use of the company car when its use is not directly related to the job. This list includes both earmarked and general consumption items. They differ from the first type in that they are restricted to the privileged few. The Royal Commission observes that "they are provided to attract and retain staff and have expanded considerably over the years of income policy to combat the narrowing of the margin of executive rewards caused by the tax structure and pay restraints."[24] The report points out that the proportion of labor costs accounted for by these payments has risen sharply, from 10 percent in 1960 to 20 percent in 1977. Of course, most firms do not try to cost out the value of these benefit schemes that are designed to attract and retain staff. Hence, very little information about them is available. It does seem clear, however, that the very intention of these benefits is to widen the distribution of earnings.

The above typology of fringe benefits is crude because it excludes a number of important types of fringe benefits such as discretionary cash grants and preventive forms of social protection. Aside from shelter, time, and consumption, the firm also makes available cash bonuses, both on an *ad hoc* and a regular basis. These lump cash payments have their origin in in-kind benefits such as the turkey for Christmas, which eventually became transformed into the Christmas bonus. Essentially these benefits were gifts. Of course, over time these discretionary gifts came to be expected as part of the routine privileges attached to a decent job. Thus, the line between informal and formal bonuses tends to erode eventually. Cash fringes take many forms, from holiday gifts and 13th-month bonuses to stock investment plans, in which fringes take the form of a capital asset.

If the firm is mandated by the state to provide protection for the worker against the risk of illness and accidents, should the cost of these preventive programs be regarded as a fringe benefit? More generally, should the cost of making occupational health and safety measures available be treated as a fringe benefit? This is obviously a fuzzy category, because we conventionally regard fringes as a direct benefit to the individual, not merely conditions surrounding employment. Prevention of morbidity and mortality seems to be an elusive benefit; very few systems of classification treat prevention as a fringe benefit.

Rationales, Entitlement, and Distribution

This review of the substance of fringes (what they are, who initiates them, and why they are initiated) makes it clear that there is no single rationale that can en-

compass the diversity of benefits, whose character and purpose change over time. That no single principle unifies them is perhaps the distinguishing characteristic of fringes—they serve as the legitimate arena in which the redefinition of social relations is worked out. They therefore represent the flexible aspect of the system of economic rewards, in which social change occurs without a compelling drive for internal coherence. Social confusion represents social change.

Fringe benefits are both an extension and a deferral of wages and an instrument for meeting the social needs of the worker and his/her family. In the case of each specific type of fringe we face an indefinite boundary between compensation and social obligation. But whatever rationales are fashionable at any point in time, an expansion of fringes is accompanied by their transformation from an informal, discretionary gratuity provided by employers as a gift to the formal, contractual, "vested contract rights" we identify as legal entitlements the courts will protect against diminution or revocation. Benefits can be arrayed on a continuum from a gratuity to a vested contract right in which the benefits are treated as property and the courts act as guarantor of entitlement.

This transformation from gratuity to rights brings with it a new set of problems. "To an extent, these reactions against bad old gratuity interpretations have already gone too far, locking in against statutory alteration benefit-inflating gimmicks such as . . . New York City's calculation of lifetime pensions on the basis of a final year wage doubled by overtime."[25]

Whatever intellectual rationales are advanced to justify fringes and the principle of entitlement to them, the growth of fringes as an economic resource has a substantial effect on the distribution of income. Sometimes fringe benefits can narrow inequalitites. Consider the situation of sick benefits in West Germany. As in most countries, Germany had a sick benefit and a parallel sick pay system. The former was administered and financed by the state and the latter by the firm. In 1973, new legislation mandated that the firm pay the total cost of the first six weeks of sickness benefits. The effect of this move from a public to a private system of payment and administration was to narrow inequalities. After all, white-collar workers had always been entitled to 100 percent of their salaries during periods of sickness. The new scheme extended those benefits to blue-collar workers. As a result, after the new law had been introduced, the total earnings of blue-collar workers increased by 2 to 3 percent.

Although the German case of sick pay is interesting, it is atypical. Many fringe benefits do not reach workers with low earnings or those in part-time employment —hence, they tend to widen inequalities in society. Most of the empirical evidence seems to suggest that the scope of the coverage and the adequacy of benefits vary sharply with the earnings of the workers. Peter Townsend argues that in Britain employer welfare benefits "are distributed more unequally than either gross or net earnings, and a substantial proportion of low-paid employees had no benefits at all or benefits of very small annual value."[26]

Timothy Smeeding reaches the same conclusion for the United States: "In the private non-farm economy, 37.8 percent of all workers and 54.6 percent of all

full-year, full-time workers receive both employer provided health insurance and pension benefits."[27] The value of the fringe benefits for this group of workers accounts for 44 percent of their wages and salaries. Smeeding then ranked all workers according to ten wage and salary levels and computed the value of fringe benefits as a proportion of each earning level. He found that legally required benefits exert an equalizing influence on compensation, because all workers receive them and because employer contributions are at a constant percentage of earnings up to a certain ceiling.

In contrast, some of the other fringe benefits show a regressive effect by earnings level and by employment status, i.e., full-time, full-year versus part-time workers. For example, pension contributions increase sharply with earnings because they are computed as a constant percentage of earnings for all workers, without a ceiling. On the other hand, health insurance contributions by employees are allocated equally in terms of dollar amounts and thus are proportionately more valuable to the low-income earner. However, the percentage of workers with low earnings who are covered is low. This "cancels the pro-poor distributional impact of health insurance contributions." These contributions are only pro-poor "if we look at those workers fortunate enough to be counted." Smeeding concludes that "there is a more unequal size distribution of total employer compensation than of wages and salaries alone."[28]

CONCLUSION

The welfare literature takes for granted that there is a particular, identifiable kind of society called "the welfare state" that is distinguishable from other societies. From this perspective, we are led to ask questions such as which societies are evolving into a welfare state and whether the rate of development of welfare state activities exceeds that of economic growth. Of course, embedded in this analysis are normative concerns about identifying the limits and possibilities for further development of the welfare state as a social instrument for social protection against the uncertainties of a market economy.

I believe that the focus on the welfare state is not a helpful way to understand modern industrial societies. Many well-known facts are not easily interpreted in this framework.

1. Every mature welfare state contains social provisions that are distributed and financed through the private sector. Thus, we are always dealing with, at the very least, a two-tier system of government and private initiative.

2. Many developing countries that have little direct welfare state protection nevertheless have an extensive system of government-mandated social protection, attached to employment. Even when the state's direct role in providing a fall-back system of security is very modest, it can nevertheless be an active agent in promoting such welfare in the private sector.

3. The state, in all modern societies, manages the economy to some degree, welfare goals being among the purposes it pursues.

These considerations lead to the conclusion that it is not the evolution of the welfare state that needs to be studied, but the political economy of industrialized and industrializing societies. This requires a detailed, systematic study of the interaction between public and private sectors. I start with the premise that industrialized societies must be viewed as unified or joint systems in which the state and the market are seen as different aspects of political economy. The state is actively involved in shaping the system of social protection that exists in the private sector; and the private sector is deeply involved in determining what the government does. More specifically, government is actively involved in determining the structure of social protection, including what risks are to be covered, which groups are to be protected against these risks, and how much protection they are to enjoy. Government influences private decisions through a variety of means, including mandating, tax exemption, and regulation. Private enterprise, in turn, through the activities of management and unions, influences government initiative.

The detailed ways in which the public sector and the private sector interact in the provision of social protection is critical to an understanding of industrial society. We need to think of the welfare society in a more precise way, namely, as a structure of rules and institutions in which the state and the market interact as instruments for protecting the members of industrial society against the uncertainties of that society. The distributional effects of welfare societies must always be considered problematic rather than given. The extent of egalitarianism produced by a political economy concerned with social protection must itself continue to be the subject of empirical inquiry. However, systematic understanding of the distributive effect of provision in the welfare society requires information on the scope and character of social protection in the public sector. In the United States, fringe benefits are impressively large, accounting for about one-third to over 40 percent of total labor costs for the third of private-sector workers who receive both pensions and health insurance; hence, they provide an important window to look through in our efforts to understand the modern industrial economy.

NOTES AND REFERENCES

1. Lester C. Thurow, "Equity, Efficiency, Social Justice and Redistribution," Paper prepared for the Conference on Social Policy in the 1980's. Paris: OECD, 23—25 October 1980 (mimeographed).
2. G. L. Reid and D. J. Robertson, *Fringe Benefits, Labor Costs and Social Security*. London: Allen & Unwin, 1965. P. 21.
3. G. L. Reid, "The Concept of Fringe Benefits." *Scottish Journal of Political Economy*, 1961, *9*, 208—218.
4. Even if wages have part of their origin in meeting need, this does not imply that they do not reflect productivity. Typically, decisions about the capital-labor ratios treat the wage as a socially defined given; capital investment treats wages as the constraint.

5. Rudolph Klein, "Public Expenditures in an Inflationary World." Paper prepared for the Brookings project on the politics and sociology of global inflation. November 1978. Pp. 5,6.

6. These figures were calculated from statistics presented in recent National Income Accounts by subtracting all taxes (income, Social Security contributions, indirect, etc.) from all wages and salaries plus entrepreneurial income.

7. Richard M. Titmuss, "The Social Division of Welfare." In *Essays on The Welfare State*. Boston: Beacon Press, 1969. Chap. 3.

8. Bernard Cazes, "The Crisis of the Welfare State in the Western Economies." Paper prepared for a conference in Mexico City supported by the Fondation de Sciences Humaines, August 1979. We can, of course, also question the focus on civilian expenditures. The military performs an important social welfare role; for example, it provides an apprenticeship system for working-class youth. Moreover, enrollment in the military increases when unemployment rises: when young people cannot get jobs, they may stay in school or join the army. Also, military spending in the civilian sector has a significant effect on employment rates. This is especially the case in certain key sectors of the economy.

9. Tax expenditures are "a reduction of expenditures for those who benefit from them and a loss of revenue for the body which grants them." *Accounts of Social Protection in the European Community, 1970–75*. Brussels, Belgium: European Economic Community, 1977. P. 23.

10. Charles Schultze argues that in the United States, ". . . in the short space of twenty years the very nature of federal activities has changed radically, the newer programs are different; and the older ones have taken on more ambitious goals" that traditional explanations do not measure. Charles L. Schultze, *The Public Use of the Private Interest*. Washington, D.C.: The Brookings Institution, 1977. P. 9.

11. Civil public consumption equates current expenditures for goods and services, excluding defense expenditures; and social transfers include current transfers to households and Social Security benefits plus social assistance, but exclude subsidies, interest on the public debt, and other transfer expenditures.

12. Public employment as a percent of the labor force, excluding nationalized industries, varies by country. The figures are 25 percent for Sweden; 20 percent for Great Britain and the United States; and about 13 percent for Germany and France.

13. Such examinations can, of course, be used by the firm as part of its own personnel policies in getting some workers to change jobs within the firm or to impose early retirement on other workers. Thus, the regulatory process can have perverse and unintended effects on the well-being of the worker in the firm.

14. *Financial Times* (London), 14 July 1980, p. 8.

15. These imputed contributions "represent the counterpart of social benefits granted directly . . . by employers to their employees . . . irrespective of whether these obligations are paid in pursuance of a legal or other statutory obligation, a collective agreement . . . as employer/employee agreement within an undertaking, the contract of employment itself, or even, in certain cases, on a voluntary basis." *The European System of Integrated Social Protection Sta-*

tistics. Part I, "Methodology." Luxembourg: Office for Official Publications of the European Community, 1981, P. 16.

16. Royal Commission on the Distribution of Income and Wealth, Report Number 8, Fifth Report on the Standing Reference. London: Her Majesty's Stationary Office, 1979.

17. Timothy Smeeding, "The Size Distribution of Wage and Non-Wage Compensation: Employer Cost vs. Employee Value." Paper prepared for the NBER Conference on Research in Income and Wealth, December 1981.

18. " 'Perks' Rise with Inflation." *The New York Times,* 27 August 1980, p. D-5.

19. A. M. Skolnick, "Twenty-five Years of Employee Benefit Plans." *Social Security Bulletin,* September 1976, p. 4.

20. *Profile of Employee Benefits.* New York: The Conference Board, Inc., 1974.

21. Smeeding, Op. cit. P.5.

22. Flexitime extends the privilege of organizing one's work time downward to the rest of the occupational structure. The flexible use of time permits the worker to respond to demands made by the family for errands and crises and to civic demands such as jury duty and other public obligations. We need to distinguish privilege from fringes, but there is no sharp dividing line. Part-time work may itself be regarded in some situations as a fringe.

23. Royal Commission on the Distribution of Income and Wealth, Op. cit. Paragraph 9.20.

24. Ibid. Paragraph 9.21.

25. Correspondence with Lance Liebman, Professor of Law at Harvard University, June 1980.

26. Peter Townsend, *Poverty in the United Kingdom.* London: Pelican Books, 1979. P. 223.

27. Smeeding, Op. cit. P. 26.

28. Ibid. P. 42.

Chapter 2

Claims, Claiming, and Claims Structures

How shall we understand modern industrial societies? Two general modes of understanding have emerged. One is represented by the powerful abstractions of formal economic analysis; the other is a more descriptive, "institutional" view that sociologists, anthropologists, and political scientists might have toward the same phenomena.

The division arises in large part from sharply different methodologies employed by the different disciplines, but it has consequences for the boundaries of the subject matter. Economic analysis centers on individual choices among competing goods. It does not usually inquire into the sources of preference; furthermore, it has trouble dealing with actions taken because of coercion or commitment. Thus, it has serious difficulty with the complex combinations of coercion, commitment, group belief, and value structure that make up human institutions. Because it deals most easily with monetized human activities, in which the ambiguities of transactions have been smoothed over by reduction to price, economic analysis tends to set off monetized human activities as "the economy." The institutional view, on the other hand, may treat monetary transactions as an aspect of a much larger field of interactions describable under such headings as family and kinship, social institutions, and power.

The development of a science of economics and the delineation of an area of action called "economic," to which it might refer, constitute an element in the history of the development of industrial society itself. As Karl Polanyi has pointed out, before what he terms the "great transformation," there were not thought to be such things as pure "economic activities." Making a living and the distribution of goods and services were embedded in the general institutions and activities of society and were thought of as aspects of the interplay of specific social groups. This was the perspective of Adam Smith's *The Wealth of Nations.*

In his book *The Great Transformation,*[1] Polanyi described the radical transformation of society as the development of a market economy, the appearance of a new kind of societal organization in which an "economic sphere" became sharply separated from other institutions in society. But it also had a normative element: it played a role in particular efforts to shape society according to distinctive visions of the proper role of the state in the new order. The conception of a separate "economic realm" seems, oddly, to have served the purposes of both Left and Right. On the one hand, the understanding of the "operation of the market" as the sum of myriad transactions among individuals, each seeking to maximize his own well-being, assumed an adjustment of interests through the Invisible Hand more perfect than any state intervention might possibly achieve and justified the unrestricted pursuit of self-interest by business firms. On the other hand, the collectivists' view that the "market economy" did daily violence to human life served as the rationale for a demand that "politics take command" and that society reassert its humanizing control over the economic process.

The conceptualization of society as containing an "economic sphere" distinct from the political and social spheres served the interests of business, which fought to keep labor in the market, that is, to regard the purchase of labor as part of the self-regulating market mechanism. It remained only for the marginalists to exploit this vision theoretically, to place economics, the "Queen of the Sciences," in a dominant position among the social sciences and to separate its formulations very sharply from the more descriptive and institutional picture of reality arising from sociological and anthropological field work.

Certain difficulties arise out of this separation, however. The first lies in the recognition that within advanced industrial societies there persists a segment of firms (the "traditional sector") that does not conform to the oversimplified image of larger, more capital-intensive firms pushing out smaller, less economically efficient ones. On the contrary, such societies continue to utilize, even to import, "secondary workers" who are relatively unskilled, work for lower wages, and have little job security.

But the "logic" dictating that small firms must be completely overpowered by large ones has proved faulty. It focused on economies of scale and ignored the cost-cutting strategies available to small firms—their ability to pay lower wages and to expand and contract in response to market conditions. When the original image failed to be borne out in reality, "new" theoretical reasons were sought for the persistence of the traditional sector, with its secondary workers. In this "new" view, there were political and social functions to be served by the perpetuation of this sector; and public policy itself became the reason for its existence.[2]

A problem also arises from the attempt to integrate the powerful abstractions of economic theory with the real world of interests and institutions so as to deal effectively with the latter. The gap between the two, present from the beginning of formal marginalist theories, could only intensify as economic entities became larger, the "market" more and more subject to their management, and the role of government in the economy more extensive. Dense institutional reality and formal models were too far apart for the models to serve conveniently as the basis for working policy and program design.

One response to this difficulty is to reject the issue. In the words of Frank Knight, "Economics, in the usual meaning, as a science of principles, is not, primarily, a descriptive science in the empirical sense at all. It 'describes' *economic* behavior and uses the concept to explain the working of our modern economic organization and also to criticize and suggest changes."[3] For economists interested in making a contribution to policy formation or policy criticism, this sort of position is not very helpful; and these economists generally follow the strategy of trying to incorporate into their models some representation, if only rather schematic, of the characteristics of economic institutions. Theories of wage determination have to take account of labor unions and collective bargaining; theories of inflation have to take account of monopoly and of the goals of the modern firm other than that of profit maximization.

The difficulty arises from the separate consideration of the "economic sphere" when an attempt is made to reconcile the ideas of necessity and functionalism—which seem to be implied by some economic analysis—with the evident variability of economc systems. Although differences among the economic institutions and managerial forms in various societies are sometimes explained as the residues of differing pre-industrial bases, bound to be further eroded by processes of development seen as inherently convergent, there are contrasting pieces of evidence. The finding that French and German firms producing the same good or service with the same technology consistently do so with strikingly different managerial structures and different assortments of skills[4] suggests, for example, that "industrial society" constitutes not a single type, but rather a series of types. Hence, there must be considerable scope for institutional variability across societies characterized by the same economic structure. These difficulties are widely recognized, and one can identify a recently revived interest in Marxism and "political economy" as an attempt to respond to them.

A NEW CONCEPTUAL LANGUAGE

One way of coping with this conceptual problem is to build a descriptive language around the notion of *claims*. The aim of doing this is to reject explicitly the placing of claims from work—called "earnings"—in a special status as given by economic process; rather, the attempt is to develop a language within which "earnings" may be seen to be as institutionally determined as claims on consumption arising out of kinship relations or the welfare system. In this way of looking at the world, "economic" processes are seen as but one part of a world of political rules and social conventions.

Up to a point, this perspective is that of the Marxists. But it clearly parts company from them in treating the system of earnings as centrally problematic, rather than as given by the structure of production. It is possible to treat "work" itself as part of that body of conventions Polanyi saw as the construction of a new social reality. In this extended view, "work" is no more self-evidently a claim on consumption than any other; the concepts of "work" and "wages" may be seen as social conventions that, rather arbitrarily, give some institutionally determined claims on consumption a special status.

From this point of view, we would treat "earnings from work" as one component in an institutionalized system of claims on consumption, along with other sets of claims generated in the kinship system (as in the case of wives and children) or against the state (as in the case of welfare). This indeed seems to be the sort of view that emerges from looking at the way low-income households cope with this situation; it is not a question of work *versus* welfare so much as a problem of assembling, from various sources, what we have come to call *packages* of income.

I use the term *claims* because I want to call attention to two aspects of what people receive in society. There is an element of right, entitlement, or "just desserts"; however, these are not always automatically forthcoming, and there is also an active process by which individuals within institutions demand, extract, request, or enforce their bids for resources. Groups and individuals continue to press to extend their entitlements; thus, claiming is an ongoing, always incomplete, process.[5] *I* believe that when the entitlement is granted as a right, this must be understood as the outcome of an earlier process of claim-pressing. It is a kind of truce in an ongoing struggle that has taken the form of requests, bids, bargains, or negotiation. Because there is no sharp line of demarcation in this ongoing process, the terminology is often confusing.

The attempt to develop a vocabulary around the concept of claims has been a response to the need for a language to describe political economy at the level of the individual and the household. However, as we begin to lay out the system of categories arising from the idea of claims, we find that it leads us back to the "macro" level—to the system as a whole. Claims and claiming have an individual aspect; but individual claims are made, necessarily, in terms of social conventions, systems of legal and customary entitlements, collective institutions by which claims are asserted. We find that we want to look at claiming as a social and political process, with complex and specific histories in particular societies, and at claim structures as wholes.

When we look at the distribution of economic resources as depending on the overall structure of society, not merely on the performance of the economy, to what kinds of issues do we direct our attention? These issues may be described as falling into three broad categories: the nature of claims, claiming as a process in which claims evolve over time, and claims structures viewed as the outcomes of this process.

In looking at the nature of claims we note that they can take at least two forms:

first, a claim for stability and security; and second, a claim for adequacy. Claims for security against interruptions of economic well-being include, for example, seniority rights, severance pay, pension arrangements, and unemployment insurance. Claims of this nature are directed at the continuity of life-style. In the "modern sector" some groups have the ability to win shelter from economic fluctuations[6] by shifting the uncertainty to other groups. Other claims are focused on the issue of adequacy, ranging from the bid for a wage increase to the demands of organized welfare groups to have special grants for school clothing or equipment to furnish a new household. In struggles over such issues, the concept of "adequacy" is given different content by different participants in the dialogue: changes in the conventional meaning of adequacy are part of the struggle over claims. Even the concept of nutritionally defined subsistence poverty, which might appear to be beyond the realm of political opinion, is part of the process of negotiation.

CLAIM SYSTEMS

Industrial societies seem to have four major systems within which claims are generated and honored: family, work, government, and capital. Each system provides an avenue for establishing claims. The principles on which claims rest are different in each of these systems. But each system is also sufficiently differentiated so that within it one finds many principles concurrently operating. Thus, in practice, the principles underlying each of the claims systems become blurred at the margin. Therefore, it is at the margin that the most interesting questions lie, because it is there that we find the possibility for redefinition and change.

The *family* is bound together by the principle of solidarity. Reciprocal obligations within the family derive from the sense of community bound together by blood. The entitlements and the obligations derive from these blood ties. Thus, the principles of filial responsibility of a daughter or son to her or his parents differ sharply from the responsibility of spouses for each other. But the established principles for support of a mother or for support of a wife change over time with the growth of other institutional arrangements (such as pensions or nursing-home care) and the long period of time elapsing between the emptying of the nest and the economic dependency of parents on their children. Marital separation and divorce and patterns of cohabitation are also redefining the claims of spouses against each other. Of course, the children's claim against the family differs yet again. Perhaps, at one time, children were seen as an investment, in the quite literal sense of providing the child with resources when he is in need so that as he grows up he will, in turn, feel obliged to provide for his parents when they are no longer able to care for themselves. Here, too, the view of children as an investment in the future is undergoing change. Today, children are more likely to be seen as an item of consumption. In summary, then, although the family may be described as resting on a system of solidarity claims, these principles undergo change over time, and are highly differentiated within the family.

Work as a system of claims for economic resources rests largely on the principle of productivity, that is, compensation for producing goods or rendering services. Productivity claims express themselves in quite different ways. A contract between an employer and an employee may be based on piecework, or the worker may be employed by the hour to deliver a product. This contrasts sharply with a pattern of employment by the year, or by the lifetime. There are, of course, traditional distinctions between salaried and wage workers, between workers who have sheltered employment, as in the case of those with lifetime tenure, and those exposed to the constant and immediate market demand for their product.

In addition to claims for compensation for productive work, a variety of other claims are made against the work situation. Two such claims produce inherent conflict.

There is a claim to security, in which workers are concerned primarily with protecting themselves against the economic uncertainties of the market. If, however, we accept that uncertainty is an inherent characteristic of industrial society, then it would appear that when some workers secure "shelter," others will be exposed to uncertainty, because markets will always fluctuate in response to shifts in demands and thus create instability in employment.

There are positional claims resting on the view that the well-being of individuals depends not only on the material goods they have but on their *relative* positions within the workplace. Here the gains of some workers must be offset by the losses of other workers.

Government as a system for providing economic resources may rest either on the principle of economic need, deriving from the view that a society has a moral obligation not to permit any of its members to starve, or on the principle of contributory entitlement, according to which government acts as a conduit to redistribute their own savings to individuals. This is, of course, the classic distinction between assistance and insurance. But in fact, the boundaries between these two principles are vague, since the pure principles serve as a myth to mask social practice.

Government distributes its largesse on principles other than wage-related contributions or means-tested needs. In Workmen's Compensation, for example, we find the principle of compensation for personal injury decided on the basis of the accident as interpreted by a civil court. An alternative principle is that of compensation based on the condition of the victim rather than the circumstances of the accident.

Capital or property represents the fourth system of claims. Here we need to distinguish between the right to have property in the first place and the right to a rate of return from the property, however it was acquired. We may acquire capital from the three claiming systems reviewed above, namely, through inheritance from the family, through one's own work, or from some lump-sum remuneration from the state, perhaps because of an accident or death. People's attitudes toward capital differ depending on whether it is acquired by inheritance, by effort, or by compensation for an accident. Governments are more willing to confiscate or heavily tax capital when it is inherited and less willing to do so when it is acquired from the other two systems. But here, too, we need to distinguish between principle and practice; although governments may be willing to tax inherited capital at a very high rate, in practice they often tax only symbolically and permit the individual to retain his wealth by a system of legally sanctioned evasions or loopholes.

Although capital may be seen as a residue of prior claims systems that takes the form of deferred consumption, capital and/or property also becomes a claims system in its/their own right. That is to say, individuals have a right to a return from that capital or property. Return from capital enjoys a special position in the claims system, partly because it is believed that capital provides an investment that makes the development of other resources possible. Thus, if the well-being of a society as a whole depends on the availability of capital for investment, then government has a special responsibility to promote its availability. On the other hand, its strategic importance leads many critics to the view that more control over capital is required so that it can be brought to bear to achieve collective purposes. At issue is the question of the right to exploit resources.

These subsystems are not independent of each other. Not only do they interact but the state and its specific agencies take an active role in enforcing claims; for example, parents are taken to court for child neglect. The state allows claims against it with a view to the interaction of this claim system with the needs not only of families but of firms, as in the example of forbidding striking workers to receive welfare.

CLAIM PACKAGES

A *claim package* is the unique assemblage of claims a household puts together in attempting to maximize its welfare within a given claim system.[7] This claim package involves, at least at some level, the selection from a range of possible alternative income sources. In modern industrial societies, individuals and families can derive income from such sources as earnings by a principal wage-earner, earnings by other members of the family, income from assets, income from private retirement plans, income in the form of gifts or recognition of legal obligations (child support) by relatives, and income from a number of public transfer sources, of which the three major types seem to be social insurance programs, means-tested programs, and universal benefits (such as family allowances in most European countries and Canada). Welfare in the United States is our principal means-tested income program, along with food stamps. Welfare reform has to be understood in the context of the other kinds of claims that families are able to make on society for income. One of these, claims from participation in the labor market, has received a great deal of attention in policy research on welfare reform over the past decade. But it is only one of several kinds of income sources.

Claims confer more than income: they also confer position and status. The claims that an individual can reasonably assert are determined by his or her previous position in society. For example, as Charles Reich points out, within the variety of claims against government, some, such as various kinds of licenses and mortgage rebates, are available only to persons who already enjoy some measure of social and economic resources.[8] Such claims against the state constitute a way of multiplying the privileges of position. At the other end of the spectrum are claims such as welfare, food stamps, and public housing. It appears that claims both confer status and are determined by previous status.

Therefore, the way in which claim packages are put together varies according to choice and to social placement. Different systems provide different possibilities (the variegated street trades of the developing countries represent, in part, a response to the absence of a "welfare system" in the American sense); city and rural patterns differ; there are marked regional variations; and there are differences among classes. The fact that variation exists within classes suggests that choice as well as constraints is important: low-income families with the same level of income have quite different packages depending on work—welfare choices, on the husband—wife earning choice, and on headship choices—willingness to become a female-headed family, for example.

Claim packaging is itself a dynamic process that extends beyond an individual's position in the income distribution. Packages change as individuals move up from one family structure to another and as their needs and preferences vary over their life cycles. It would be useful, therefore, to study how individuals reassemble claim packages. This would parallel studies of how individuals move across the occupational structure. Such an approach would extend mobility studies not only to occupational mobility, which provides a particularistic description of labor market experience from the perspective of the job and the career path of an individual, but also to claim mobility as individuals vary their claim packages on the basis of their position in the income distribution, stage in the life cycle, and family structure.

Broader economic forces also influence claim packaging, as a matter of explicit governmental policy. Income packaging is sensitive to changes in the business cycle. Culture plays a role as well. A "macho" husband may not permit his wife to work; poor but independent farmers may be too proud to accept the welfare to which thay are entitled. But these preferences of individuals must be seen in relation to options made available by the society and the local community in which they reside. Culture cannot be viewed independently of the structure that anchors it.

The claim packages assembled by households today are the product of a long evolutionary process of *claiming* that parallels the history of industrial development. The political history of the eighteenth through the twentieth centuries in Europe has as its major theme the emergence of new claims against the state and against the firm and the redefinition of claims against kin. To cite some conspicuous examples: the legitimizing of labor unions in the hard-fought struggle for the right to organize established a new claiming group and a claiming agenda, which it promoted; the obligation of the United States federal government to provide jobs or, failing that, to provide income for families of long-term unemployed workers represented the emergence of a claim against the state inconceivable in a previous age; there has even evolved with time a much less specific, but nevertheless real, claim against the state that it should so manage the economy as to produce a reasonable level of stable well-being for its citizens. In these and other ways we continue to create new claims against government (such as day care) and against the economy (as in job splitting or career lines for women), and claims within the family (as in change of sex roles). This political process also creates reactions against these claims—the backlash against welfare and against the women's rights movements, for example.

HOW CLAIMS ARE ESTABLISHED

The processes of claiming by which new claims are asserted and come to be established, and older claims and claimants adjusted, account for societal transformation over time. Anthropologists and sociologists have made much of the contrast between the role of kinship in preindustrial societies and in the industrialized ones, in which other institutions come into being and play powerful roles.[9] This is a process in which claiming within the family, while still important, loses its dominant position in the structure of claims, and institutions organized on other principles come to dominate society. It has been pointed out that the legal systems of Western industrial societies have experienced several successive waves of new kinds of "property rights," which represent, in effect, new claimants and new possible foci for assertion of claims. The development of business law, which made possible claims in the firm, was paralleled by the development of a structure of claims to the job system, such as seniority rights, which established bodies of claims for the new bourgeoisie and the newly established working class, respectively. More recently, the legal system has seen the evolution of a body of claims and entitlements in the welfare system, relevant to persons at a social level below that of the established working class.

The processes by which such claims come into existence, and in some cases come to be established as legitimate, are themselves complex. Alessandro Pizzorno distinguishes several distinct phases. The first is a state of "formation of collective identities," during which "action is not oriented toward the maximization of individual gains, but toward the aim itself of forming the new collective identities.... During this phase, actions (like conflicts, polarization of positions, preference for ideological coherence, for 'unrealistic' goals) that would appear 'irrational' from the point of view of individual gains acquire a meaning if seen from the point of view of identity formation." This is then a phase of heightened participation and militancy. But when the goal of identity recognition is achieved and the claims are legitimized, participation will subside and ideological affirmation recede (Pizzorno).[10]

Organization by itself is not sufficient to enter effectively into the direct claiming process. What is needed is resources that compel others to recognize the claim. These resources take many forms. When the Chartists organized to make a claim for the vote, the resource they made use of was numbers. Now the power to vote in large numbers has become a resource. Yet another resource, one especially available to groups with little power, is the capacity to disrupt the flow of wanted services, or the capacity to excite a sense of shame for the failure to honor a claim that appeals to widely accepted moral principles of social justice. (See Gunnar Myrdal's *An American Dilemma*[11] for an example applied to racial discrimination.)

But not all claiming arises from this direct process of groups' organizing to make the claim on their own behalf. This is an indirect process: one group claims something on behalf of another group. For example, social workers who want to make services available to the retarded, the mentally ill, and the otherwise disabled will lobby and proselytize for the entitlement of their potential clientele to services of this sort. The motives inspiring these claiming processes are varied, usually combining self-interest and altruism in arguments that appeal to the claims rationales existing in society. Once a claim is established—as, for example, in the entitlement of old people to social security benefits—groups of claims managers come into existence to manage this body of claims, and they promote their interpretation of the best interests of the claimants.[12] Some analysts see this indirect process in which claims managers intervene and reinterpret needs as a usurpation of the democratic process of interest group negotiation.

The discussions about these indirect claiming processes—the self-interest of social workers, the role of "outside agitators"—make it clear that there are within societies implicit standards with respect to the claiming process.

An aspect of the process of claiming is the development of *claims rationales*. Whereas claims are established by a process of pressure, leverage, and/or bargaining, they are asserted by normative argument. The rationales employed typically include both elements of factual assertion as to the nature of society (inevitability, efficiency) and elements of assertion concerning the ethically proper (justice, compassion, right character). Although the claims made within the family and against firms and the state interact, they are also, to a substantial degree, segregated from each other, in large part through the separation of the rationales underlying each. Thus, for example, the rationales for claims against the state are embedded largely in law and legislation and in political theory; economic theory centering on concepts of productivity plays a substantial role in developing the rationales for claims against firms; and claiming within the family is played out against a background of loyalty and social custom and the sociological and psychological theorizing that attempts to make sense of this behavior. The demand for "wages for housework" has the power to shock partly because it violates the traditional separations between claims rationales.

Since the various sets of claims against kin, against the state, and against firms, and their various rationales, can never be completely segregated, but are bound to interact with each other, the outcome of the various historical processes of claiming is what may be described as a number of distinctive *claims systems*. These claims systems may then be compared as wholes, not only with respect to the distribution of claims on quantity of economic resources (as in income distribution studies) or security resources (as in divisions between primary and secondary workers) but also with respect to the placing of claims. One might, for example, compare societies in which the dominant claims subsystem is that of claims against firms with those in which the dominant subsystem is that of claims against the state or against kin. Such a comparison would cut across the usual socialist—capitalist division, placing Yugoslavia, for example, in a category with some capitalist states and in contrast to more centrally managed capitalist and socialist economies.

CLAIMS AND THE ECONOMIC PROCESS

This perspective enables us to see the various systems of claims as both internally negotiable and culturally variable. A given system of claims appears in this view as a system of social conventions, or an always evolving system of power relations.

An economist confronted with this perspective would immediately raise two issues:

1. Claims cannot exceed the total amount of goods produced by society. Since a society cannot for long distribute more than it produces, some mechanism for keeping the two accounts in balance is needed. A self-equilibrating mechanism is preferable, so that neither a manager nor a political overseer need worry about the process.

2. Distribution systems are not neutral; there is a close relationship between the structure of claims and the total production of the society. The way we slice up the pie influences the size of the pie. Moves to distribute resources according to criteria of welfare or social justice that fail to take "proper" account of incentives to produce run the risk of undermining the vitality of the economic system and reducing the resources available for everyone.

With respect to the first problem, neoclassical economic theory proposes a solution. The marginal productivity theory of wages proposes that a myriad of individual transactions between workers and employers in a competitive market, in which each is trying to maximize the ratio of return to costs, will tend toward the economically efficient outcome in which workers everywhere will receive wages equal to the value of their marginal products. Thus, the amount of wage claims and the supply of goods and services against which claims are made are self-calibrating.

Barbara Wootton pointed out some time ago that it stretches faith much too far to apply this kind of reasoning to the managerial salaries in the "high tail" of the income distribution,[13] and few economists would indeed try to carry it into these higher regions of the claims structure. Nevertheless, the theory does provide, for those who find it helpful, a rationale for wage differentials that allows inequality to live comfortably with both maximum efficiency and social justice. In theory this comes about because all wage differentials are understood as payments for productive capacity. If wages are determined in this way, it follows that the prevailing inequalities arise because these differentials must contribute to aggregate production. Therefore, a society that was, according to John Rawls's[14] criteria, a "just society" might still embody substantial and persisting earning inequality—provided the inequality made possible increases in production that especially improved the position of the disadvantaged.

The theory is marvelously flexible. It is willing to accept the rough-and-tumble reality of groups negotiating and struggling for claims. It does this by acknowledging that there is a prior historical process by which wages have been set and which must be taken as a given. Marginal productivity is nevertheless rescued from this disorderly process by the view that capital adjusts to the reality of the wages it faces. This reciprocal process of adjustment has the net effect of adjusting the payment of various categories of labor to their marginal productivity. In this view there need not be any conflict between marginal productivity and claiming theories.[15]

Nevertheless, if we turn from theory to practice, we recognize that the marginal productivity of wages, with its self-equilibrating functions, is a postulate of particular and general equilibrium, not an observation about reality. As Frank C. Pierson put it, "The marginal-productivity theory of wages . . . was arrived at almost wholly by deductive means many years ago; yet to this day it lacks any solid factual underpinnings, since it embodies concepts which defy empirical verification."[16] We continue to object to the marginal productivity view of wages, because focusing on the metaphysical assumptions of self-calibration leading to a state of equilibrium obscures the role of power as a force for deciding whether it is labor or capital that does the adjusting, and equally obscures the power struggle among different classes of labor. This focus also obscures the fact that there can be many workable arrangements and that the existing arrangements are the products of particular historical struggles and are subject to change by similar processes in the future.

Once we concede that social factors influence the distribution process and recognize that distribution and production are linked in theory, but not in fact, we have broadened the scope for claiming in the political arena. After all, claimants are not interested in determining the truth of the theory, which appears to be immune against refutation, but in using the theory to solve the practical problems of claiming that they face.

Now we are talking not about individual claims in a market system, but about the claims of organized groups in the political arena. Even if individual claims in a market system are seen to be self-stabilizing, the same cannot be argued for the claims of organized groups. When groups compete to get more of the social product for themselves, they do not give back either more work or more sacrifice. They get more if they are able to threaten more. When society grants them benefits, it is buying "consensus" from them. "What is at stake in atomistic competition is the distribution of the social product in return for contribution to it. What is at stake in group competition is the distribution of the social product in return for social consensus. This gives the groups a larger portion of the social product than their members contribute (in market terms)."[17]

Nevertheless, we recognize that these "politically derived" claims structures, constituting the social and the moral framework within which economic activity takes place, must have their consequences, and important ones, for the size of the pie. But here, instead of a clear and dominant theory, we have various competing and partial theories, providing no clear guidance.

As political claims against large-scale corporatism expand, leading to more job security for some, improved quality of the work environment, and the growth of fringe benefits, from pensions to medical care to educational grants, we are beset with a puzzle. Shall we interpret these trends as a sign of success or a cause of failure? Do these claims erode or nourish productivity? Do they lead to less worker alienation, more collective identification, and hence to larger output (Japanese corporatism), or do they lead to the undermining of incentives? What kinds of corporatism lead to productivity and self-calibration—state corporatism, which we know as the welfare state, or business corporatism,with its tenure and fringes? If production and growth affect the structure of claims, then is it true, as Irving Kristol[18] has argued, that in time the claims arising out of the growth society will erode the structure which made that growth possible?

We have now shifted, in the discussion of incentives, to a level on which micro-economic theory will not be particularly helpful. We are now dealing with claims systems as providing, as wholes, frameworks for action that will be expressed in what is produced and how it is produced. R. H. Tawney opposes the argument that a degree of income inequality is necessary to bring about the savings and reinvest-ment necessary for long-term growth by holding that the lessening of social tension and hostility produced by greater egalitarianism would be reflected in increased output.[19] Fidel Castro speaks of "creating wealth with political awareness and more collective wealth with more collective political awareness."[20] The opposite view is that it is only "material stimulus that is indispensable to the increase in work pro-ductivity, the essential key to Cuban economic recovery."[21]

Once we see claims structures as relating to output as a whole and as political and social systems as well as in the form of strictly "economic incentives," it is dif-ficult to generalize, because each such claims system must be grounded in a partic-ular set of historical circumstances. The Yugoslavs' resort to a system built around claims on the firm was grounded in a combination of economic problems con-nected with their break with the Soviet Union and the applicability of enterprise de-centralization in an extraordinarily heterogeneous country. The Cubans' move to "moral incentives" and the centering of their claims system around the national revolutionary economy is hardly explicable except in the context of material short-ages in an isolated society. Thus, discussion tends to take the form of arguing not for one strategy against another at all times, but for the relative merits of incre-mental changes in a given system at a given time.

The discussion is made even more complex because the relationship between production and distribution is reciprocal. From this perspective we recognize that the level of affluence and the rate at which it grows influence the way in which the pie is distributed. In periods of economic growth there is more to distribute. Be-cause it is not necessary to take from some to give to others, it is not necessary to worry about relativities. As Fred Hirsch has written, "The growth alternative is inherently less divisive . . . it offers the possibility of consensus action, of a game with winners but no absolute losers, of leveling up without leveling down; limiting the political choice to distributing the increment, rather than demanding the more fundamental political act of redistributing existing resources."[22] Hence, the character of the claiming process changes radically with the curve of production.

We are left with the understanding that the structure of claims on distribution is not given through some kind of economic inevitability, that there is scope for rearrangement. But the problem still remains of having a structure that will produce the output to honor the claims when they fall due. There is certainly no infinite freedom to rearrange the distributional system. Both "economic necessity" and institutional intransigence set limits, but we argue about what the limits are. Those who see the limits as tight, and as being defined in terms of largely economic constraints, focus on a concern with "overload." The notion here is that the government is coming to have more claims made on it than it can honor, given its current level of economic resources. Others press to rearrange the system to make resources available rather than to trim programs to fit the available resources. The process of claiming takes place within the context of this kind of indeterminacy concerning the limits of possibility.

Although there is an argument about the resources available, and ongoing economic growth very much alleviates the sense of struggle over scarce resources, it is always recognized that resources are not infinite and that, therefore, claims compete. For example, when affirmative action opens jobs for blacks and women, whites and men feel threatened. The claim of women for pay equal to that of men for similar work conflicts with the press for equality of income among families—since better-paid women are quite likely to be married to better-paid men.

This problem, in turn, surfaces as an issue of latent conflict between two sorts of rationale that have been applied to earnings: the economic rationale of payment for a factor of production, and the welfare rationale expressed in the phrase "a living wage," related to the concept that earnings should be sufficient to support a family.[23]

Not only do claims conflict but the legitimating rationales of claims systems are potentially competitive. In the capitalist United States, conservatives express concern that a rise in welfare benefits will erode work incentive. The debates within socialism over "moral" versus "material" incentives center on the understanding that the use of the classic "bourgeois mechanisms" of career openings and consumer goods to shape the quantity, quality, allocation, and discipline of the labor force leads necessarily to a more private conception of social life and away from general commitment to the polity and to the life of politics. Systems such as the Cuban and the Chinese, which have invested heavily in the construction of politicized claims structures, have necessarily restricted the role of classic "economic" claims even while focusing closely on the role of work.

CONFLICT AMONG CLAIMS STRUCTURES

One view of culture and society sees no necessary problem in the coexistence of quite different value systems and different legitimizing rationales for claims—provided these do not conflict in daily practice. This view would have it that rationales do not derive from the necessity of consistency, but are better seen as an accommodation to situationally specific behavioral demands. In this view, because institutions serve different purposes, they embody different rationales of justification. The same individual, needing all these purposes, will accommodate perfectly to the competing demands each rationale makes.

Consider a concrete example. The law steadfastly refuses to treat husbands' obligation to support and wives' responsibility to render wifely services in a contractual framework. The rationale for reciprocal relations in marriage does not derive from economic exchange. The legal system recognizes the different rationales that justify action in business institutions and the institution of marriage. As a result of this differentiation of rationales, some troubling paradoxes arise.

A woman who does not marry can treat the services she renders as the basis of economic exchange and can sue for support. (The famous Lee Marvin case provides a clear illustration of the principle at work in the law.) A wife, however, cannot bring a similar suit, because marriage is based on the rationale of solidarity, not exchange. As the legitimating rationales have become clear, some people have proposed that women would get a better deal if they did not marry but instead signed contracts, which the court would be required to honor.

To the degree that there is a drive toward consistency within cultures, there will be competition among legitimizing claims rationales. A set of values presented strongly in one sphere of life will penetrate into other spheres. R. H. Tawney's[24] criticism of capitalist society was that material values dominate the culture and subordinate spiritual and relational values. The rationale for competition in economic life overwhelms other spheres. The modern fear seems to be unlike Tawney's: it seems to be that the claims against the state, rationalized as the citizen's right to live, hence the obligation of the state to provide livelihood, will come to dominate other spheres.

Scholars argue vigorously that the availability of claims against government has eroded claims against the family and that this, in turn, has threatened the social solidarity of society. They say that we must attempt to revitalize the intermediary structures (the family, the church, the voluntary association, etc.), or the integrative fabric of society may become weakened.[25] An alternative argument might suggest that the availability of claims against government has revitalized claims against kin, especially for low-income families. There cannot be an exchange system without something to exchange. Welfare provides low-income families with resources that can be distributed among kin. Thus, public transfers may strengthen the ties of social solidarity rather than undermine them.[26]

This process of intersystem accommodation and the creation of claim structures generates a considerable amount of friction and conflict, from which the policy debate and the agenda for reform emerge.

The conflicts and interdependencies among claims structures bring in response complex forms of claiming that try to take account of these conflicts and interdependencies. In the United States and Europe, organized groups have recognized that their well-being depends not only on the wages they receive but on the direct benefits they can secure from government, such as the indirect concessions they can win in the form of rebates and subsidies, and the burdens that can be relieved in the form of lower taxes. Unions in Britain and, to a lesser extent, in the United States, in recognition of these interdependencies, have bargained for a "state firm" claim package. As these interdependencies become the subject of bargaining, it becomes clear that we are enmeshed in larger issues about the structure of society as a whole, which we have called the claims structure. When bargaining takes place at a local or sectoral level, the issues of interdependencies are obscured because there is no national framework to give them coherence. This is the situation that prevails in the United States, where we have a highly segmented system of bargaining by interest groups. When bargaining takes place at the national level, as in Britain and Sweden, then the implications of the claiming process for inflation and income distribution become more evident. (Off in the wings is yet another issue: the future of claims within the kinship structure, and how this influences claims against the firm, as in lower wages for teen-agers, and claims against the state, as in affirmative action.) A struggle between government and national interest groups thus ensues, mediated by public opinion and other interest groups—but with government as both mediator and actor. The character of this struggle is central to the problem of liberal democracy in an industrial state.

In the course of the negotiations concerning these issues of claims structure, the political, the economic, and the social come to be seen as interconnected, or as aspects of a single system with respect to which policy is to be made. A theory of the economy cannot be separated from a theory of the state and a theory of the family. In moving toward this view of the field of policy, the capitalist welfare states come to a kind of convergence with the socialist countries. At the same time, within each of the categories—capitalist and socialist—there are particular national forms of claiming and claims structures, grounded in the choices and necessities of particular histories and particular situations. I propose the notion of claims, claiming, and claims structures as an intellectual framework for making some crosscutting comparisons regarding issues of policy. I shall return to this theme in a later chapter.

NOTES AND REFERENCES

1. Karl Polanyi, *The Great Transformation*. Boston: Beacon Press, 1957.
2. Suzanne Berger, "The Traditional Sector in France and Italy." Unpublished. Cambridge, Mass.: MIT, 1980.
3. Frank Knight, "Anthropology and Economics." *Journal of Political Economy*, 1940, *49*, 247–68.
4. Laboratoire de l'économie et la sociologie du travail, "Comparaison de l'hierarchie des salaires entre L'Allemagne et la France." Unpublished. Aix-en-Provence, 31 December 1972.
5. Joel Feinberg, "The Nature and Value of Rights." *Journal of Value Inquiry*, 1970, *4* (4), 243–57.

6. Marcia Freedman, *Labor Markets: Segments and Shelters*. Montclair, N.J.: Allanheld, Osmun, 1976.
7. Martin Rein and Lee Rainwater, "Sources of Family Income and the Determinants of Welfare." Cambridge, Mass.: Joint Center for Urban Studies of MIT and Harvard University, May 1976 (mimeographed).
8. Charles Reich, "The New Property." *Yale Law Journal*, 1964, *73* (5), 733–86.
9. Robert Redfield, "The Folk Society." *American Journal of Sociology*, 1947, *52* (4), 293–308.
10. Alessandro Pizzorno, "Civil Society, State and Pluralism." Unpublished. Princeton, N. J., 1978.
11. Gunnar Myrdal, *An American Dilemma: The Negro Problem and Modern Democracy*. New York: Harper & Row, 1962 (rev. ed.).
12. Martha Derthick, *Policy-making for Social Security*. Washington, D. C.: Brookings Institution, 1980.
13. Barbara Wootton, *The Social Foundations of Wage Policy*. London: Unwin University Books, 1962.
14. John Rawls, *A Theory of Justice*. Cambridge, Mass.: Belknap Press, Harvard University Press, 1971.
15. In our understanding of marginal productivity theory, we were substantially assisted by discussions with John Harris and Robert Solow.
16. Frank C. Pierson, "An Evaluation of Wage Theory." In G. W. Taylor and F. C. Pierson, eds., *New Concepts in Wage Determinism*. New York: McGraw-Hill, 1957.
17. Pizzorno, Op. cit.
18. Irving Kristol, *Two Cheers for Democracy*. New York: Basic Books, 1977.
19. R. H. Tawney, *Equality*. London: Allen and Unwin, 1952.
20. Fidel Castro, "Creating Wealth with Political Awareness, Not Creating Political Awareness with Money or Wealth." Havana *Granma*, 28 July 1968.
21. René Dumont, *Cuba: Socialism and Development*. New York: Grove Press, 1970. P. 140.
22. Fred Hirsch, *The Social Limits to Growth*. Cambridge, Mass.: Harvard University Press, 1976. P. 174.
23. Gertrude Williams, "The Myth of 'Fair' Wages." *Economic Journal*, 1956, *64*, 621–34.
24. Tawney, Op. cit.
25. Nathan Glazer, "The Limits of Social Policy." *Commentary*, 1971, *52* (3), 51–58.
26. Carol B. Stack, *All Our Kin: Strategies for Survival in a Black Community*. New York: Harper and Row, 1974.

Chapter 3

Social Services: Purpose and Form

It is generally accepted in theory that the starting point in the design of social service programs should be the objectives we hope to realize. From the logic of this argument it follows that purpose shapes form. But reality is more complex. When we turn from theory to practice, we find that the reverse is more nearly true: form shapes purpose. It seems best to think of the relationship between social aims and program design as reciprocal rather than unidirectional. We pursue this theme in the next three chapters, giving particular attention in chapter 4 to the question of the coordination of social services.

The terrain we need to cover is muddied. Social services are extremely difficult to define as a set of activities and tasks abstracted from their purposes. Specific activities are not merely neutral instruments of broad objectives: the activities themselves, and the way they are implemented, act to alter our intentions.

Joel Handler, commenting on federally financed services, observes that the lack of knowledge and the lack of agreement create a situation in which "statutory criteria are vague, ill-defined, ambiguous, and subject to conflicting and competing interpretations . . ."; vague language in the statutes, the administrative rules, or the guidelines "creates a 'downward flow' of discretion, [in which] . . . the lowest field officer interprets rules and guidelines for specific cases."[1]

Although we cannot hope to define these services in any complete way, we can at least illustrate what is meant by them, recognizing that the most interesting and difficult questions for program design arise when we try to generalize the activities and assign purposes to them. Let us start with a distinction between upper- and lower-case services.

Upper-case social services refer to activities such as housing, medical care, and education. We call them "upper-case" because they represent the established, high-cost segments of the social services. There is a large degree of consensus that individuals and families need places to live, surgery and drugs when ill, and specialized knowledge and skills to help them get jobs. Education is regarded as so valuable to society that children are required by law to be exposed to this service. We customarily think of services in terms of *universal entitlement*, but for many programs a more relevant concept is that of *universal requirements*. More than education is involved. For example, building codes have a compulsory element of obligation to conform to housing standards; and medical services carry an obligation, especially with regard to children, to provide proper care.

It is important to understand that these service activities are financed by a variety of means and administered in a variety of settings: the public sector, the non-profit sector, and the market. In practice, however, the pattern is often a subtle mix of public financing and private administration.

Lower-case social services are more personal and play an ancillary role, supporting the main duties of the upper-class services. For example, social workers employed in a housing authority or hospital or school are performing lower-case services; they help their respective agencies carry out their functions by dealing with the people who find it difficult to adjust to the mandates and routines imposed by the upper-case services. Increasingly, lower-case services are carried out in "freestanding" specialized settings, such as those devoted to family planning, child protection, and family counseling. Here they may also aid people to adjust to other institutional demands, such as those made by schools on students for work and discipline, those made by employers on workers for productivity, and those made by law enforcement agencies on citizens for law-abiding behavior. But the link to these institutions is indirect. The specific activities carried out in ancillary and freestanding settings include: clarification of the client's state to himself (counseling); the provision of information about community resources that he might require (information and referral); and the distribution of concrete "life-line" services (such as day care or meals-on-wheels). Note how difficult it is to distinguish the setting, from the activities provided, from the social objectives.

We cannot hope to clarify the meaning of these activities and the setting in which they are carried out without referring to their purposes. We can, however, identify two competing interpretations of what the purpose of personal social services "should be." Before discussing these conceptions of purpose, I want to stress that the distinctions cannot be held too rigidly. It is not simply a matter of choosing one or the other of the purposes discussed below. In this area there are no "pure" cases: most situations involve a subtle blend of both objectives. Hence, in practice, attempts to design social service systems that draw on one or another conception are always unclear. The lack of clarity arises partly because the conflicting purposes reflect a broader philosophical disagreement (which is more than an intellectual issue), but also as a practical question concerning the distribution of power. Services are not only what people want, as they define it (in other words, a response to consumer demands), but also what others (social managers) believe is good for those people. Thus, the design of social services is not simply a matter of social choice among unambiguous purposes but a struggle for position, which must be viewed against a backdrop of competitive conceptions of purposes that turn out in practice to be complementary.

Before turning to the question of design, let us start with a review of the two main purposes of social services and the broader intellectual tradition of which they are a part. Although these traditions do not exhaust the range of competing aims, they do illustrate the recurrent sources of definitional ambiguity and conceptual confusion.[2]

COMPETING PHILOSOPHICAL TRADITIONS

We can identify two conflicting service philosophies: the universalist-formalist and the selectivist-discretionary. These traditions have their roots in the legal system of our society. Albert Venn Dicey's book on the law of the Constitution, written in 1885, offers a similar distinction. He compares the English commitment to the "rule of law" with the system prevailing on the Continent, where the executive exercises far wider discretionary authority. He explains that the rule of law means "the absolute supremacy . . . of regular law, as opposed to the influence of arbitrary power, and excludes the existence of arbitrariness, prerogative, or even of wider discretionary authority on the part of the government. Englishmen are ruled by the law, and by the law alone; a man may with us be punished for a breach of law; but he can be punished for nothing else."[3]

Dicey's characterization of the sharp dichotomy between the rule of law and rule by discretion may be overdrawn when is applied to current situations. Experience with discretion becomes codified and develops into administrative law, which is a rule of law followed by discretionary agencies. There does appear to be a strong tension between formal reliance on the law and administrative reliance on discretion. In Dicey's analysis, the principle of universal and selective provision of services can be identified, because equality before the law means "equal subjection of all classes to the ordinary law of the land administered by the ordinary Law Courts; the 'rule of law' in this sense excluded the idea of any exemption of officials or others from the duty of obedience to the law which governs other citizens."[4] Dicey's comments refer to the situation in which on the Continent, government officials were beyond the sphere of the civil courts and were dealt with selectively by special bodies. Thus, the law was universally applied in Britain but selectively applied on the Continent.

In this chapter we are concerned with this tension between formal rules and discretion as applied to universal or selective programs. The tension between these principles influences the design of social services.

The Universalist-Formalist Position

According to the universalist-formalist perspective, those who utilize social services engage in a transaction that is essentially no different from acquiring any professional good or service. Since services are viewed as commodities, the legal rules that apply to commodities apply to services as well. Because the users of social services and commercial services have common problems, Rosalind Brook and L. Syson[5] have proposed the development of "consumer shops." These shops are to be administratively decentralized and charged with handling requests and complaints relating to both social and commercial consumer goods.

The reason for emphasizing this similarity between commercial goods and social services is to make use of the principle that individuals are considered to be the best judges of their complex and varied needs, as they define these needs. In this context services should be publicly available universally to all who might want to make use of them. Administrative and financial barriers that inhibit access to these services should be eliminated or reduced so that all citizens, regardless of income, may have the opportunity to utilize them. One way in which this can be done is to provide services free of charge for the total population by financing them from general revenue. This ideal was approximated in the British medical care system, in which the idea of a free-on-demand service for the entire population was not only accepted in principle but implemented in practice. A different way in which public polity can serve as the guarantor of the free exercise of preferential choice is by making available a level of income adequate to enable people to purchase in the market the services that they have determined they need or want. Thus, either an administrative or a financial arrangement, or some combination of both, can assure that the principle of universal entitlement is realized in practice.

To this universalist doctrine is added a formalist position in which rule by case law, exercised through the courts, is designed to replace arbitrary administrative decisions with rule-making procedures. The use of formal rules reviewed by courts is designed to preserve individual autonomy against dependence on legislative will (and shifting, invidious, social attitudes) and against willful or gratuitous administrative discretion.[6]

This formal reliance on rules of law is designed to protect citizens against what Alan Keith-Lucas has described as the intrusion of public morality into administrative practice through the "law of anticipated reaction," which arises because of vaguely defined administrative guidelines and professional vacillation between the ideals of "client self-determination" and the realities of community agencies' imposing "adjustive" goals on those who seek their services.[7] The formalist doctrine provides a way of protecting the client against becoming dependent on the administrative goals of professionals and officials. In brief, then, formalism assures the rights of the clients against administrative discretion.

The writing of Charles Reich, a professor of law at Yale, has influenced the formalist doctrine applied to social service. Reich, writing in the mid-1960s, argued that there had been an extensive growth of government largesse, which in turn had created new and extensive dependency relationships between the citizen and the government. New legal protections were devised to protect the citizen from the arbitrary exercise of goverment power. Since World War II, government largesse had been extended to the provision of income and benefits, direct government employment or indirect employment through government's right to provide licenses or franchises, government contracts, and an extensive system of subsidies to reduce the price of goods and services. These forms of government largesse had traditionally been regarded as a gratuity or a privilege, on the grounds that the citizen was free to accept or reject whatever the government offered or that the right to give was inherently a right to withhold and a right to attach conditions. Government, therefore, was free to impose whatever condition it wished on the service, benefit, grant, subsidy, or contract it made available. The principle of a gratuity contrasted sharply with the principle of property law, in which formal rules and legal protection prevailed. It was the business and professional community that first pressed for clearly defined legal standards and the use of due process requirements to protect themselves against the arbitrary action of the government in dispensing contracts, subsidies, and grants. Reich argued that a body of law and precedent slowly developed that eroded the traditional distinction between property and gratuity.

The protections that had been granted to business and professional interests were gradually extended to the income classes that were dependent on government social services for their economic well-being. The first inroads into this doctrine of "new property" arose in the specific area of welfare and in the general area of the public provision of income support. Eventually, the legal protection against arbitrary discretion and administrative abuse went beyond income support to the provision of personal social services.[8]

The formalist doctrine had its roots in the protection of clients' legal rights by the redefinition of the principle of gratuity. It is more difficult to trace the origin of the universalist ideal. I believe that universalism appeals to those who work in professions such as social work. These professions are caught in the tension between bureaucratic efforts to get clients to adjust to the normal standards of society and the principle of self-determination, by which clients are expected to be free to choose their own life-styles so long as they are law-abiding. This tension arises, in particular, in work with disadvantaged groups.[9] Universalism provides a broader constituency that can tame the arbitrary imposition of professional standards on client behavior. The ideology of universalism asserts that society can be made better by introducing a structural reform to promote community solidarity. What is needed is not merely a way of distributing charity effectively. Practical reasons reinforce the argument: the prestige of the professional depends on the social class of the clients he or she serves.

Universalism not only serves the professional and protects the client: it also improves the quality of the services. It was widely believed that a program only for the poor or only for the disadvantaged was likely to be an inadequate program, because the poor were too dependent on the service and could not effectively use the strategies of "exit" (the sanction provided by declining to participate) and "voice" (the sanction provided when one argues, complains, or praises) to change the behavior of the service provider. For all these reasons, it was important to make services more broadly—or, as an ideal, universally—available to all who needed them. This naturally required redefining the purpose of social services so that they could deal with normal developmental problems of growing up and adjusting to economic uncertainty and change.

The Selectivist-Discretionary Position

From the selectivist-discretionary position, services are viewed as fulfilling some purpose defined by someone other than the user of the service in order to help the user achieve a standard of behavior that may not reflect his own preferences. Social services must then be seen as being part of a broader area of activities that Robert Vinter has called "people-changing" or "people-containing" activity.[10] These services are directed at promoting compliance with social norms. They promote controls that are "necessary for the protection of a man for himself against himself, for the protection of his dependents, or for the protection of a wider public."[11]

The selectivist-discretionary perspective seeks to impose external standards of control and to restrict freedom of choice. In this model the preferences of the consumer are subordinated to the purposes and intent of the provider of public largesse. The emphasis is more on community prerogatives than on citizen rights and individual self-determination. In this context it is interesting to note that the preamble to the Social Security Act of 1935 declares that the purpose of the legislation is to "provide for the general welfare [and] to promote the well-being of the nation."

In summary, selectivity is the critical premise of this perspective. According to this view, it is essential to select those groups that threaten community prerogatives or that require protection from themselves. Thus, the emphasis is not on universal entitlement, but on selectivity, i.e., reaching the poor, the dependent, the deviant, and other groups requiring protection.

To make the general principles more concrete, let us consider the example of the welfare recipient. According to the universalist-formalist position, the recipient of welfare largesse needs to be protected against the exercise of arbitrary administrative discretion and abuse so as to be assured legal rights and entitlement to public benefits. In the selectivist-discretionary perspective, the recipient of welfare is dependent on the state for his economic sustenance. This dependency is generalized into a more fundamental inability to cope effectively with his social and economic environment, on the assumption that competent people can economically provide for themselves. Accordingly, the state has the obligation to provide such people with services that will enable them to alter their work-oriented behavior in order to reduce their economic dependency on government.

Of course, social services provide only one approach to changing the behavior of those who are economically dependent. *Governments may also resort to coercion when services fail to promote compliance or seem too costly.* Society has an obligation to maximize the protection of one class of people when threatened by the behavior of another. In such situations it is inappropriate to use an individual standard to judge the program when a collective standard is more appropriate. Social services are assumed to have external effects, i.e., people other than the direct consumers are expected to derive benefits from the consumption of these services.

Discretion, in this framework, becomes a necessary means for working with selected populations to achieve communal aims. " 'Discretion' is the opposite of fixed, clearly defined, and precisely stated eligibility rules and conditions. Discretion gives officials choices . . . it refers specifically to the conditions imposed by social workers upon the recipients of social services . . . In most programs, and especially in a social service program, officials are allowed great latitude in imposing conditions as part of the price for the delivery of social services."[12] The exercise of discretion is understandable when we consider the legislation that finances federal social service programs. Here we find a clear statement of communal objectives: "achieving or maintaining self-sufficiency," "preserving, rehabilitating, or reuniting families," "preventing or reducing inappropriate and institutional care," "the reduction or prevention of dependency." What is ambiguous is how precisely these aims are to be realized. It is the lack of knowledge that encourages the exercise of discretion. "In these situations the legislature defines the problem in general terms and delegates the task of finding solutions to an administrative agency."[13] On-line workers respond by defining "problem areas" and developing "service plans" for working with their clientele.

Applications and Ambiguities

In summary, then, we find that according to one tradition, services are for everyone, and formal (usually legal) procedures are necessary to assure that those eligible get what they are entitled to receive. According to the other tradition, services are good for some people because they serve the broader collective purpose. At issue is whether services are imposed by one class on another or elected as a free choice and understood to be a legal right. Although this dichotomy as I have tried to present it may be compelling, it is not without its own ambiguities.

Particularly troublesome is the question of how to classify compulsory education. It is a service that is imposed on young people in order to socialize them to the dominant norms and customs of society. At the same time, people feel their children have a right to be educated, because education provides choices that can broaden life chances. It may appear paradoxical that people have a right to a service they are compelled to receive. This naturally raises the broader question of how these two seemingly contradictory traditions can be combined.

The problem is even further complicated. Programs such as citizen participation and decentralization are supported both by those who passionately advocate selectivist and by those who advocate universalist objectives. American public policy bypasses these questions by leaving purposes indeterminate.

Although both perspectives enjoy a long intellectual tradition, each is incomplete, and hence neither can provide an adequate framework for considering how services should be distributed, financed, and administered.

Holders of the universalist-formalist position have avoided the problems associated with the high cost of a universal program and have neglected to take account of the costs of a program that is flexible and adaptive to the complexities of the human condition. Moreover, if they run the risk of offering a service they believe clients demand, they may have failed to gauge the market correctly and inadvertently lapsed into the role of reformers and shapers of the way people should organize their lives. For example, designers of recreation facilities for teen-agers often misgauge the receptivity of youth to organized or supervised activities, and social workers may promote the service as part of their developmental strategy for young people in transition.

Those who adhere to the selectivist-discretionary position seem reluctant to accept the implications of a substantial body of literature that shows the limited effectiveness of lower-case social services in promoting compliance or in encouraging achievement. In many situations people enjoy or choose or accept their situation. They are unwilling or unable to alter their behavior. Moreover, an extremely selectivist position runs the risk of creating two classes of citizens—problem families and those ordinary families that can avoid the problems faced by families by assimilating into the normal society.

These conceptual and practical ambiguities surface when we examine the question of program design.

THE SERVICE DELIVERY DEBATE

The above-described philosophical traditions serve as a policy paradigm for the delivery of social services in that they declare objectives, imply a theory of intervention to achieve those objectives, and propose a set of organizational means of translating the theory into specific action. But why choose between these incomplete and complementary perspectives? It is not difficult to see that we need both personal choice and social control, both universal and selective programs, both formal legal protection and professional discretion. Why should policymakers be forced to choose between artificial dichotomies that, in the effort to simplify policy options, also distort reality?

Each perspective can be understood as a way of simplifying reality and making it manageable and controllable. It is a policy paradigm that provides meaning and action because it contains aspirations, ideals, and objectives and sets a program of specific activities to be carried out in time. The choice of a paradigm "presumes a different framework, steers attention to different variables, poses problems of a different order, and suggests different methods of approach to solve these problems."[14] For these reasons artificial policy dichotomies that offend common understanding have vitality in policy debates. Yet, as we turn from theory to practice, we find that policies are pragmatic compromises between competing ideals. Any specific program of action embodies compromise and is the result of bargaining about the conflicting paradigms that are taken as given at the level of theory.

Decentralization and Participation in Social Services

The intellectual tradition that hopes to encourage free expression of individual preferences has sought to do so by both financial and administrative approaches. The financial strategy emphasizes the provision of an income adequate to make it possible for individuals to exercise their own choices, and the administrative approach calls attention to alternatives in the delivery of services that would enable the individual's preferences for publicly provided goods to be revealed. It is in this context that citizen participation and decentralization have played a prominent role. Both are part of the same intellectual tradition, which places the rights and preferences of individuals at the center of concern.

Yet, as we move from abstract argument to real cases, conceptual issues emerge that blur the vision required to translate clear purposes into a programmatic design. As a result, it becomes difficult to distinguish priorities assigned to the competing traditions of individual preferences and community prerogatives.

Part of the reason that the conceptual issues remain fuzzy or blurred and that clear priorities are not affirmed in practice is that the strategies of exit and voice serve as imperfect instruments for the declaration of preferences. Exit as a strategy does not work. Refusal to use unwanted services does not achieve its desired aim, because the market leverage against social services is weak. Many services are independently funded by government and private charity, fees for services accounting for only a portion of the total financing. Exit provides some leverage for altering priorities, but not enough to control what service providers do.

Voice (the demand to be heard) is also imperfect. This does not mean that the call in the late 1960s and early 1970s for decentralized services so that citizen inputs could be made did not work to some extent. But the rhetoric of participation did raise the question of who, in practice, does get to be heard. We know that at some periods, such as the early 1970s, blacks successfully exercised their voice; but other ethnic and racial groups were not heard (witness the Hispanic discontent with New York City's Community Action Program). Moreover, it is probably true that it is the neediest groups that manage the politics of voice least well.

Although there is no ideal way for people's preferences to be incorporated into the system of service provision, it is nevertheless useful to review the kind of intellectual argument designers and theoreticians have developed concerning how consumer preferences could enter the social services.

One interesting approach to this subject is found in the work of Charles Tiebout, who tries systematically to link personal preferences to decentralized services. In a statement before the Joint Economic Committee, Burton Weisbrod has summarized the approach as follows:

The substance of the Tiebout doctrine is essentially as follows: in the modern world, each metropolitan area contains a [sufficient] number of local goverment jurisdictions such that each consumer-voter may actually reveal his preferences for local public goods by moving into that particular jurisdiction whose differentiated tax expenditure package is best adapted to his wants. Note that revealed preferences are not detected or exchanged voluntarily by use of prices for individual public goods, but rather by what may be described as a single, collective price for a package of public goods—in the form of a local property tax payment.[15]

According to Tiebout's model, governmental units provide packages of alternative services. It is assumed that families have unrestricted mobility and that residence is determined by preference for these service packages rather than by proximity of work to residence. Individuals and families express their preferences by moving into subunits that offer them the service packages they want. The more varied the individual preferences, the larger the number of subunits of government that are needed to express them, even to the point of having a one-person government. In addition to assuming complete and unfettered mobility, the model must also assume a homogeneity of residential interests that leads people to want to band together to create subunits of government to have their service preferences satisfied.[16]

But the Tiebout model is too cumbersome to reflect faithfully individual choice. In practice people cannot select pieces of the service package—it is a case of all or nothing. To remedy this situation, another exit strategy is to permit individuals to choose specific service packages by shopping around. The most obvious way to do this is by duplicating services and having them compete for clients. One means by which this form of exit can be expressed is by a voucher program. Medicaid and Medicare are examples of voucher schemes that specify the kinds of services for which government will reimburse clients while permitting them to seek out their own package of medical requirements. This principle has also been applied on a demonstration basis to other areas, such as educational services.

The one-stop, multiservice center has also tried to demonstrate how ease of access facilitates choice. Such public, multiservice, neighborhood centers blossomed during the late 1960s. They were designed as programs to prevent delinquency and alleviate poverty. One form that such centers took can be traced back to a speech given by President Lyndon Johnson in August 1966 in which he called for the creation of 14 Neighborhood Service Programs.[17] Each center was to include participation by residents (voice); linkage agreements with local social, economic, and core services, including intake, diagnosis, and referral; and federally assisted component programs to fill locally determined gaps in service. Although the terms *core*, *component*, and *linkage* are different from *service packages* and *vouchers*, the basic ideas they express about social services are broadly similar. The critical assumption is that the spatial reorganization of services is presumed to widen alternatives in choice of policies.

Exit as a strategy of choice is expressed by dropping out of the service. This strategy is used by low-income clients, as evidenced, for example, by the inability of family casework agencies to hold onto their clientele. Mark Fried explains the low holding power of social agencies by the hypothesis "that discrepancies between clients and agencies are core issues in service outcome."[18] Low-income families see the source of their difficulties in terms of lack of money, jobs, housing, and medical care. Typically, social service agencies lack access to these resources[19] and, driven by the desire to do what they can, tend to redefine their clients' problems in more personal terms, such as personal competence or emotional stability. This discrepancy in the definition of social troubles leads clients to exit from the service by simply not returning after two or three sessions.

We turn next to the strategy of voice. Citizen participation and decentralization are presumed to be closely interrelated strategies, each reinforcing a common commitment to discover local preferences and to transform them into specific programs. Alfred Kahn has usefully termed this process "participatory administration," which he describes as a call for "locally shaped and controlled organization, with few guidelines and directives from higher levels, employing local people where possible, with local administrators (and/or line staff) hired by and subject to approval of 'the community.'"[20] He counterposes this approach to one that calls for "professional responsibility, competence, efficient organization, standardization, [and] accountability for funds" and argues that there "can be neither a fully centralized nor fully decentralized strategy"—hence some mix or combination of the two is necessary.

How can voice strategies be made acceptable to the service providers? As social service bureaucracies are given broader, more open-ended, and less clearly defined mandates, formal-legal principles of entitlement are weakened. To succeed, these services must secure legitimacy, public support, and a better understanding of what people want; and this can require more citizen participation.[21]

Such recognition of the complementary contributions of political action and professional services is important at a time when the controversies generated by participatory strategies seem to have undermined those strategies' acceptability. In addition to direct citizen participation, perhaps the most common voice strategy is that of advocacy.

The idea of advocacy derives from the legal system, in which there is a world of legal procedure that defines issues in a specialized way by rules, procedures, and precedent. To plead one's case one has to redefine one's problem to fit the rules of argument in the legal world. Therefore, persons or groups at risk need specialists to present their grievances in a way that can be appropriate to the rules of argument in the legal world. This idea has been carried over into the social service world. A clear-cut case must be pleaded in the right way, to the right person, at the right time, and in the right form. The person who performs this role is an advocate, who specializes in the exercise of leverage in the social service system to get his or her clients what they need and want. By its very nature the advocate's voice must support the rules of the system. To change the rules of the system, voice must take other forms, such as protest or anarchy, which can lead to the destruction of the system.

Exit and voice as strategies for realizing entitlement have limitations. The short-coming of exit is obvious—people cannot always exit. This is especially clear in the Tiebout model, in which the service package is spatially bounded. If we assume that a service-saturated community is most likely to be created when people do not have jobs, then people must choose between jobs and services. What is at issue in their choice is the question of whether the poor will be better off if clustered together where they can get the services or dispersed where they can get jobs, but few services.

Exit as a strategy of choice is often not realistic, however. This is the case when the service is needed as a lifeline to survival. Economic necessity prevents withdrawing from this service. For example, most welfare clients simply are unable to choose not to be on welfare.

The most obvious limitation of voice is that people cannot acquire the things they most cherish—for instance, low-wage earners cannot get stable, adequate, and satisfying jobs. The efforts to implement this solution only create a new "green light" problem when no corresponding expansion in the volume of community resources occurs. "Green light" is the opposite of red tape. Since the amount of service is fixed, the capacity of some groups to get a green light for the services they want must mean that some other group is deprived of the services. The purchase-of-care approach only redistributes scarce resources, thus exacerbating the problem of access in some other part of the service system. Increased efficiency in one sector can result in declining efficiency in another. In the absence of national mechanisms for the expansion and redistribution of social services, the effectiveness of advocacy in promoting reform and reallocating resources has proved limited. This reformulation of the problem brings to the surface the limits of voice as a strategy for redistribution when the economy is weak and needs for services are strong.

Social Service Integration and Coordination

Those who follow the intellectual tradition that holds that discretionary services should be provided to a select portion of the population who have special needs or problems have tried to increase the rationality of this suggestion by encouraging the coordination and integration of social service agencies.

At the end of the century it was widely believed that the organization of private charities contributed to the problem of pauperization, which was then defined as public aid for those in economic need. The existence of many uncoordinated, private, and autonomous social service agencies providing charity created a situation in which the slothful and the indolent were able to exploit the social service system by securing income from private charities sufficient to enable them to avoid the need to work. To solve this problem, a Charity Organization Society was formed and a central clearinghouse developed to prevent the same people from receiving charity from more than one agency.

Voluntary organizations regarded their function as preventing public destitution. This was defined as the receipt of public funds administered by local poor laws. It was believed that private charity administered separately from the public system, through a program of friendly visiting and cash payments when needed, would avoid the necessity for public aid (pauperization). The guiding philosophy was that those who were economically dependent needed "not alms, but a friend" if they were to avoid relying on government as a source of income.

Those who saw themselves as economically independent defined the problem as one of self-reliance. They rejected the idea that people were entitled to an income made available through public largesse. The idea of a general counselor was invented to promote conformity to this ideal of economic independence. The task of the counselor was to promote the ideal of "good behavior." The very denial of a service was interpreted as a service. The rationale was that the receipt of a cash grant would itself promote dependency. This theory accounts for the Charity Organization Society's vigorous opposition to the public financing of old-age and other pensions from general revenues.

In the period following World War II, the Charity Organization Society was renamed the Family Service Association. It initiated the use of modern methods of casework. The ideology of this new approach has been perceptively described by Joel Handler:

> . . . the connection between the theory of casework and the organization of social service delivery is that since presenting problems are only symptoms of more fundamental underlying problems, an effective social service has to be able to treat all of the problems and to reach back into the underlying causes if necessary. Therefore, service cannot be restricted to a single problem, but must be comprehensive or capable of treating all the problems of a family. . . .only insofar as specific services are considered part of a general rehabilitation program is there a need for comprehensiveness and integration.[22]

During the course of the century the intellectual argument for the coordination of services within the selectivist-discretionary tradition has changed. At first, coordination was interpreted as a way of protecting the agencies from being exploited by clients. Within this framework, duplication and fragmentation contributed to the problem of pauperization. During the post-World War II period, it has been thought that the problems of dependency, delinquency, mental illness, and other forms of "marginal" or problematic status could be dealt with by "reaching the whole person." However, "under the existing structure, families with multiple problems visit several agencies. As a result, there are gaps in the total services delivered . . . and the various agencies work at cross purposes. Thus, to make service delivery efficient, there must be comprehensiveness as well as integration."[23]

The logic of a selective-discretionary social service system, therefore, is to provide integrative, comprehensive care by a social worker and, more recently, by a case manager. As distrust of the social worker has grown, the manager has acquired considerable discretion in distributing social services to a select group of clients with multiple problems. This distrust of social work runs deep in society. One interpretation of its pervasiveness is the feeling that individual effort to bring about change is not very effective. Social workers therefore claim to deliver more than they actually can. By contrast, a manager has no pretensions. He or she is concerned primarily with efficiency and is not troubled by the lofty aims of personal reform. Managers deal not only with counseling but also with those other commodities that are essential to the lives of the poor, such as income eligibility for food stamps and, more recently, for fuel subsidies. In addition, they serve as conduits for the delivery of medical and child-care services. In brief, they deal with "lifelines" of the poor.

All of this obviously places managers and caseworkers in a position of considerable power over their clients. Historically, this type of power was placed in the hands of political ward heelers, who used it to buy political loyalty. But the professionalization of social work has "neutralized" these servants of power. One of the striking characteristics of modern social workers is their self-definition as being powerless despite their ability to influence the command of resources that shape the lives of the people they serve.

In Joel Handler's opinion, exercise of official discretion creates a problem of client dependency. He explains:

> I have defined client dependency in terms of discretion, that is, the extent to which a client needs and wants goods that may be granted or not by an official's discretion, with or without conditions. . . . The principal eligibility officer . . . receives the application, he evaluates what is necessary, and he defines the casework plan. . . . From a legal and administrative point of view, comprehensiveness and integration . . . means a centralization and monopolization of discretionary power in one agency and one official and thus a significant increase in power over clients. [24]

The title of Handler's book—*Protecting the Social Service Client: Legal and Structural Controls on Official Discretion*—suggests that he is concerned with "protecting the social service client" against the exercise of official discretion because such discretion must imply the arbitrary exercise of power over people's lives. I think that servicing the "whole person" in a highly selective, discretionary system would soon confront contradictions and drive the system to a more universal-formalist position. Moreover, in practice, this system of discretion is also likely to be neutralized. Let me elaborate my reasons for reaching these conclusions.

A truly comprehensive, selectivist system requires distributing a considerable amount of services among a very small segment of the population. It is interesting to note that this principle of "a lot to the few" has served as the ideal of political conservatives. For example, in the struggle for medical care in the United States in the 1960s, conservatives favored a comprehensive system of medical care for the needy. They rejected the idea of "a little for the many" embodied in the liberal proposal of hospital insurance for a large segment of the aged population.

Any effective comprehensive and integrated selectivist program must mean that the life of the multiproblem family is cared for in virtually every respect if the ideal of dealing with the "whole person" is to be realized. There are two obvious drawbacks to such a scheme. First, it is very costly; and second, the program creates a wedge between the service recipient and the rest of society, thus becoming self-defeating. Let us consider each of these arguments in turn.

The high cost of whole-person service may be illustrated by the experience of a demonstration program in Portland, Oregon, proposed by the Office of Economic Opportunity (OEO). This program added 1,200 low-income families to an established Kaiser Permanente prepaid insurance program. The demonstration accounted for 4 percent of the total enrolled clientele of the program. In the Kaiser Permanente approach, the cost of the prepaid plan depended on the range and cost of services included and reliance on supplementary charges for credit, office visits, laboratory services, etc. Different membership groups and individuals could specify the coverage they wanted. The OEO health program for the poor, however, costs 25 percent more than the most comprehensive plan available to the regular Kaiser membership. Part of the increased cost is attributable to the program's greater reliance on social services such as mental health care, home health service outreach workers, and health education (including teaching the value of health care and the importance of continuity and prevention).[25]

This experimental program was only an example of a comprehensive health care program, not of a fully integrated program that tried to bring together the education, recreation, health, employment, and income-support needs of people who required medical care. Yet even in the case of this truncated comprehensive program, costs proved to be astonishingly high. This experience supported the argument that social services and other ancillary services inflate medical care costs. Critics then proposed that a "stripped down" model be developed in which ancillary services would be eliminated from the basic medical programs (which we have called upper-case services). This experiment showed that a fairly modest program of comprehensive care proved costly and also created tension between upper- and lower-case services.

Even if we assumed that society was willing to bear the financial cost of such a program, a second, unnoticed problem emerged. A comprehensive-integrated selectivist program would soon create a social stigma for those who received its benefits, setting this group of service recipients apart from the rest of society and making it more difficult for these multiproblem families to function normally. In such a situation, practice would create pressure to blunt the differences between the two communities—those with multiple problems, and ordinary people whose needs arise from the "normal" problems of contingencies and "normal" transitions individuals experience over the life cycle.

After all, the boundary that separates conventional personal problems from those labeled deviant or pathological is only a matter of degree. Margaret Rosenheim makes this point in an important discussion about the juvenile court approach to delinquency. She observes that courts have a strong tendency to deal with actions—such as truancy or petty vandalism—that she describes as nuisances. She argues that there is considerable evidence to suggest that this form of delinquency is both normal and temporary, and that the very act of intervention amplifies rather than nullifies the problem it seeks to redress: "All people have personal problems, but whereas the better-off have the means to sort out their troubles privately, the poor become involved in some kind of 'problem formulation' process. If they need more help, they then become known as a multi-problem family, which . . . is an artifact of the organization of services."[26]

In brief, then, practical experience leads to the redefinition of the problem and to the rejection of a model that defines two communities—one composed of people with problems, and one of "ordinary" people. The situation is best described as that of a continuum of problems needing no sharp, rigid lines of demarcation between the problem family and the rest of society. The logic of this argument supports policies designed to increase the number of clients served so that service becomes less selective and more universal. The therapeutic ideal of rehabilitation is retained, but the framework of argument shifts to therapy as a process of helping people to adjust to conventional standards of society. The treatment of "normal" problems is obviously less costly.

This review of practice suggests a remarkable feature of the call for coordination—namely, that resistance is so strong that most coordination strategies fail. Commenting on the operating realities of coordination, Janet Weiss has observed, "The activity of coordination is itself fraught with peril. Amid all of the attempts and all of the species of coordinating mechanisms, this message is clear. Many devices are tried, but few human service programs designed to do so ever result in more coordination."[27] The service system remains highly fragmented while the rhetoric of reform continues to call for programs that treat the whole person through comprehensive, integrated services.

Given the reality of "service delivery problems," the mismatch between routing and arrivals, discontinuities of interrelated services, and an indeterminate accountability system that fails to isolate the causal agents of organizational failure conflicts with the ideals of a highly integrated system. Pressure to invent mechanisms of integration persists. When we review the efforts to respond to these "delivery problems," we recognize that the boundaries separating the formalist and the discretionary intellectual traditions begin to become blurred.

One strategy for managing these delivery problems is the purchase of services agreements. Here, too, we find a continuum. On the one hand, we have the model developed by the Vocational Rehabilitation Administration (VRA), which buys services it regards as necessary for the rehabilitation of its clientele. In effect, it seeks comprehensive integration through financial rather than administrative devices. At the opposite end of the continuum are programs that seek to provide vouchers to individuals to purchase the services they require. The individual, however, does not have full scope to choose services; rather, his or her choice is restricted in a narrow range. It is only the provider of the service whom he or she is free to choose, but in this he or she is restricted to a small list of acceptable providers. Those who support voucher schemes rather than direct service provision do so on the grounds that they can promote competition among agencies and thus improve the quality of services by encouraging freedom of choice among consumers. But a review of actual experience suggests that a highly restricted voucher system serves both the rhetoric of the formalist-universalist tradition and the realities of the selectivist-discretionary tradition.

A cross between these two approaches has been proposed for public discussion by Hartford Process, Inc., a nonprofit organization whose board comprises the business and civic leadership of Hartford, Connecticut. It has proposed that social services be handled on a "purchase for service basis." Under this scheme neighborhood residents would go to a neighborhood "life counselor," and counselor and client together would agree on a package of services that would appropriately satisfy the needs and wishes of the client. In this scheme it is the counselor who controls the flow of money and ultimately must agree on the package of services; hence, discretion is reintroduced through a middleman.

At this point we come full circle, with the argument that neighborhood residents could serve as members of the board of this independent corporation and, in their role as citizen participants, could influence the hiring of neighborhood life counselors. Resident influence would, it is hoped, reduce the unbridled exercise of discretion by these counselors, encouraging them to serve the needs and preferences of the community residents.

CONCLUSION

It seems unlikely that program design will develop from policies that explicitly articulate coherent positions. More likely, we shall continue to support programs with multiple policy aims whose definition of services and purposes will remain ambiguous. Those who will operate social services in the future may be better able to carry out their mandate if they better understand the conceptual and political issues that surround the problems of decentralization and citizen participation in service delivery systems for lower-case social services.

One conclusion from this analysis is that each approach has its characteristic strengths and limitations. The weakness of the universalist-formalist position is its failure to resolve the problems presented by a larger universe of eligible clients that available resources can accommodate, creating a situation in which it is difficult or impossible to reach those in greatest need with quality services. Although the selectivist-discretionary position may be designed to serve as a blunt instrument for promoting compliance and thus runs the risk of leading to compulsion, it has limited effectiveness in promoting these aims and avoiding the problems associated with the effort. On humane grounds, it can be argued that the preferences of clients should be honored. Policies to promote alternative service delivery models can be understood as an attempt to resolve the dilemma that each service reform entails.

NOTES AND REFERENCES

1. Joel F. Handler, *Protecting the Social Service Client: Legal and Structural Controls on Official Discretion.* New York: Academic Press, 1979. Pp. 8–9.

2. The ghost that haunts conceptualization in this area is the inability to come to terms with the meaning of performance. The units of activity to be performed cannot be specified or made comparable among different programs. This makes it difficult to study the more important relationship between performance standards and behavior outcomes. The failure to standardize services has made efforts to evaluate their effectiveness indeterminate, since countercriticism absorbs the imputed failure and attributes it to the low quality of the inputs. The problem approach seeks to avoid these difficulties by defining services as activities appropriate to any particular problem.
3. Albert Venn Dicey, *Introduction to the Study of the Law of the Constitution* (10th ed.). New York: St. Martin's Press, 1959. P. 215.
4. Ibid. P. 216.
5. Rosalind Brooke and L. Syson, "The Vocie of the Consumer." In B. Lapping and G. Radice, eds., *More Power to the People.* London: Longmans, 1968.
6. Charles E. Gilbert, "Administrative Responsibility in Public Welfare." Paper prepared for the 1964 American Political Science Association Conference (mimeographed). P. 3; and Richard Titmuss, "Welfare Rights, Law and Discretion." *The Political Quarterly,* 1971, *42*(3).
7. Alan Keith Lucas, *Decisions about People in Need.* Chapel Hill, N.C.: Univerof North Carolina Press, 1957.
8. For a useful discussion of Charles Reich's contribution, see Handler, Op. cit. Pp. 5–7.
9. A United Nations team of experts defined social services as the "mutual adjustment of individuals and their social environment." They hoped that acceptance of the principle of mutual adaptation would avert the danger that professionals might seek to impose individual adjustment to unjust and intolerable institutions. United Nations Social Commission: Report by a Group of Experts, *The Development of National Social Service Programmes* (Sales No. 60. IV, 1). New York: United Nations Social Commission, 1959. P. 6.
10. Robert Vinter, "Analysis of Treatment Organizations." In Paul E. Weinberger, ed., *Perspectives on Social Welfare.* New York: Macmillan, 1969.
11. A. M. Rees, "Access to the Personal Health and Welfare System." *Social and Economic Administration,* 1972, *6*(1), 12.
12. Handler, Op. cit. P. 8
13. Ibid. P. 9.
14. Roland L. Warren, "The Sociology of Knowledge and the Problems of the Inner Cities." *Social Science Quarterly,* 1971, *52*(3), 473.
15. Gilbert, Op. cit.
16. Jack W. Dyckman, "Decentralization: A Challenge to Planning and Governmental Organization." Paper prepared for a Conference on Centrally Planned Change. Durham, N.C., April 1972 (mimeographed).
17. Edward J. O'Donnell and Otto M. Reid, "The Multiservice Neighborhood Center: Preliminary Findings from a National Survey." *Welfare in Review,* May-June 1971, pp. 7, 8.
18. Mark Fried, "Client–Agency Discrepancies in Problem Definition." Unpublished manuscript, Boston College. Pp. 120, 121.
19. Genevieve W. Carter, "The Challenge of Accountability—How We Measure the Outcomes of Our Efforts." *Public Welfare,* 1971, *29*(3), 271.

20. Alfred J. Kahn, *Social Policy and Social Services.* New York: Random House, 1973. P. 164.
21. David Donnison, "Micro-Politics of the City." London: Centre for Environmental Studies, February 1972 (mimeographed). Pp. 6, 21.
22. Handler, Op. cit. P. 134.
23. Ibid. P. 34.
24. Ibid. P. 135. Instead, Handler favors a system in which market forces operate—that is, in which there is competition among agencies for clients and an economic payoff to providers to serve the poor.
25. May Hipshman, "The Kaiser Foundation Medical Care Program of Oregon." Cambridge, Mass.: Harvard/MIT Joint Center for Urban Studies, June 1970 (mimeographed). P. 11.
26. From Joel F. Handler's interpretation of Margaret Rosenheim's article entitled "Normalizing Juvenile Nuisances." *Social Service Review, 1976, 50,* 179. Handler's discussion of this article is on page 141 of his book *Protecting the Social Service Client. . . .*
27. Janet A. Weiss, "Substance vs. Symbol in Administrative Reform: The Case of Human Service Coordination." *Policy Analysis*, 1981, 7(1), 21.

Chapter 4

The Plea for Coordination of Services

In the preceding chapters I have examined how design questions centering on participation, decentralization, coordination, and earmarking of funds are related to the competing purposes of the social services. In this chapter I reexamine the questions of purpose from a different perspective, namely, as a response to problems that arise out of practice. In this context, coordination is viewed as a remedy for a problem that arises in practice. One of the puzzling questions in the design of social programs is how to account for the mismatch between coordination presented as a remedy and the problems that grow out of practice, i.e., action. To illustrate the difficulty, consider the following two statements:

—"Human services for young children must be better coordinated." This popular position has been enthusiastically endorsed in many countries by many people in a variety of positions—parents, social workers, doctors, teachers, legislators, and local and national administrators of service delivery networks, for example.

—"Attempts to coordinate human services for young children are seldom successful." Researchers and analysts have found that in all the places where coordination is so popular, coordination efforts repeatedly fail, amid widespread frustration.

This chapter explores the route from the first of these themes to the second. It begins with an examination of the heterogeneous sources of the plea for coordination, which are seldom made wholly explicit, even by its active advocates. But the qualities and number of these sources have broad implications for the eventual outcomes of coordination programs. Next, the ways in which these pleas for help are translated into practice, policies, and programs are considered. In some cases, the tacit, unacknowledged nature of advocates' motives interferes with the development of sensible remedies; in others, the very problems that prompt the call for coordination make it difficult to create workable programs. Thus, remedies are often designed in response to misrepresentations of the original problems. The third section surveys the consequences of these distorted or inarticulate pleas and the faulty transitions from problem to solution. Here some of the reasons why coordination programs have had such disappointing outcomes are explored. The final section contains cautionary lessons for the would-be coordinators.

SOURCES OF PLEAS FOR COORDINATION

Successful initiatives for policy change do not spring unsolicited from the void. Coordination policies, like all others, emerge from particular concerns of influential participants in the process of policymaking. Consider as an example the development of policy for children. What is remarkable in this case is how many diverse "particular concerns" seem to lead to advocacy of increased coordination as the solution. Indeed, this unusual degree of convergence on a policy direction has made coordination the dominant strategy for improving services in many countries. Clients, professional practitioners, administrators, planners, and politicians may all want to see more coordination in the delivery of services, each group for its own reasons, from the vantage point of its own positions. Any general movement toward coordination is likely to be an amalgam of the various motivations and definitions of the problem that these groups bring to their advocacy. It is often difficult to clarify and separate these motivations and therefore to understand just what problems coordination is expected to alleviate. It is necessary to examine the sources of coordination reform in order to discover what motivates the plea.

Some pleas for coordination grow out of concern for administrative efficiency. The staggering number of agencies, the multiple sources of funding, the elaborate division of labor among agencies and among professions, the overlapping lines of authority deriving from local, regional, and national administation of policy for children—all contribute to a felt need for order and rationality. Coordination is often sought as the key to rationalizing the disorder of duplication and overlap. The diversity of child-care programs under different auspices with a variety of sources of funding led the U.S. Government in 1968 to create a program for "Community Coordinated Child Care," sometimes referred to as the 4C program.[1] It seemed sensible for different day-care agencies to share in purchasing equipment and supplies, training staff, and hiring specialists.

The seeming rationality of the solution may even be invoked when no problem has been identified. An account of policy for young children in Norway reports a number of initiatives at national and municipal levels for improved coordination—

among the Ministry for Church Affairs and Education and the Ministry for Consumer Affairs and Government Administration and a Government Commission on Youth Policies at the national level; and among child welfare committees, kindergarten committees, school boards, health councils, and cultural boards at the municipal level.[2] But in no case is it clear that failures to coordinate have created any difficulties; in fact, there appears to be much successful informal cooperation. As in the 4C case, the justification for seeking improved coordination seems to rest on no more than a presumption that more coordination can only be a good thing.

But an inchoate longing for control and certainty in a disorderly environment is too vague an explanation for the enormous amount of attention now being devoted to coordination. The literature suggests that more concrete circumstances often evoke the argument that more coordination is desirable. In this section I shall consider seven such circumstances: (1) the sense of working at cross-purposes; (2) perceived overlap and duplication of coverage; (3) gaps or discontinuities in available services; (4) felt need for comprehensive or holistic treatment for clients; (5) frustration with limited service technologies; (6) clients' desires for more resources; and (7) political and organizational needs for reform and control. Not all motives are present in any one case of coordination advocacy, but neither are they mutually exclusive. The seven are discussed here not only to illuminate the diverse motives behind the call for coordination but also to explain in part why the call is sounded so frequently.

1. *Cross-purposes.* Coordination is called for to solve the problem of agencies' or policies' working at cross-purposes.

For example, a welfare department caseworker urges a young mother to go out and seek a job to become economically independent and offers assistance in doing so. Meanwhile, a school attendance officer, more concerned with the children than with the mother, urges the latter to stay at home and take care of the children in order to further their education or to help keep them out of trouble. There are fundamental conflicts in these two sources of pressure on the parent, and the advice from the two agencies is to some extent irreconcilable. When this kind of push—pull pressure arises, as often occurs when several agencies impinge upon a multiproblem family at once, some kind of coordinated or integrated case conference may be called to negotiate the competing positions and to offer unified guidance to the family.

In the late 1960s, in the United States, different kinds of child-care programs flourished in the federal bureaucracy. The Office of Economic Opportunity (OEO), the spearhead antipoverty agency, viewed child care primarily as one way to promote community control, because local communities had an interest in managing their own child-care services. In contrast, the then Department of Health, Education, and Welfare (HEW) viewed child care as a strategy to encourage adult welfare recipients to enter the labor force and thus, by increasing the employment of female heads of households, to decrease welfare costs. The 1967 amendments to the Social Security Act instructed OEO and HEW to coordinate day-care programs in the hope that the agencies could establish a common set of program standards, regulations, and objectives.[3]

The belief that the activities of government nullify each other and undermine family life has led to sentiment in favor of a national family policy in the United States and many other Western countries. This presumes that coordination could provide a basis for the discovery of shared purposes and that, given this underlying allegiance to common ends, the cross-purposes that characterize present agency practice could be eliminated.

2. *Duplication.* Because of the patchy, cumulative nature of legislation and agency creation over the past five or six decades, it is by no means uncommon to find nominal service functions replicated again and again across different funding sources and agencies. For example, at a time when the United States was trying in vain to pass two national day-care bills, one already could find on the books some 23 different provisions for day care. Housing, health, labor, military, education, and other agencies were independently financing day care for preschool children, although the amount of such care that was actually provided is uncertain.

The experience of duplication at the federal level is readily reflected in counterpart experiences at the local level. Individual service providers involved with a child or family may find themselves competing to administer nearly identical services. Such experiences naturally raise questions about the reasons for these redundant authorizations and agencies. Of course, the redundancy may be more apparent than real. A careful analysis of the meaning of "same" and "different" when dealing with human services would suggest that the case for redundancy is overstated. It is difficult to categorize accurately either the nature of problems or the nature of services offered in a practical world to a "whole" child and a child's "whole" family. Nevertheless, duplication of effort offends our sense of order and efficiency.

3. *Gaps and discontinuities.* Agency policies are often based on the belief that effective delivery of services involves a flow or continuing process. Gaps or discontinuities in the flow thus seem to interfere with the achievement of therapeutic goals. One kind of gap occurs when services offered to children at one age are thought to be ineffective because they are not maintained during later stages of the children's development. An obvious example is the creation of a preschool program for children aged three to four in a community that lacks kindergarten programs for its five-to-six-year-olds: there is thus a disruptive gap between the preschool programs and elementary education.

Some clear-cut examples of coordination designed to fill gaps are found in the policy statement of the Cheshire Central Consultative Committee for the preschool child and family: "Although full day care is provided for the preschool child, as soon as he/she becomes of school age then day care ceases. A child of 4 years 8 months can have full day care. A child of 4 years 10 months may well become a latch key child. From the foregoing it can be seen that there must be a considerable amount of joint local planning to ensure that the roles of the Education Service and the Social Services department are complementary to each other."[4] Another gap is to be filled by coordination among children's departments and education and health agencies: "For many years the day nursery was regarded as an agency primarily concerned with the physical care of children. Recently more attention has been given to their emotional and educational needs, but the lack of teachers in day nurseries hinders the development of a good educational programme."[5] The expertise of several agencies is deemed necessary to produce "a combined effort of care and education."

Discontinuities may be equally effective in prompting a call for relief in the form of coordination. The effects of preschool programs may be wiped out by primary schools that actively or passively contradict the lessons taught earlier. Discontinuity may arise when schoolteachers act against some of the freedom or creativity allowed to children in the preschool years. The benefits of a high-quality elementary education should not be interrupted by requiring that children pass through a rigid or discriminatory junior-high-school system.

4. *Felt need for comprehensiveness.* Service providers often believe that only simultaneous multiple interventions will alleviate the problems of a family beset by multiple ills. A comprehensive program of care may be required if the child of such a family is to derive benefits from any one service. Teachers or others working with a child often feel that they cannot deal with an education problem unless there are simultaneous improvements in the family's treatment of the child or in the child's health.

The perception of missing pieces of service may be inflated by the wistful belief that more comprehensive approaches might help the child. If lack of coordination is a useful way to think of the plight of individual children, it must be overwhelmingly the case for groups of children who are in trouble. The many specialized agencies serving disadvantaged children with medical care, recreation, emotional guidance, education, and income support have not been able to harmonize their efforts effectively. The problem does not seem to be duplication of services, nor serious gaps in available services, nor agencies working at cross-purposes. Rather, the problem has been a failure of timing: services have not reached the child when they were required. In crowded urban service sectors, overlapping agency mandates have made it difficult to determine who is responsible for a particular child. If services were orchestrated, coordination advocates assert, a more harmonious blending of efforts would naturally follow. Thus, coordination is believed to remedy discontinuity.

5. *Limits of technology in the human services.* A critical but far less obvious source of pressure for coordination arises from the limited efficacy of the human service professions. The roles of the human services are grounded in the human sciences; and these are, as everyone knows, weak in stipulating the regularities and predictions necessary for successful engineering. Human service professionals deal with people in grief or pain, with abused or neglected children, with the crises of the human spirit that attack the weak, the aged, and the infirm of any society. Their main business is to help other people adapt, develop, and adjust to the complexities, inequities, and uncertainties of modern life. We cannot assume that these service occupations are the equivalent of those occupations that operate on things. We cannot assume that failure betokens lack of effort, that more resources will lead to more output, that division of labor will increase efficiency. The knowledge base

of these professions is too fragile to support such assumptions. Professionals and administrators alike are placed in the immensely frustrating position of trying without necessarily succeeding, of investing more resources without necessarily operating any more successfully, of expanding and specializing only to feel dissatisfied because the parts somehow do not add up to a whole.

The limited efficacy of the human service occupations may lead to calls for coordination in two ways. First, at the level of practice, practitioners experience a measure of grief in being "whole child professionals." Armed with uncertain scientific competence, it is their everyday experience to encounter pain and suffering that they do not know exactly how to fix. Professionals may call for "coordination" because they feel the service they provide is inadequate to the human problems they are charged with solving. Second, at higher levels of intervention, a manager may use traditional assumptions about the synthesis of occupational roles in his or her approach to the human service professions. If social problems persist, there is a natural tendency to believe that either more resources or better coordination of activities will more effectively attack those problems. Managers are held responsible for making the system work, but they are frustrated by the constraints on them in fulfilling their responsibilities. Faced with severe resource constraints, their impulse is to cast about for ways to do more while spending less. As a result, coordination is frequently seized upon as a primary management strategy.

It is convenient for practitioners and administrators to reinterpret their problems as failures of coordination. Concerns about their inadequate performances are difficult to acknowledge to themselves, much less to the world. Facing up to a persistent lack of technological competence would mean admitting to their clients, their funding sources, and their professional peers that they may not be able to do their jobs. It is far preferable to admit to the lesser sin of administrative disorder.

Each of the five motives for coordination that I have discussed thus far—the sense of working at cross-purposes, duplication of services, gaps and discontinuities in the flow of services, felt need for comprehensiveness, and limits on service technologies—must be interpreted as a hypothesis that better coordination might eliminate or alleviate each of the five conditions. Some rearrangement of services might produce a critical mass or a critical conjunction, or permit a disentangling that would create or allow more effective treatment of children's problems. These arguments for coordination are based on plausible, but hypothetical, assumptions about the working of the service network. They all make some untested critical leaps: the problems in service delivery are simply organizational; the system is made up of efficacious laborers, each with a contribution to make to children and family well-being; no important competence is missing from the system; therefore, if each unit can be properly coordinated with all the others, the problems of gaps, fragmentation, cross-purposes, and the like, will be neatly erased. As should be obvious when these unspoken assumptions are articulated, they are occasionally correct, but also are occasionally far from the mark.

Each of the five may thus represent a correct or an incorrect hypothesis about the appropriateness of a coordination solution as a remedy for a problem as formulated. Another characteristic of each of these five sources of pleas for coordination is that each may represent a direct practice worry or a detached calculation. The various participants in the service delivery system frequently experience the need for coordination in different ways. For example, a professional's sense of working at cross-purposes with another agency may result from an infuriating emotional experience stemming from interference that, in turn, may lead to a plea for coordination. But this is quite different from the case of a planner who extrapolates the likely impact of several social policies, detects potential contradictions, and rationally proposes coordination to smooth over the incipient conflicts.

The "hot knowledge" of the practitioner is firsthand, the result of primary encounters with children. The "cold knowledge" of administration is more remote from children's pain; it belongs to those who manage services at a distance. Some hypotheses about the benefits of coordination seem to be motivated by hot knowledge, by direct emotion, passion, and anger. Others seem to come from cold knowledge, from reason, analysis, and controlled concern. In my example, a sense of working at cross-purposes may emerge out of hot or cold knowledge, and either form of knowledge may lead the policymaker to hope that better coordination will solve the problem. But the plea for coordination takes on a different sound and shape when it originates in hot rather than in cold knowledge: it is less orderly, less articulate, more unruly, more emotional. A particular situation may provoke either type or both types of pleas simultaneously, and the hot—old distinction cuts across the five sources of pleas that I have outlined. Even the fifth, the limited technology of the service professions, may either be experienced out of personal dismay and frustration or discovered in the process of analysis and calculation. Understanding the difference between them helps clarify some of the independent sources from which coordination programs emanate.[6]

The last two factors to be considered represent a somewhat different leap of faith from problem to solution. Coordination is invoked as a tactical move toward coping with fundamental, ongoing concerns both by clients and by legislators and general-purpose government officials. The concerns—more services for clients and more power and influence for politicians—are not susceptible to solution once and for all, nor is coordination seen by its advocates as more than a temporary means of achieving short-term progress toward the desired end.

6. *Clients' demands for more resources.* Families receiving social services have a primary interest in getting adequate help when they need it. For example, Martha Baum and Alan Coleman have summarized the findings of a county survey as follows: "In the main, those who saw a need for change in the service system perceived available services and personnel to be in short supply and wanted essentially more of the same. What comes through is more a feeling of service shortage rather than duplication or gaps."[7]

Clients may see coordination programs as one path to overcoming these shortcomings. When budgetary constraints foreclose the possibility of new programs or more staff, clients may support coordinating efforts as a way of sustaining social or organizational momentum toward more effective service delivery. The increased efficiency that is assumed to result from coordination may be seen as a means of generating more resources to devote to service delivery. Alberto Melo documents a case in the city of Coventry in which public demands for improved preschool facilities played some role in the establishment of coordinating councils that included social services, health, and education officials.[8] The emphasis on comprehensiveness in many coordination programs may also appeal to clients, either for the sake of improvements in the number or variety of services available or for the convenience of co-location or improved access and intake. A variety of client needs may lead parents and families to advocate coordination—not necessarily for its own sake, but as a route to improved services.

7. *Political and bureaucratic needs for reform.* Coordination (like other kinds of reorganization) can become a tool in outright power struggles over control, priorities, or resources within the social service system. Each group with a stake in how social services are organized is interested in coordination linkages that operate to its own relative advantage. Naturally, ideas about appropriate and effective coordination conflict.[9] Conflicts among any combination of interested parties over control of service priorities may be acted out in the arena of coordination reform, each group trying to impose its vision of a better-run system on all other groups. Sidney Gardner, among others, discusses the battles between general government acting as coordinator and the entrenched categorical interest groups and service professionals: "Line agencies, their legislative allies, and associated interest groups frequently resist any administrative services integration changes which may decrease the importance of categorical program managers . . . Their resistance is wholly predictable, for categorical interests are usually fighting in their own territory, which generalists invade with some proposed intervention and then move on to new priorities in other areas."[10]

Sometimes these conflicts are really over questions of coordination. At other times the call for reform premised on the assumption of coordination is simply a way to fight other battles. The organizational changes involved in most coordination plans offer opportunities for shifts in control over many aspects of organizational life. The political nature of the funding decisions provides interested parties with ways to enter into these power struggles. The result is that coordination becomes more than an administrative issue, more than a professional issue. It is embedded in political issues, and becomes a political issue in its own right. As Harold Seidman has written, "Organizational arrangements tend to give some interests, some perspectives, more effective access to those with decision-making authority."[11]

Laurence Lynn provides a good example of political motivations in his analysis of the attempted coordination of all social services in Florida.[12] A confluence of political forces on the state legislators led them to impose a massive, unwanted reorganization on the service delivery agencies in the state. Most potent of these forces was the political fashion of accusing large bureaucracies of incompetence, coupled with the allure of programs that claimed to improve the quality of care within existing budgets. One net effect of the mandated service integration was to remove some control over the huge budget of the Department of Health and

Rehabilitative Services from the state's governor and his appointees and to give it to the legislature's oversight committees.

As Murray Edelman has noted, a strategy of coordination often has symbolic political implications that are as important as, if not more important than, the content of the coordination initiative.[13] In this case, as in the others, the expression of pro-coordination sentiment by political officials may be motivated by no more than a play for political advantage.

TRANSLATING PLEAS INTO REMEDIES

As our seven categories illustrate, the pleas for coordination can come from a remarkable variety of sources, and may take many forms. When coordination programs are proposed by diverse constituencies to fill different needs, the effort to translate the theory into administrative and professional practice becomes complicated.

First, a pro-coordination coalition may have multiple goals for coordination and integration programs. Under the rubric of coordination, reformers hope to achieve increased efficiency, accessibility, accountability, advocacy, comprehensiveness, participation, and numerous other objectives. All of these are worthy goals, but they are by no means the same, and different objectives may well imply contradictory courses of action in any given instance. For example, setting up a coordination program to eliminate overlap in no way guarantees improvement in comprehensiveness of services. To the extent that a coordination reform attempts to accomplish inconsistent tasks, the reformers may be unable to achieve any of them. The vague hypothesis that coordination will be effective often camouflages the multiple, conflicting hopes that parents, politicians, administrators, and professional service providers and interest groups impose on the program. The result is a persistent lack of both consensus and clarity about what the program is supposed to accomplish.

Even when the ostensible goals are agreed upon, a second sort of confusion often disrupts efforts at effective reform. Goals have to be translated into specific proposals for change. In a social system as complex as a network of social service delivery organizations, knowing where one wants to go does not mean that one knows just how to get there. Eliminating fragmentation and discontinuity is a highly desirable goal, but there are many possible ways to attack it, and no very good way to know which is most likely to work. In the reigning ignorance and confusion, administrators often put into place specific administrative changes that do not have much connection with their long-term goals—that is, they try methods of attaining their objectives that turn out to be ineffective or irrelevant.

Consider an example. A superintendent of a school district in Philadelphia, Pennsylvania, was disturbed by the prevalence of functional illiteracy among school dropouts in low-income areas of the city.[14] He decided that mental health could be improved within the schools by bringing mental health specialists to work in the school system. These specialists were to provide screening, consultation with teachers, and some direct service. Coordination between them and the teachers seemed to be the crucial requirement for altering the climate in the schools. What remains obscure is how such linkages could, in fact, reduce the problem of illiteracy or lower school dropout rates in the ghetto schools. There is not much logical congruence between the initial professional concern about illiteracy and dropouts and the "solution" of coordinating mental health specialists and teachers. The hypothesis that coordination would solve this problem clearly rested on faulty premises.

Administrators may know just what they want to accomplish but, because of constraints of resources or lack of knowledge or technology on how to effect desired change, may not be able to accomplish it.

Coordination reforms must be implemented in complex settings, with the participation of a number of interested people who have a stake in the outcome of the reforms. To the extent that these people fail to understand their own and each other's motives, they may fail to participate effectively; they may be angered at having their expectations violated,or they may end up working at cross-purposes. In any case, effective reform will be difficult to achieve.

The problems of clarity are exacerbated by the difficulties of translating hot knowledge into cold. There is a gap between the passion and emotion experienced as hot knowledge and the cognition and rationalizations embodied in cold knowledge. There can be serious distortions in communicating across this gap. The feelings of outrage, empathy, and grief aroused in those who deal with young children in trouble may make it difficult to deal rationally or articulately with service delivery problems. The pain of clients and practitioners does not travel very far in the networks of administration, planning, or analysis. The wires of such formal communication systems carry only translations, imperfect as they inevitably are, of that hot knowledge into cold. Such flawed renditions of the source of the plea can only make it harder to apply a remedy appropriate to the malady.

Thus, the many sources of coordination advocacy and the nature of those sources create problems in the design of programs capable of curing the offending symptoms. The tacit nature of the motivations and the many constituencies that may be mobilized make it hard to understand just what drives the plea for coordination in any given instance. This fuzziness obscures central questions about what should be done. For example, it is possible to coordinate at many levels, but there is far from unanimous agreement about what type of coordination is most important.[15] Some call for coordination of all services (Gary Brewer and James Kakalik[16]); others, for coordination of all service delivery to families living within limited geographic areas (Sidney Gardner[17]); others, for various strategies of coordination at the administrative level (some contributors to the symposia reported by the ASPA,[18]); and still others, for coordination by the mutual adjustment and readjustment of policies initiated by autonomous agencies, with no centralized coordinator (Charles Lindblom[19]). Unless coordination advocates can specify precisely the condition they hope to change and the purposes they hope to realize (see chapter 3), they can have little notion of what should be coordinated—people, facilities, policies, resources, information, or control. In practice, the frequent result is that coordination is aimed at the wrong level. Michael Aiken and his co-workers have described attempts in five projects to coordinate services for mentally retarded children and adults.[20] They found each project coordinated at a level that was mismatched to its purposes. It is not unreasonable to suppose that such tactical errors could be avoided if programs had a firmer fix on their goals and purposes at the outset.

A final concern in the design of remedies is that the remedy will not be simply "a bit off," but will be wholly inappropriate. There are many problems in the delivery of services that are not problems of coordination and therefore cannot be solved by improving coordination. There are problems of fit or congruence when client needs do not match up neatly with available services. There are problems when services are stigmatizing, when the very effort to provide treatment by special labeling of those who are treated (as in special classes for the mentally retarded) exacerbates or even creates the condition the treatment seeks to relieve. There are problems of high dropout rates, of clients not wanting to continue in programs that professionals want to provide. There are problems of professional conflict in which doctors, teachers, social workers, and psychologists see the need for different sorts of treatment and each is unwilling to subordinate his or her concerns to alternative philosophies of treatment. There are problems of poor-quality services, of burned-out service providers and inadequate staff resources, of uncertain political support, and of shrinking budgets. But none of these is a coordination problem, and we should not expect coordination to be a broad-spectrum solution to such urgent but unrelated concerns.

Unfortunately, there are many cases in which coordination is invoked reflexively, on the mistaken assumption that a plea for coordination must indicate a corresponding need. When the Joint Planning Team in Britain asked eight local authorities for examples of intergovernmental problems requiring improved coordination between local and central government, they were astonished to find that the local officials had no concrete problems to report. A county in Pennsylvania revamped its social service system to create comprehensive, integrated, and coordinated service delivery despite an internally commissioned survey that concluded: "The problems associated with a need for services integration did not manifest themselves to any marked degree in our samples (of households and of active clients). . . . The conclusion has to be that, from this limited perspective at least, service integration attempts are quite unlikely to lead to any very great positive impact on consumers."[21]

In such instances coordination is unlikely to be useful. A plea for coordination remedies may rest on mistaken hypotheses; many problems *cannot* be ameliorated by a shift in organizational arrangements or an admonition to cooperate. Coordination is no substitute for clear, focused objectives, high-quality services, or adequate resources. We squander our scarce energies when we assume that our guesses about the beneficial effects of coordination will always be correct.

SOME CONSEQUENCES OF FAULTY TRANSLATIONS

We often find little congruence between the original practice problem and the coordinating mechanism that results from the plea. As noted in the first section, the plea for coordination often misrepresents its many sources and usually appears less speculative and better defined than it really is. And as indicated in the last section, the translation of pleas into operating programs is a second source of confusion and peril, with further distortion of the original problem introduced into the process. In far too many cases, we settle on programs and practices that are badly connected to our objectives.

In this section several consequences of such faulty translations will be explored: difficulties in implementing coordination programs because they are mismatched to their settings; unanticipated negative consequences of coordination programs because they are not carefully thought through; and, most tellingly, failure to achieve our policy objectives through coordination.

Some of the ambiguity and confusion in pleas for coordination is reflected in legislation designed to establish coordination policy. When the formal mandate for a program provides unclear or contradictory guidance, the process of implementation is hamstrung from the start. Anne-Marie Foltz illustrates this dilemma in the case of the Early and Periodic Screening, Diagnosis, and Treatment Program (EPSDT), a program that was designed in 1967 to be the most comprehensive child health care effort the United States had ever undertaken.[22] The failure of the initial legislation to specify how state health and welfare agencies should work together on the program led to a delay of over six years before the program could be implemented, and even then EPSDT served far fewer children with less comprehensive services than its sponsors had provided for. Another example is Alan Orenstein's account of Massachusetts's programs for handicapped children.[23] The legislation set up multidisciplinary teams within the school system to diagnose and provide services to handicapped children. But the teams did not have the legal authority to provide or purchase all the necessary services, nor did they have jurisdictional authority over which agencies—mental health, welfare, or education—should take responsibility for a particular child. The lack of clarity in the legislation in this case, as in the EPSDT case, led to delay, struggle, and sabotage in implementation, together with a decline in the morale of members of the coordinating teams.

A clear, formal mandate is desirable, but is not in itself sufficient. Coordinating never proves to be an easy task. As students of organizational change have known for some time, the organizational procedures of service delivery agencies become entrenched, partly through habit and partly because they are sustained by internal and external incentives. The incentives that sustain current service delivery networks are not trivial considerations. Change in and of itself has costs. It creates uncertainty; it threatens the positions of key members of the organization; it disrupts organizational effectiveness. Any executive who has tried to rearrange organizational boxes to achieve greater coordination knows how personally threatening it is to alter the organizational turf an individual has acquired. Individuals in organizations are unwilling to change their position relative to others unless the benefits of a proposed change are perceived to outweigh the costs. Change will not occur unless the system of incentives is revised so that new operating procedures are seen as more effective, more convenient, more efficient, or more rewarding than the old. Coordination reformers cannot simply point out more rational ways for organizations to behave and expect them to change. Agencies must be shown that it is in their own interests to bear the costs of change. No matter what the source of the original pleas for coordination, these organizational needs must be recognized if effective implementation is to result.

The need for incentives is especially acute in interorganizational coordination. Coordination programs usually require individual organizations to surrender some of the resources, power, or autonomy that they have traditionally controlled to other organizations or to a coordinator. This constitutes a cost in the usual sense of a loss of resources. But it is also costly in that it threatens the organization's basic needs for maintenance and survival. Control over resources or expertise enables an organization to continue to function, gives it goals and boundaries and claims on additional resources that distinguish it from other organizations. One of an organization's most important objectives is to perpetuate itself. When coordination programs seem to jeopardize survival, either through the immediate prospect of absorbing the organization or by forcing it to give up some of its autonomy, resistance must be expected.

Just as existing organizations of service deliverers have needs, so, too, do the professional groups that staff these organizations and the governmental groups that pay for them. The professional service providers, as the final links in the service delivery process, are the people who must change their daily work behavior if the service delivery system is to be changed in any meaningful way. It is they who feel the primary impact and make the essential difference in attempts at systemwide reform. Those coordination projects that provoke the least resistance seem to accomplish that feat by setting up appropriate incentives for the professional service providers. When service providers believe that coordination will make it easier rather than harder to provide high-quality services, they are much more likely to cooperate fully.

Several kinds of incentives may be offered, some more effective than others at providing help to the service providers. Coordination and integration programs may offer increased funding, various types of comprehensive information systems, the availability of more and more varied professional expertise, increased planning or analytical capability, or physical facilities, as in a multiservice center.[24] In general, service providers tend to see money and some kinds of information as more helpful than planning or buildings.[25] Thus, coordination reform sweetened with more funding and more comprehensive information seems more likely to evoke support and cooperation from professionals than coordination without them. To the extent that professionals feel helped and supported by the reorganization, they are likely to contribute to successful coordination. To the extent that they feel threatened and undermined, they are likely to resist. Again, regardless of the primary impulse for coordination reform, the concerns of professionals for quality services must be satisfied if genuine change is desired.

Those who carry out programs are equally aware that social service systems are created and paid for by governments as embodiments of political and social purposes. This political context of service delivery makes it legitimate for each group—clients, professionals, administrators, special interest groups, general-purpose government officials—to pursue its own interests through coordination reform. Hence, coordination, like other political issues, must be the product of compromise, bargaining, and negotiation among the power centers. Douglas Henton's data on the feasibility of implementing coordination linkages in 33 different settings showed that projects that were the outcome of bargaining and negotiation among interested parties were more successful in achieving coordination links than projects that were the result of a technical planning process.[26] No one group, no matter how passionate its plea, could expect to impose its vision of who was to coordinate whom on all others.

All these difficulties—ambiguous legislation, organizational inertia, professionals' resistance, and political bargaining—dramatically affect the rate of successful implementation of coordination programs. In their detailed evaluation of 35 services integration projects, Sheldon Gans and Gerald Horton found that coordination linkages were not common even among the most highly regarded projects.[27] None of the projects had fully developed a majority of the linkages that they had planned; indeed, many had abandoned their plans for coordination in favor of an emphasis on service delivery. William Lucas and his co-workers have reported a similar phenomenon.[28]   Not only did implementation fail to meet expectations but in 8 of the 40 coordination projects they evaluated, they could not find evidence that any linkage—fiscal, personnel, locational, organizational, or administrative—had been created. A national review of the Neighborhood Center Pilot Program conducted in 1969 concluded that although efforts at coordination had been mounted by interagency mechanisms, they had died because of lack of local departmental interest or support; and extensive interagency coordination had failed to materialize.[29] Each agency acted unilaterally in the program, and there was no intragovernmental coordination.

Another consequence of the unreflective adoption of coordination procedures is programs that have not been thoroughly thought through, which then have unanticipated and unwanted side effects. An example of such unintended effects is provided by Adrian Webb's account of the reorganization of personal social services in Britain.[30] The Seebohm reforms in England, named after the chairman of the committee that recommended them, attempted to increase coordination; but the experience seems to have resulted in decreases in coordination at some levels. This happened because the reorganization stimulated a massive demand for social workers and administrators and thus made possible considerable upward mobility into the newly created senior positions that the law required. As practitioners became administrators, inexperienced workers were hired to work in the field. Even those with little experience were promoted. The result of this growth and mobility was to create a situation in which many workers lacked training, experience, and familiarity with the local areas they served. This contrasted sharply with the earlier period of stability, in which workers had acquired considerable contact from living and working for many years in the same area. Writing at the turn of the century, Adrian Webb observed that the influx of inexperienced generalist caseworkers has eroded the established pattern of cooperation between doctors and social workers. In part the restructured organization of services removed the doctors from their former positions at the center of the day-to-day delivery of services. Cooperation dissipated in part because the inexperienced generalist social workers may have been less useful to doctors than their experienced specialized predecessors.

Another sort of unintended consequence stems from the political context of the social services. Social services are the expression of diverse political purposes and values that must compete for scarce resources. Under such circumstances attempts at coordination may actually be dysfunctional.[31] The elimination of overlap, duplication, and waste may mean the elimination of diversity, the homogenization of services. For example, central intake and referral systems may provide clients with increased access to services, but may eliminate clients' freedom of choice among treatment types or philosophies. Overlap may encourage experimentation with alternative methods of treatment, because professionals, administrators, and clients all know that traditional help is available elsewhere. By discouraging overlap, coordination programs may discourage innovation. As expressions of our political purposes, social services reflect the pluralistic character of those purposes. Rationalizing the system through coordination may destroy some of this pluralistic character.[32] Fears of such results may motivate some of the resistance to coordination by clients, special interest groups, and politicians sensitive to these constituencies.

Instead of lowering costs, harmonizing the crowded service environment may reduce the rate of growth in the overall volume of resources available. Services proliferate as new programmatic initiatives find constituencies to support them. Coherent policy might actually reduce the extent of political support. This suggests that an adequate level of resources may require some measure of complexity and redundancy.

As noted earlier, hopes and concerns for people in need of services are complex, diverse, and redundant—and they are also inconsistent and contradictory. In a fragmented system these contradictions are not directly confronted and thus do not have to be resolved. Attempts to coordinate social services across categories may lead to the surfacing of many such inconsistencies in our social values. It may be socially useful in some ways to be made aware of the contradictory messages that our social policies convey, but there is some social danger in making these conflicts explicit in ways that provoke confrontation or sharpen divisions among segments of society. The more comprehensive the coordination, the more likely it is to require direct and explicit decisions about such uncomfortable trade-offs.

If coordination efforts are so difficult to implement, and if they generate such undesirable secondary consequences, it should come as little surprise that their overall success rate is disappointing. Murray Meld develops this argument as follows:

Efforts to achieve human services integration over the past decade have not been

notably successful . . . No organizational model had been found which demonstrates its effectiveness in achieving human services integration . . . despite
some rhetoric to that effect . . . There is no evidence, for example, that cost
savings and efficiencies have been accomplished. Nor can one claim significant
institutional or system change. . . .Resistances to change in the *status quo* of
the service structure . . . [have a] tendency to thwart the human development
potential of human services.[33]

Systematic data on costs show that such programs almost never achieve cost
reductions, and in most cases the commitment to change serves only to increase
aggregated costs. Morrill sums up the results of the Department of Health, Education, and Welfare's analysis of the experience. "Services integration seldom reduces
costs in the short term . . . Services integration at the delivery level most often
requires shared information systems that are often expensive."[34] Sheldon Gans and
William Horton conclude their analysis of 30 coordination projects with this
statement: "Although there are some cost savings resulting from economies of
scale and reduction of duplication, they do not appear (at least in the short run) to
equal the input costs of administrative and core service staff required to support
integrative efforts."[35] Most administators claim that these are short-run increases
with long-run decreases to follow, but there is little evidence that direct long-run
financial benefits ever materialize. Analysis of coordination efforts over a long
period of time in the areas of mental retardation[36] and child care[37] have shown
no significant changes in efficiency. But, as Meld notes, it may be unfair to draw
definitive conclusions on this point in the context of overall retrenchment in social
service outlays and programs in many countries.[38]

Costs provide a direct measure of the impact of a coordination program, but
evaluating change in the continuity, comprehensiveness, or quality of services reaching the client is far more difficult. Self-reports of client satisfaction with services are
generally agreed to be an inadequate representation of quality, and this is especially
the case when children are the clients. There is no adequate way to evaluate the
effects of coordination programs on service delivery. Research has so far not produced any systematic data to show that coordination makes a difference to the
well-being of the client. Anecdotal and impressionistic accounts of service integration and coordination projects show mixed results. A few projects claim to have
had some positive impact; many admit that impact seems to be minimal. Depending
on who does the reporting (i.e., proponents or opponents of the coordination plan
or neutral outsiders), the same story may be told in different ways; and the lack of
hard data makes it difficult to judge the relative merits of the competing versions.
But the sense of the literature is that few coordination projects have made an
important contribution to client well-being. It has proven much more difficult than
was generally anticipated to change the ways in which services are delivered to
clients at the local level.

CONCLUSIONS

I have argued thus far that many diverse and not wholly consistent forces inspire the advocacy of coordination. These forces do not translate neatly or easily into practice; in fact, some of them cannot even be captured effectively in words. As a result, we frequently adopt policies and programs with little relevance to our initial concerns. The inevitable result is that the coordination programs we launch seldom satisfy our purposes. The logic of this argument suggests several ways for policymakers to avoid this grim progression.

It is not always possible, nor is it strictly necessary, for would-be coordinators to understand the true sources or motives of their plea for coordination. What does seem to matter is that policymakers agree on what is to be coordinated. "Coordination" by itself is too vague to be a guiding principle for action. As we have shown, people want coordination for a variety of reasons, to address a motley set of needs. Reforms promoting coordination do not want the same thing when they ask for coordination. Choices must be made. Policies and programs must aim at improving some specific coordinative strategies (by client group, service function, geographic area) even at the potential cost of less coordination somewhere else. Policies inevitably fail if they try to be all things to all people. When the multiple objectives of all relevant constituencies are negotiated into a focused, limited set of purposes, planners and administrators are in a much better position to create workable programs with appropriate targets.

Embedded in this last suggestion is a second recommendation: that policymakers take seriously the claims of multiple participants in the delivery of services. This means that policies should accommodate the political and organizational milieu of services delivery and include provisions for responding to the needs of client, community, and interest groups with a stake in the efficacy of those services. Only through the mobilization of the joint efforts of several constituencies can sufficient energy be summoned to overcome the inertia and potential opposition to change in a complex system of services.

My final admonition in this unromantic guide to coordination reform is to be skeptical about the ultimate effects of better coordination. There are numerous avenues for reforming services, and many have no coordination element at all. These should not be neglected simply because coordination may happen to be in fashion. Coordination, as I have tried to argue, can be a useful, but limited, remedy. Experience with efforts to promote coordination to date has not been overly encouraging, and there appear to be many compelling reasons why this has been so. I do not mean to deny the obvious fact that some efforts to promote coordination are sensible and that many programs could perform better than they have thus far if they were more effectively integrated or coordinated with other efforts to achieve similar aims. I do mean to suggest that coordination has been, and continues to be, oversold. At this point the most productive strategy may be to determine the circumstances under which the goals of high-quality, cost-effective services can and cannot be achieved by this type of reform.

NOTES AND REFERENCES

1. Gilbert Y. Steiner, with Pauline H. Milius, *The Children's Cause.* Washington, D.C.: Brookings Institution, 1976.
2. Arnstein Finset, "Childhood Policies, Local Coordination, and Citizen Participation." Unpublished paper prepared for the Center for Educational Research and Innovation/OECD. Paris: Organization for Economic Cooperation and Development (OECD), 1978.
3. Steiner, Op. cit.
4. Barbara N. Rodgers, John Greve, and John S. Morgan, *Comparative Social Administration* (rev. ed.). London: Allen & Unwin, 1971.
5. Ibid.
6. I do not intend to suggest that "hot and cold" modes of knowing are mutually exclusive. I present them here as a rough dichotomy, but they may shade into each other, and each into other modes of cognition as well.
7. Martha Baum and Alan Coleman, *Research for the Allegheny County Human Services Bureau: Findings from the Community/Client Surveys.* Pittsburgh: Social Research Associates, July 1976.
8. Alberto Melo, "The Under-fives and the Corporate System of Coventry." In *Intersectoral Educational Planning.* Paris: OECD, 1977.
9. Harold Seidman, *Politics, Position, and Power.* New York: Oxford University Press, 1970.
10. Sidney Gardner, "Roles for General Purpose Governments in Services Integration." In *Project SHARE. Human Services Monograph Series,* 1976, No. 2, p. 27.
11. Seidman, Op. cit. P. 14.
12. Laurence E. Lynn, Jr., "Organizing Human Services in Florida." *Evaluation,* 1976, *3,* 58–78.
13. See Murry Edelman, *Political Languages: Words That Succeed and Policies That Fail.* New York: Academic Press, 1977. Pp. 26–29. The symbolic appeal of coordination is frequently powerful. An extended analysis of the causes and consequences of this potency may be found in Janet A. Weiss, "Coordination of Human Services: Substance vs. Symbol of Reform." Working paper 805. New Haven, Conn.: Yale University, Institution of Social and Policy Studies, 1978.
14. Philadelphia Alliance of Specialized Mental Health Agencies, "Mental Health and Mental Retardation Workshops." Philadelphia, 1978 (mimeographed).
15. Martin Rein, "Decentralization and Citizen Participation in Social Services." *Public Administration Review,* 1972, *3,* 687–700.
16. Gary D. Brewer and James S. Kakalik, *Handicapped Children: Strategies for Improving Services.* New York: McGraw-Hill, 1979.
17. Gardner, Op. cit.
18. American Society for Public Administration (ASPA), *Human Services Integration.* Washington, D.C.: ASPA, 1974.

19. Charles E. Lindblom, *The Intelligence of Democracy.* New York: Free Press, 1965.
20. Michael Aiken, Robert Dewar, Nancy DiTomaso, Jerald Hage, and Gerald Zeitz, *Coordinating Human Services.* San Francisco: Jossey-Bass, 1975.
21. Baum and Coleman, Op. cit.
22. Anne-Marie Foltz, "The Development of Ambiguous Federal Policy: Early and Periodic Screening, Diagnosis and Treatment." *Milbank Memorial Fund Quarterly,* 1975, *53*, 35–64.
23. Alan M. Orenstein, "Chapter 766: The Massachusetts Special Needs Law." Unpublished. Paris: OECD, 1976.
24. Sheldon P. Gans and Gerald T. Horton, *Integration of Human Services.* New York: Praeger, 1975; Robert E. Quinn, "The Impacts of a Computerized Information System on the Integration and Coordination of Human Services." *Public Administration Review,* 1976, *36*, 166–74; Douglas G. Montgomery, "Strengthening a National Network on Aging to Serve the Elderly." In *Human Resource Administration.* Washington, D.C.: American Society for Public Administration, 1976.
25. American Society for Public Administration, Op. cit.; William A. Lucas, Karen Heald, and Mary Vogel, *Census of Local Services Integration, 1975.* Santa Monica, Calif: Rand Corporation, December 1975.
26. Douglas Henton, "The Feasibility of Services Integration." Department of Health, Education, and Welfare Interagency Services Integration R&D Task Force, 1975. Washington, D.C.: DHEW (photocopy).
27. Gans and Horton, Op. cit.
28. Lucas, Heald, and Vogel, Op. cit.
29. Stephen T. Fitzsimmons, Abt Associates, Inc., *A Study of the Neighborhood Center Pilot Program.* Vol. 1. *Summary B, Prepared for the Executive Office of the President, Bureau of the Budget.* Washington, D.C.: U.S. Government Printing Office, 1969. Pp. 27–29.
30. Adrian L. Webb, "Coordination between Health and Personal Social Services: A Question of Quality." *Eurosocial Reports,* 1975, No. 4.
31. Martin Landau, "Redundancy, Rationality, and the Problem of Duplication and Overlap." *Public Administration Review,* 1969, *29*(4), 346–58.
32. Roland L. Warren, "Alternative Strategies of Inter-Agency Planning." In Paul E. White and George J. Vlasak, eds., *Interorganizational Research in Health.* Washington, D.C.: National Center for Health Services, 1970.
33. Murray Meld, "Human Services Integration: Toward a Humanistic Approach." *The Social Welfare Forum, 1976* (Proceedings of the National Conference on Social Welfare). New York: Columbia University Press, 1976. Pp. 101–103.
34. William A. Morrill, "Services Integration and the Department of Health, Education, and Welfare." *Evaluation,* 1976, *3*, 52–57.
35. Gans and Horton, Op. cit. P. 48.
36. Aiken et al., Op. cit.
37. Steiner, Op. cit.
38. Meld, Op. cit.

Chapter 5

The Design of In-kind Benefits

This chapter will focus on those public benefits that fall between services provided directly by government and the distribution of cash grants. These in-kind benefits pose challenging design questions.

At an abstract level, we can identify two critical design questions of design: (1) To what extent should policy involve a mix of unrestricted cash grants and in-kind benefits? (2) To what extent should policy combine income-tested benefits and universal entitlement? Let us consider each in turn.

When a new program is designed, we either make available earmarked services, such as education, medical care, or public housing, or we provide cash to purchase these and other goods and services.[1] At any point in time, however, we have a mix of both. These cash or in-kind benefits can be distributed to all citizens or residents of the society on the basis of universal entitlement or selectively to those in economic need according to some accepted criterion of need. The concept of need restricts entitlement to low-income families by establishing several levels of family income to serve as a standard of eligibility for families of different sizes and compositions. There are clearly many other rules for distinguishing eligible from noneligible groups. When we make use of the dichotomy between universal and selective, the term *selective* means that economic factors (income and/or assets) serve as a test of eligibility.[2]

Policy analysts assume that these dichotomies are conceptually interesting and administratively useful in designing programs. They then set out to provide intellectual arguments for and against each choice. Superficially, these choices seem clear and self-evident. In practice, however, all kinds of ambiguities emerge at the boundary separating these programmatic forms. It is seldom simply a matter of choosing between cash or in-kind benefits; rather, there is a "continuum of transfers ranging from unrestricted cash, cash with advice, earmarked vouchers, in-kind provision, and finally, compulsion."[3] When we examine the actual net receipt of resources and give our attention to one aspect of this question, namely, selectivity by income testing, we find that this principle can be thought of either at the point of consumption, in the allocation of expenditures (who gets what), or at the point of financing, where the role of taxation becomes critical (i.e., who pays for it). Viewed from this perspective, all programs are income tested at either the taxation or consumption expenditure level; but they can be antagonistic or complementary. They are antagonistic when selectivity on the consumption side is undone by other programs in the system. (For example, a program that subsidizes the families of university students also taxes the same families to cover the cost of the subsidy.) They are complementary when they reinforce each other.

Even when we agree to restrict our discussion to the expenditure side, we find more than a simple dichotomy between universal entitlement and income testing. There are at least three different principles of distribution. Benefits can be distributed neutrally with regard to income (allowances for children are an example); they can be distributed positively in relation to income, i.e., the more you earn, the more you get (this is the principle on which wage-replacement insurance principles rest); or they can be distributed negatively in relation to income, i.e., the less you have, the more you get (this is the principle on which welfare-type programs are based).

These complications are, of course, recognized by everyone who has seriously thought about the design of income-support programs. My particular purpose is to identify three circumstances in which the policy dichotomies of cash versus in-kind benefits and universality versus selectivity become most meaningful. The first is when the choices are embedded in the economic and political context in which decisions are taken, that is to say, when choices are examined within the context of the institutional events from which they arise; it is futile to search for general rules of program design stripped of their context. The second is when it is recognized that there are many different ways of selecting the population eligible for benefits, so that the specific form of the program as well as the general principle behind it becomes important. Because the different ways in which income-tested programs can be designed have different effects on participation rates and stigma, it is not obvious that it is the principle of selectivity that unifies variations in program form. Third, there is often a sharp discrepancy between theory and practice. This discrepancy is particularly striking—and, I might add, disturbing—when we contrast the intellectual arguments for in-kind benefits (based on theories of purely public goods, merit goods,[4] external benefits to donors) with the practice by policy analysts of assigning a cash value to in-kind benefits in order to determine their contribution to the distribution of real economic well-being. In practice, procedures for assigning cash values to in-kind benefits completely disregard the benefits to donors on which the theory of in-kind benefits so critically depends.

By focusing on *context, form*, and *practice* I shall distinguish between analysis, which tends to be abstract, and real life, which tends to be bound by situations. This approach has implications for the practice of policy analysis, which has neglected the institutional setting in which program design is created.

THE CASE FOR INCOME TESTING

Before examining how context influences decisions on income testing, I shall review the general case for income testing of benefits. I have already suggested that in practice we make use of a continuum of in-kind benefits and that the dichotomy between cash and services is a stylized simplification of a more complex reality. Housing benefits provide an example of this continuum. At one extreme we find unrestricted cash grants for those below a specified poverty level. On the assumption that rent is a component of living expenses, the value of the grant is computed by estimating the cost of housing. This general welfare grant becomes more restricted when it provides people with an earmarked grant to cover the actual cost of rent as it is incurred. Next on the continuum are rent supplements, which protect people from a housing burden, defined as some ratio of housing cost to total income (usually one quarter). Yet another approach seeks to reduce the cost of the housing unit by subsidies that lower the cost of borrowing money for the builder and thus make the unit less expensive. Finally, we note the use of public regulations that compel people to "consume" a given standard of housing, even if they might prefer cheaper housing of a lower standard. These forms of direct and indirect cash grants to the tenant, landlord, or housing unit can be contrasted with the direct provision of public housing, in which housing aid is viewed as a service.

By implication, the different types of in-kind benefits require different intellectual justifications. I cannot hope to cover here all the programs along the continuum, and will therefore limit my discussion to earmarked or restricted cash transfers that are distributed on the basis of income. Between unrestricted cash grants and public provision of compulsory in-kind benefits (as in the case of presecondary education) we find cash grants allocated for specific purposes, such as housing allowances, university grants, and reimbursements and exemptions for items such as drugs, eyeglasses, dental care, and food. What is the intellectual rationale for these unrestricted cash transfers? There are two general arguments for earmarked and income-tested benefits.

The strongest general case in favor of income testing is equity. The equity case applies in situations in which the per capita value of benefits is greater for higher-income than for low-income groups. In this situation, inequalities in the per capita distribution of services exacerbate the income inequalities of society.

Educational benefits are an example of a benefit that serves the better-off more than it does the poor, since the young in lower-income groups are less likely to secure a university education than those in higher-income groups. The lower participation rates are widespread, and some societies have debated ways to address this problem. For example, in 1978 there was a British proposal, later aborted, to provide educational maintenance grants for students 16–19 years of age attending secondary schools. Proponents of the idea argued that a generous means-tested grant would enable working-class children to continue school and that many more would therefore take the advanced examination (A levels) needed to get into a university.

The second general argument for income-tested benefits is that they can prevent, or compensate people for, undesirable externalities. In a thoughtful paper, Brian Abel-Smith offers some examples in the field of housing.[5] Housing allowances can protect children from having to live in bad housing because their families' incomes are inadequate. The allowances also protect workers in tight markets from exorbitant rents that might force them to relocate to low-rent, job-scarce areas where they would be likely to become unemployed. So important are these and other externalities to society, Abel-Smith argues, that it is legitimate to disregard the use value of the benefits to the consumer. I shall return to this important observation later, in my discussion of the relationship between theory and practice.

Income testing also has disadvantages. These disadvantages became evident in the U.S. Congressional debates about the Family Assistance Plan (FAP), introduced by President Nixon more than a decade ago, in 1970. FAP was designed to encourage welfare recipients to work by permitting them to keep half of the earnings they secured from work. The FAP program by itself had a 50 percent marginal tax rate. But in the crowded policy environment of the 1970s, FAP was only one of many programs. When FAP was considered in combination with the tax rates of other programs (food stamps, 30 percent; public housing, 25 percent; the positive income tax, 14 percent; Social Security, 6 percent; etc.), potential recipients faced a combined marginal tax rate that could exceed 100 percent. This meant that a person who worked would be economically worse off when the value of all the benefits and taxes was taken into account.[6] No politically acceptable solution to this problem was found during the 1970s, although various forms of negative income tax were debated in Congress.

The main problem is that any given income-tested program adds to both the marginal and the cumulative tax rates, thus creating, in principle, problems of work incentives and a sense of unfairness (it is wrong to subject the poor to very marginal tax rates even if this does not affect their willingness to work). We need, therefore, to be extremely cautious about using this potentially egalitarian tool, since redistributive aims can conflict with efficiency and fairness. Abel-Smith has suggested an interesting criterion for deciding which programs should be income tested, namely, that the service be one that everyone uses. In other words, the case for income testing is strongest when the goods and services to be distributed selectively are ones that are universally used. Thus, housing subsidies can serve as a prototype for income testing. By contrast, education at the postsecondary level provides a good example of a program that reaches high-income, but not low-income, groups, i.e., there are vertical inequalities. Since not everyone makes use of advanced education, the program meets only one standard of income testing—that of inequitable distribution, but not that of widespread use. In the case of housing, the two principles—widespread use and unequal distibution—reinforce each other.

It is useful to turn next from general principles to an analysis of experience. A review of data on the per capita distribution of educational expenditures in Britain and in the United States suggests some interesting contrasts. Grants to students at the postsecondary level are distributed in Britain to all students who qualify for advanced education. The size of the grant, however, depends upon parental income— i.e., it is income tested. Before 1977 all students received a minimum award of 50 pounds a year regardless of parental income,[7] and an income-tested supplement was added onto this base. The system produced subsidies that were four times greater for low-income students than for higher-income students.[8]

In the United States, Burton Weisbrod "cashed out" the costs of education in California and then related these costs to the parental income of university students. He found that the children of better-off families got a larger per capita subsidy than those of lower-income families. The main reason for this was that parental income was positively correlated with participation rates (the children of well-off parents were more likely to go to college), staying power (they were more likely to complete their education), and selection (they were more likely to be enrolled in the high-cost sector of both public and private education).[9]

It is not clear whether these data suggest that Britain has a more egalitarian educational subsidy system than the United States. The findings do, however, call attention to two different institutional arrangements for distributing in-kind subsidies—directly to the student, or to the university. Student grants subsidize individual students, permitting them to go to any institution they can get into, without concern for fees and maintenance expenditures. Subsidies to individuals look universal, because all students who are not from abroad get their fees paid and receive a minimum grant; and means testing appears to be egalitarian by concentrating additional resources for full maintenance of those in need. But the situation is more complicated if the number of students in the high-benefit group proves to be quite small. To determine whether this system is egalitarian, we also want to know how the total amount of money spent by government for student aid is distributed to students who come from different income groups. The share of total expenditure by income class might be a more revealing measure of vertical inequalities than per capita benefit.

The choice of a measure of inequality is particularly important because it implies a model of equality. At least three models are relevant. The first is the concept of equality as a means of improving the real welfare level of a whole income class. From this perspective we want to know what percentage of the total class makes use of the benefit and what proportion of the total money they receive. The second concept is equality of opportunity. Here the per capita measure seems important. The underlying rationale for this model is to increase individuals' chances of moving out of their income class, rather than to improve the position of the class as a whole. The idea is to reach those who are "best off" within a class in order to equalize their opportunity to leave the class. The third concept of equality seeks to distribute resources to those who are "worst off" within a given income class. The model is that of compensation for misery and misfortune rather than equalization of opportunity or the reduction of class inequalities. In this concept, the sous-proletariat is the target of reform. This is essentially an "anticreaming" concept of equality.

Discussion of models of equality raises questions about whom income test programs should seek to reach and what the intellectual justification is for wanting to reach any particular group. The discussion above suggests that egalitarian aims can be realized by reaching three quite different groups: the low-income class as a whole, the best-off within an income class, or the worst-off within an income class. Simply focusing on vertical per capita inequalities obscures the target of means-tested programs.

In addition to paying attention to the question of who gets benefits, we need to understand why we want to reach any particular group. The conventional rationale for equalizing subsidies in education and housing is that of investment.[10] We hope that the subsidies will help each person contribute to society his or her maximum potential human capital. Educational subsidies can also contribute to a stable society by encouraging upward mobility across income classes, thereby creating the sense that society is not divided along rigid class lines. When the investment objective is primary, the aim of reducing vertical inequalities becomes subordinate to it, and income-tested programs multiply. For example, children in low-income households are more likely to suffer from poor nutrition than children in other households; this reduces their capacity to study, and investment objectives are therefore threatened because of the strong relationship between poor nutrition and poor learning. One implication of this argument is that we should develop a means-tested school meals program. Indeed, the case for income testing based on an investment argument can lead us to search out all of the negative consequences of low income—poor health, bad housing, etc.—and to justify means testing as necessary to improve human capital. Such meritocratic considerations are more likely to emerge when the aim of public policy is to increase individual productivity.

The argument that income-testing is justified whenever vertical inequalities exist is interesting. But what about the special case when the cost of the service is much higher than the actual user is prepared to pay for it? Let us call this phenomenon "discounting" and have it refer to situations in which people value the service below the actual cost incurred by government in providing the service.[11] The basic argument appears to be that when the goals of investment and subjective use value are in conflict, the principle of investment should override that of the users' preference, because someone besides the individual is also benefiting from these services. But this answer is unsatisfactory for several reasons. There is a considerable amount of cynicism with respect to the distribution of public services and a deep feeling that services are not provided with uniform quality across income classes, that they are not effective in meeting investment aims (however these may be defined), and that people in all the income classes may not be getting their money's worth from the in-kind benefits provided by the government.

The primary justification for discounted benefits is that donors as well as users derive benefits from the services. If this rationale for program intervention is accepted, then the case for in-kind benefits rests on some theory of donor satisfaction. I shall return to this issue later.

THE CONTEXT OF INCOME-TESTED PROGRAMS

It is useful to move from general theory to concrete case. In what follows I shall compare the development of income-tested programs in Sweden and Denmark. My purpose is to show that the institutional context in which programs develop must be taken into account if we are to appreciate why income-tested programs were introduced and if we are to understand what consequences follow from their introduction.

Swedish social policy during the 1960s was heavily biased in favor of rental units.[12] The key tool of equalization was an income-tested housing allowance that reduced the rent burden and protected families from rent increases.[13] Eighty percent of a marginal rent increase was covered by the allowances. Half of all families with children received allowances, and virtually all families with one earner received these benefits, In 1970 the program was extended to all families with children. The value of the benefit varies with the size of the family, the level of rent, and family income. This type of comprehensive income testing seems to be designed to exclude the top of the income distribution rather than to include the bottom.

In 1973 the level of means-tested programs offset the level of tax exemptions to homeowners, creating a situation in which public subsidies between rental and owned units were broadly similar.[14] On a per capita basis, owners received an average of 250 Swedish kroner, while renters received 220 kroner.

Why, then, did Swedish policy turn to income testing? The income-tested housing allowance, which was inspired by the belief that everyone should have access to good-quality housing, was developed largely to correct inequities within the rental sector. Later this aim was further redefined, when the quality of the unit was dropped as a condition of entitlement and the allowance became a general cash subsidy. The active manpower policy, which encouraged geographic mobility to get jobs, created housing shortages in areas of high employment. The housing allowance facilitated the implementation of labor market policy; this, in turn, contributed to the prevention of unemployment. Finally, in the late 1960s, concern about poverty and low income among families with children led to an interest in making child allowances more selective. But there was strong resistance to modifying these universal benefits, and the cost of sharply increasing the benefits seemed prohibitive. An income-tested housing allowance was an alternative to universal children's allowances as a way of reaching low-income families with children. In practice, concern about inequities in the per capita distribution of public subsidies in housing played only a minor role.

Dissatisfaction and restlessness with the housing policy and the feeling that policy should not be biased in favor of home-ownership have been growing since 1975. The housing market seems saturated, and people are dissatisfied with the large suburban rental units. "Specific criticisms were that increasingly the buildings were too high, too close together and too stereotyped in appearance . . . What was being produced . . . was a hard, anonymous and anti-life environment."[15] Since there is virtually no population growth in Sweden, any shift in policy may lead to abandonment of the existing rental units, which would be an enormous waste of resources. It would appear that extensive means testing and a bias toward rental units led to a policy stalemate and a shift in practice. By 1978, single-family homes almost totally dominated new construction.[16] There is now a surplus of flats in high-rise buildings. In this context a possible remedy might be to increase the bias to renters further through an even more generous means-tested housing allowance that would decrease the cost of rental units and compensate renters for the disadvantages of suburban block living.

Danish housing policy, by contrast, provides a clear example of a policy biased in favor of home-ownership. Owners receive a per capita subsidy of 500 Danish kroner; renters receive per capita subsidies of only 60 kroner. At the same time, rent controls were abolished in the 1970s, thus further reinforcing the bias in favor of owners. The bias in favor of home-ownership reinforces the traditional values of the ownership of small property.

In the United States, home-ownership represents a kind of modern Jeffersonian argument. Owners, like farmers, have a stake in the community and thus serve as ballast for political stability. Ownership contributes to the more effective rearing of children by giving children a sense of stability as well as additional space in the home itself. In Danish housing policy, it is the concern for privacy rather than the American celebration of ownership that seems to have played the critical role in the development of the policy.

The review of housing policy in Denmark by Gösta Esping-Andersen[17] suggests that the ownership bias had the effect of undermining the welfare state and producing considerable economic and political disruption. Economically it led to land speculation and the fueling of inflation by the use of productive capital in this non-productive sector. Politically it divided owners and renters and created a strong movement of discontent in the left wing of the Social Democratic group, who are largely renters. To redress the imbalance created by liberal tax incentives to private-home-owners and the elimination of rent controls, a set of compensatory programs was designed in the form mainly of means-tested rent subsidies to lower-income and large families. These subsidies provide a clear example of the intellectual arguments for means testing advanced by Brian Abel-Smith,[18] but intellectual arguments and political realities conflict. Esping-Andersen reports that rising incomes eroded rent subsidies for many families. Rent subsidy policies thus bred frustration more often than satisfaction. During the early 1970s, the pressure on the Social Democrats to adjust the priorities in their housing policy became so intense that they were forced to introduce a bill to reduce the favorable tax advantages accruing to home-owners. The policies backfired because many Social Democrats had acquired their own homes, thanks to the earlier tax-exemption policies, and they were reluctant to relinquish the gains they had achieved. The efforts to introduce more egalitarian policy exacerbated equity politics, in which groups vied to maintain their relative advantage. In brief, the introduction of income-tested programs for renters to redress the vertical inequalities created by tax-exempted home-ownership programs created political polarization, backlash politics, and a movement toward the political Right.

In Sweden, by contrast, concern about quality of housing, about bottlenecks in manpower policies, and about child poverty seemed to inspire the development of an extensive means-tested housing allowance. Policy did not try to equalize per capita inequities in housing subsidies. In this context, income testing and a renters' bias were politically acceptable. But the policies contributed to a new problem—erosion in the quality of the physical environment of suburban high-rise rented apartments.

This review of income-tested housing allowances in Sweden and Denmark suggests the following three general conclusions:

1. Countries turn to income testing for reasons other than a reduction in vertical inequalities and the avoidance of externalities.[19]

2. The introduction of income testing can produce negative side effects. In Sweden it contributed to a decrease in the quality of living; in Denmark, to political polarization.

3. Only partially did these negative reactions depend on the income-tested programs per se. A more critical factor was the emergence of unanticipated events.

THE FORM OF INCOME-TESTING AND UNIVERSAL PROGRAMS

It is, of course, a mistake to assume that the income-tested housing allowance programs in Denmark and Sweden are identical. They differ in important ways in terms of the value of the benefits, the proportion of the population receiving the benefits, and the aggressiveness with which eligible clients have been contacted. There are seven different ways of identifying the differences among income-tested programs. Following this discussion, we shall review the important variations in universal programs.

1. We need to distinguish between income- and means-tested programs. An income-tested program uses only income as a criterion for determining eligibility. By contrast, a means-tested program depends on an extensive assets test. Swedish policy analysts are eager to point out that the program for housing allowances is income tested, not means tested, which suggests that it is more politically acceptable to both taxpayers and recipients than the means-tested welfare program (Social Help). One of the ways in which means-tested programs are liberalized is to reduce assets by a series of "disregards"—that is, some assets, earnings, and income are

not taken into account in determining eligibility. When the "disregards" are very extensive, the practical distinctions between an income test and a means test disappear.

2. The size of the population covered is a critical aspect of an income-tested program. As noted, Swedish housing allowances reach half of all families with children. This contrasts very sharply with welfare-type programs in the United States, which reach less than 10 percent of the population. The extent of coverage is important because it defines the program as a social phenomenon.

3. The value of the benefits in an income-tested program is obviously important. But their value cannot be measured in absolute terms alone: it must also be measured in relation to the income of the family. Housing allowances contribute only a small part of total family income. By contrast, many means-tested programs, such as welfare, account for large proportions of the total family income.

The combination of coverage and generosity gives a program its distinctive character. For example, a program may give "much" to a few people (the American welfare system) or "little" to many people (the Swedish housing allowance).

4. Most income-tested programs use categories of inclusion other than simply income. Perhaps the most important distinctions concern attachment to the labor market. In Britain, the Supplementary Benefits program is available only to people who are out of work. By contrast, the British Family Income Supplement is available only to people who are currently working. Similar distinctions exist in Sweden between mandatory and voluntary social help programs. In brief, then, social categories as well as income categories define the universe of those who are eligible to receive benefits.

5. The extent of discretion is perhaps the most controversial of all features in income-tested programs. Discretion enters income-tested programs in order to achieve the ideal of individualization. At the same time, income-tested programs strive for a degree of uniformity. There is thus a conflict between the goals of individualized need and uniformity of benefits. The exercise of discretion is costly, however, because it takes up a great deal of staff time, is a source of grievance among recipients, and produces glaring inequities in the distribution of benefits. Moreover, it has been the critical focus around which welfare rights organizations have mobilized their efforts. Hence, discretionary grants have contributed to the politicization of income-tested benefits. Income-tested programs differ quite sharply in the extent to which they rely on discretionary grants.

6. Income-tested programs can serve as a general "safety net," providing minimum economic resources that other programs fail to supply. Alternatively, they can be restricted and directed specifically to a single item of consumption, such as education, housing, medical care, or others. Much of the general criticism of income testing is centered on general rather than specific income programs, though general programs also have specific features. In many welfare programs, for example, housing costs are paid as they are incurred; and this is, in effect, a restricted program within a general program.

7. Sometimes, general income-tested programs serve as automatic "passports" to

entitlement for specific income-tested programs. For instance, a person who receives Supplementary Benefits in Britain is automatically also entitled to get free prescriptions, milk and vitamins, dental treatment and glasses, school meals, and transportation to hospitals. The income-tested programs secured through the "passport" route have participation rates of 70 to 80 percent. By contrast, specific or earmarked income-tested programs that require a separate eligibility review often have disturbingly low participation rates.

We cannot assume that all universal programs are similar. In fact, most universal programs are not universal at all, but are confined to broad social categories of eligibility based on factors other than income. In most universal programs, citizenship or residence serves as a category of restriction. For example, in Britain, in order to be eligible to receive a serious and expensive surgical intervention, some form of residence must be established. But because emergency medical care is free on demand to both nonresidents and noncitizens, the British Health Service comes closest to the ideal of a universal program, though it is only general practitioner services that are free on demand, access to specialist services being available only on referral by a general practitioner.

Consider next the case of universal Child Benefits, which are available to all children under 16 in Great Britain, but are also selectively available to those 16 to 19 years of age who are full-time students. The selective Child Benefits are designed primarily to relieve the economic burden of parents who keep their children in school. Child Benefits in these age groups are unequally distributed when compared with the universe of all children: only 58 percent of 16-year-olds, 28 percent of 17-year-olds, and 10 percent of 18-year-olds receive Child Benefits. It is reasonable to speculate that these "universal" educational benefits are more likely to go to the children of higher-income families than to those in low-income families. In this sense universalism reinforces income inequalities.

In brief, then, it is a mistake to make a simple distinction between income-tested and universal programs. We also need to take account of the form of the particular program. Issues of design are critical in determining the political acceptability, economic costs, and social consequences of the development of each of these types of program.

ANALYSIS OF IN-KIND BENEFITS IN PRACTICE

When we leave the subject of earmarked cash benefits and the various forms of income testing and universal benefits, we confront what is perhaps the most controversial of all the issues in the design of income-support programs: in-kind benefits. In the United States, no matter what intellectual arguments have been advanced in support of unrestricted cash grants, expenditures for in-kind benefits have, in fact, grown at a more rapid rate and account for a large proportion of total social welfare expenditures. I believe that the critical question in the analysis of in-kind benefits is the problem of "discounting": how to take into account the fact that people value services at less than their actual cost to the public.

A number of empirical studies in the public sector have shown that the recipients of in-kind benefits value these benefits at less than the cost to the provider. In a study of public housing in the United States, Eugene Smolensky and J. Douglas Gomery identify two approaches to this issue: "The value approach views the subsidy from the tenant's side with the benefits valued by the tenant's taste and income. The resources cost approach takes the taxpayer's perspective and the market's appraisal of the product."[20] Although each of the two approaches seems valid, each gives us a different estimate of the value of public housing to be allocated to the individual user. These authors offer two broad conclusions: first, that taxpayers are spending $65 per unit per month to provide a subsidy that the tenants value at $27 a month, i.e., the subsidy exceeds the value to the tenant by $38; second, that it follows that the benefits to those who are not tenants exceed the benefits to tenants by $11 per unit per month ($38 − $27). Such paradoxical findings are, of course, very sensitive to the assumptions that are made, but they do not identify the nature of the problem.

There have been other efforts to estimate the difference between the direct costs of services and in-kind transfers and their cash value to the recipient. The cash value to clients of in-kind benefits for food, housing, and medical care has been estimated by Timothy Smeeding[21] to average about 70 percent of market value. In other words, when we discount the actual cost of in-kind benefits according to how people actually value the services, we are left with a "dead loss" of 30 percent. If we accept the theory of public goods and merit goods, we must assume that these in-kind benefits have considerable value to the donors of these services as well as to the direct beneficiaries.

The problem of discounting is complicated not only because of methodological difficulties but also because those who pay taxes and those who receive benefits are different people. We therefore cannot simply equate the burden of paying taxes and the privilege of receiving benefits. In everyday life, then, the policies of taxation and the policies of redistribution are separate.

To appreciate the seriousness of the "cashing out" problem, we need to understand the political consequences of this technical issue. Conservative economists such as Edgar Browning[22] have tried to demonstrate that the distribution of family income is much more equitable in the United States than is popularly believed. Whereas the Census reports that the lowest quintile in 1972 received 5.4 percent of all money income, Browning estimates that, when in-kind benefits are taken into account, this group gets 12.5 percent of "net income." Moreover, he claims that the share of the lowest quintile increased by two-thirds between 1952 and 1972. By contrast, most other studies of inequality have concluded that there have been virtually no changes in income structure in the post-World War II period.

Morton Paglin summarizes the argument as follows: "The reason that official poverty statistics show little decline in the last decade is simply that they are inadequate in measuring the real improvement which has in fact taken place in low-income households."[23] What is left out of the picture in the official definition of poverty in terms of money is in-kind benefits programs such as food stamps, Medicaid, rent supplements, public housing, etc. "Their exclusion results in a gross distortion of the poverty problem." Paglin concludes that if in-kind benefits were taken into account, in 1975 only 3 percent of the population would have been classified as poor, compared with the Census estimate of 12 percent. By 1980, according to Paglin's procedure for "cashing out," there would be almost no poverty in the United States.

Economists at the University of Wisconsin[24] have criticized Browning's and Paglin's work on methodological grounds. One of the important bases of their criticisms is the failure to discount, i.e., to take account of the difference between cost and value. Discounting and other methodological refinements show that the percentage increase in the income shares going to the bottom quintile was only half as large as Browning claimed. But even with this refinement, it is clear that, when in-kind benefits are cashed out, there has been a substantial reduction in the extent of poverty and income inequality over time. In any case, adjusting costs to correspond more closely to how the recipients value services does not solve the problem of how to treat the "dead loss" discounting produces.

While American scholars have been concerned with the problem of the disparity between cost and value of in-kind benefits, the British have been much more preoccupied with refining measures of the actual use of in-kind benefits and services. Writing in 1965, R. Leonard Nicholson called attention to the fact that estimates of the values of benefits allocated to households "would be improved if we had more information than we possess at present about such matters as the extent to which different households make use of the various health services [and] the benefits which individual households derive from housing subsidies."[25]

But the problem is still more complicated. In my earlier discussion of services, I pointed out that the value of in-kind transfers and services may lie not only in the direct use of these services but in their potential use. Thus, a person may value medical services very highly even if he or she never uses them in the course of a year; the value derives from the likelihood that if he or she becomes ill, these services will be available to him or her. Commenting on this problem, the British Royal Commission on the Distribution of Income and Wealth gloomily observes, "Where the value of the service lies partly in its ready availability and partly in the actual use made of it, there is no agreed method of valuing the benefits."[26]

An American study of in-kind benefits reaches much the same conclusion. It argues, "Unless it is absolutely required in a particular income distribution application, therefore, it seems best not to add together the measures of money income and in-kind income, no matter what valuation principle is used."[27]

Another problem that cashing-out procedures must face is the treatment of services designed to change an individual's human capital. Here the distinction between current and future welfare is critical. It does not make much sense to assign a monetary value to educational benefits and add it to a person's income, because the person cannot "consume" these benefits directly in his or her annual household budget. Education has a value in the future as well as in the present. Hence, efforts to assign a cash value to services must address the difficult question of how to treat benefits that "pay off" over a long time. Some analysts respond to this problem by making estimates in which education is both included and excluded in their definition of net income, i.e., two sets of estimates are made, one with, and the other without, education as a factor.

Both the British and the American procedures for cashing out in-kind benefits fail to take into account the value of the benefits to donors. As we have seen, the British method is to allocate current costs to individuals on the basis of age, sex, and use of programs; the Americans attempt to cash out in-kind programs as a way of measuring their effectiveness in reducing poverty. In this respect, it appears that the theory of public goods and the theory of externalities are unrelated to the actual empirical studies carried out by economists. The analytic and the theoretical work are divorced from each other. Admittedly, there are practical reasons for the problem, among them the difficulty of translating theory into practice. If the rewards to donors were acknowledged, the evidence supporting a backlash would need to be reinterpreted; the data would instead suggest an expansionist welfare state, a cycle of benign reinforcement. Of course, the problem is more complicated. Some give freely, and others feel that they are being "done in" by being forced to give. It is this conflict among donors that shapes our social program and gives it its special complexity.

Politically, the problem has been defined as one of overload and backlash. When the discount rate is high, is there a risk that a vicious cycle will (or has) set in, in which (1) taxpayers feel overwhelmed by their burden; (2) service recipients feel aggrieved because they place little value on the services received; and (3) analysts inform the society that it is corrupt because, despite high public expenditures, benefits accruing to those at the bottom of the income scale are deemed slight?

In summary, I have tried to highlight briefly some of the conceptual and methodological difficulties involved in cashing out. Many believe that the problem is intractable. Analysts who hold this view argue that it is a mistake to attempt to cash out such benefits because they are qualitatively of a different order from cash benefits. Those who take this position believe that the distribution of in-kind benefits can be better approached by a set of social indicators that measure patterns of use, quality of services, specific situations, and problematic conditions.

I believe that, despite the obvious difficulties in cashing out, efforts to do so will persist, because allocation decisions among the three kinds of benefits must be made by governments. Economists recognize that it is not possible, in principle, to make interpersonal comparisons of utility; nevertheless, social policy requires such measures, even if they are conceptually impossible.

Analysis of policy tends to be on an abstract level, emphasizing the dichotomy between universal and income-tested programs and between cash and in-kind benefits. I have argued that the analysis of program design requires that it be embedded in a context, that attention be given to the complexities of form, and that practice be related to theory. An analysis stripped of context and situation cannot provide answers to the design problems faced in real life. On the other hand, efforts to ground program design in the details of experience inhibit the capacity to develop general rules. Experience, however, does provide guidelines for understanding when general rules should be violated and when they make sense. The intellectual challenge we face is how to join abstract analysis and program design.

NOTES AND REFERENCES

1. One economist equates in-kind transfers with price subsidies and cash transfers with income subsidies. Jack Wiseman, "The Economics of Subsidies: Some Taxonomic and Analytic Problems." York, England: Institute of Social and Economic Research, University of York. Reprint Series, No. 256, p. 456.
2. When assets are included in the test of eligibility, the term *means test* is conventionally used. An income test, by contrast, relies only on current income as the criterion of eligibility. The distinction is, however, more important in European income-support schemes than in those in the United States, where assets tests are more common.
3. Lester C. Thurow, "Government Expenditures: Cash or In-kind Aid?" In Gerald Dworkin, G. Bermant, and P. Brown, eds., *Markets and Morals*. New York: Wiley, 1977. P. 98.
4. There is some disagreement about the usefulness of this distinction, but a public good generally refers to those goods that are not divisible and have to be enjoyed by everyone, such as clean air. A merit good can be consumed by individuals,but it is a good for the collectivity to a greater degree than is appreciated by the direct recipients of it, as in the case of education.

   The case for the public provision of purely public goods exists when "exclusion is impossible... consumption is non-rival. My neighbor's enjoyment... does not subtract from my enjoyment... [and] identical amounts must be consumed" (Thurow, Op. cit. P. 86). This argument is not convincing in the case of social welfare. The model applies most clearly to national defense, not to social welfare expenditures, in which services are not a public monopoly, but are sold in the market and distributed for fees and without cost in both the private and the nonprofit voluntary sector. Indeed, the history of social welfare is a history of the efforts by voluntary agencies to prevent a takeover by government. In particular, private social workers in the Charity Organization Society (COS) believed that it could provide a substitute for government authority and thus promote individual responsibility for protection against economic adversity. The Community Chest movement, which flourished in the United States during the 1920s, was inspired by the idea that voluntarism could substitute for government programs. In practice, the idea proved faulty, because COS and the Community Chests were never able to provide adequate services even in good times; and, of course, they collapsed altogether during periods of economic recession, when they were needed most. (For a discussion of these issues, see Roy Lubove, *The Struggle for Social Security*

1900–1936. Cambridge, Mass.: Harvard University Press, 1968.) The introduction of public social welfare programs had essentially nothing to do with the theory of purely public good.

5. Brian Abel-Smith, "Services in Kind." In Irwin Garfinkel, ed., *Income-tested Transfer Programs: The Case For and Against*. Madison, Wis.: Institute for Research on Poverty, 1982.

6. For an informed discussion, see Larry L. Orr and Felicity Skidmore, "Poverty Research Institute." Madison, Wis.: University of Wisconsin, March 1980 (mimeographed).

7. Since 1977 three important policies have been introduced: (1) The minimum award has been raised from 50 to 200 pounds. (2) University fees are automatically paid for all British students, whereas foreign students must pay tuition fees, which have been substantially raised. (3) The marginal tax rate on the parental means test at the higher income levels has been reduced to offset the loss of tax exemptions for students that resulted from the elimination of the tax exemption and the creation of the new Child Benefit scheme.

8. Students whose parental income represents 75 percent of the average earnings of male manual workers receive, on average, a maintenance grant, after the parental contribution has been taken into account, of 1,100 pounds. In contrast, students with parental incomes of 300 percent of the average earnings of male manual workers receive an average maintenance grant of 233 pounds. Parliamentary Debates. *Hansard*, 14 December 1978, p. 50.

9. Joseph Pechman has criticized Burton Weisbrod's findings for his failure to take into account the system of financing the educational subsidies. When taxes are taken into account, Pechman finds that the subsidies well-off families receive are offset by the taxes they pay. The striking pattern of vertical inequality and the value of subsidies to well-off families disappears when both tax and benefits are taken into account. Of course, Pechman's findings depend on the critical assumption that all income classes pay an equal proportion of tax for education. Since the tax is not earmarked, there is no way of testing this assumption. For this exchange, see: Lee Hansen and Burton Weisbrod, "The Distribution of Cost and Direct Benefits of Public Higher Education: The Case of California." *Journal of Human Resources*, 1969, *4*(2), 176–91; Joseph Pechman, "The Distribution Effects of Public Higher Education in California." *Journal of Human Resources*, 1970, *5*(3), 361–70; Lee Hansen and Burton Weisbrod, "On the Distribution of Costs and Benefits of Public Higher Education: Reply." *Journal of Human Resources*, 1971, *6*(3), 363–74; Joseph Pechman, "The Distribution of Costs and Benefits of Public Higher Education: Further Comments." *Journal of Human Resources*, 1971, *6*(3), 375–76.

10. There are other rationales based on the principles of consumption, compensation, and fairness. The individual rather than society is seen as the primary beneficiary of public intervention.

11. Most economists use the concept of discounting to refer to time delays. I do not intend that the concept refer to time, but rather to subjective use value.

12. The example is drawn from a report by Gösta Esping-Andersen, "Social Class, Social Democracy, and the State." *Comparative Politics*, October 1978, pp. 42–58. I have also profited enormously from several extended discussions with the author.

13. The Swedish Housing Allowance program does have an assets test based on the value of the home. Thus, the program is, in fact, a means-tested rather than an income-tested one. Wealth in excess of 75,000 kroner is added to income. Since the assets limit is set relatively high, this justifies referring to it as an income-tested program.

14. Even if there were no bias on the expenditure of the output side, there might be bias on the input of the financing side. To the extent that the financing is progressive, the net bias favors renters.

15. Åke Dairn, "Why Do Swedish Suburbs Look the Way They Do?" *Human Environment in Sweden*, 1979, No. 9 (February), p. 8.

16. It is interesting to note that no society seems to apply a means test to exemptions for housing allowances. This would, in effect, be a policy of giving more tax exemptions to lower earners than to higher earners.

17. Esping-Andersen, Op. cit.

18. Abel-Smith, Op. cit.

19. In Britain, the case of housing allowances (rent and rent rebates) was justified largely on the grounds that the universal subsidies for public housing, which produced low rents, was too costly. When government reduced housing subsidies and rents increased, low-income groups experienced hardships. It was not politically acceptable to let the poor suffer the consequences of raising rents without some program to protect them. The rationale for income testing was the political necessity of protecting the consumption of the poor when general subsidies were removed. It had much less to do with the broader arguments about per capita inequalities in the distribution of housing benefits.

20. Eugene Smolensky and J. Douglas Gomery, "Efficiency and Equity Effects in the Benefits from the Federal Housing Program in 1965." *Joint Economic Committee, 92nd Congress, 2nd Session*. Washington, D.C.: U.S. Government Printing Office, January 1973. P. 147.

21. For a discussion of these issues, see Timothy N. Smeeding, "The Trend toward Equality and the Distribution of Net Income: A Reexamination of Data and Methodology." Madison, Wis.: Institute for Research on Poverty, December 1977.

22. Edgar Browning, *Redistribution in the Welfare System*. Washington, D.C.: American Enterprise Institute, 1975.

23. Morton Paglin, "Poverty in the United States: A Reevaluation." *Policy Review*, Spring 1979, pp. 8–9.

24. For example, Timothy Smeeding and Sheldon Danzinger (University of Wisconsin) have criticized the way in-kind benefits and services have been cashed out, i.e., assigned a monetary value. Timothy Smeeding, "Valuing Government Expenditures: The Case of Medical Care, Transfers, and Poverty," in *Review of Income and Wealth*, September 1980, pp. 281–300; Timothy Smeeding, "Alternative Methods for Valuing Selected In-kind Transfer Payments" (U.S. Bureau of the Census, Technical Paper No. 50). Washington, D.C.: U.S. Government Printing Office, April 1982; and Sheldon Danzinger and Robert Plotnick, *Has the War on Poverty Been Won?* Madison, Wis.: University of Wisconsin Press (in preparation).

25. R. Leonard Nicholson, "The Distribution of Personal Income." *Lloyd Bank*

Review, January 1967 (this is a publication of Lloyd Bank in London, England).

26. Royal Commission on the Distribution of Income and Wealth, *Report No. 4, 2nd Report of the Standing Reference*. Comnd. 6626. London: HMSO, October 1976. P. 26.

27. Gershon Cooper and Arnold J. Katz, "The Cash Equivalent of In-kind Income." Stamford, Conn.: Cooper and Company, December 1977 (mimeographed).

Chapter 6

Value Tensions
in Program Design

In this chapter I shall identify: (1) the main elements that
enter into the design of an income-support program; (2) the
conflicts and dilemmas that arise when program elements interact; and (3) the broader context of events, purposes, ideas, and
structures that give these elements meaning and influence
choice. Similar value tensions arise whether we are dealing
with a means-tested program, in which economic need determines eligibility, or a non-means-tested program, in which the
eligible population may be defined in terms of medical status
(sickness benefits), geographic area (inner city), age (children
or the elderly), dependence status (wives, widows, children),
race (special program for Indians), occupation (farmers), or
industry (maritime subsidies), or the funds may be earmarked
for consumption of a particular type (transportation, food,
housing, education, medical care, etc.). The crucial questions
concern who (eligible population) gets what (benefit level and
form), how (administrative structure), and at what cost
(method of financing). These are the abiding issues that apply
to every program.

My discussion focuses primarily on developing a framework for examining value conflicts in program design.[1] The
analysis is limited to one program area—means-tested income-
support programs, a controversial method of intervention with
a long history about which much has been written. The salient
feature of this income-support program is that the eligible population is selected because it is presumed to be in economic
need. Some means-tested programs are concerned with general

consumption (unrestricted welfare programs); others, with targeted consumption, for example, subsidized housing, food, or medical care. Consumer choice is, in the latter case, restricted in order to promote earmarked consumption.

This discussion of the elements and objectives of program design emphasizes tension, options, and constraints with regard to values; it does not deal explicitly with the choices actually made by society at a particular time. To deal theoretically with the question of which choices are actually made would require social, economic, political, and cultural theories of preferences and priorities that are not currently available. My discussion therefore covers only a small part of a broader theory of program design. My aim is to try to develop a model that will help us understand which alternatives will be preferred by social decision-makers.

ELEMENTS AND OBJECTIVES OF PROGRAM DESIGN

Every program must first specify: (1) an eligible group; (2) the type and level of the proposed benefit; and, therefore, implicitly, if not explicitly, (3) a level of total expenditures. As an initial approximation, a program is defined by a particular combination of these elements; thus, each specification of the eligible group, the form of benefit (e.g., cash versus in-kind), and the level of benefits results in a different "program."

This simple definition of a program creates an obvious value tension between the aim of minimizing total cost and the aim of maximizing the benefits to those for whom they are intended. That governments seek to reduce cost while increasing benefits is an axiom in public policy. It obviously says nothing specifically, however, about how these conflicting aims can be realized. Providing "adequate" benefits to those in need and keeping budgetary costs low present a conflict in objectives that requires some sacrifice in one or both. Available analytic models cannot readily predict the complete political trade-offs that are accepted to reconcile these conflicting aims. These models ignore the question of who chooses, i.e., the provider, the client, or the Congressional Appropriations Committee, with its allocative and oversight roles. The best that can be done is to specify some of the kinds of choices that must be made and to estimate (often crudely) the "price" to be paid for each choice. But the ideas and events that influence the choice made are also important if we are to avoid an overly rational interpretation of why programs take the form they do.

The assertion that it is better to have a program do the same thing at a lower rather than a higher level of expenditure makes sense so long as we are dealing with economic axioms about efficiency rather than with political and bureaucratic axioms. Once these requirements have been taken into account, action is governed not only by what is good for the public interest or for the client but also by what is good for the politician and the bureaucrat. Here we are dealing not just with the traditional problem of goal displacement but with the issue of what the goals of action are and how these substantive goals can be separated from symbolic actions.

For example, congressmen want to know how Head Start expenditures are spread geographically as well as something about reading scores. Obviously, reading scores have to do with outcomes in a nonbureaucratic sense, whereas the geographic spread of expenditures is clearly an important political and economic objective. It is naive to pay attention to the former goal and ignore the latter. But to accept both goals is to obscure the differences between the substantive and the symbolic.

Thus far I have mentioned only two conflicting policy objectives: (1) minimizing budgetary cost, and (2) maximizing benefits, i.e., doing the most at the least cost. Two further conflicting objectives need to be made explicit: whether benefits should actually go to *all* persons who are eligible, or *only* to eligible persons.[2] I call this conflict of entitlement the inclusion and exclusion dilemma—the more attractive the program, the more likely it is to include not only those defined as eligible but those it prefers to exclude as well. I regard this conflict as one of the central and most critical value conflicts in program design.

It is deeply disturbing to discover that deliberate efforts to exclude ineligible people also prevent us from reaching those we want to include, because we value both objectives. It is inevitable, however, that every act of inclusion, i.e., every attempt to establish criteria of eligibility, is an act of exclusion, because all programs are categorical in some sense. For example, in Britain, nonresident children of workers from European Economic Community (EEC) countries receive child benefits (called family allowances before 1975) because of a reciprocal agreement among EEC countries, but nonresident children from India and Pakistan are excluded. The boundary defining the children who are to be included or excluded, when interpreted as a system of stratification by race, raises a very sensitive political issue.

Because the inclusion–exclusion value conflict is so important in income-support policy, I want to elaborate on the dilemma in some detail. First, we need to sharpen the distinction between those for whom the program is intended and those for whom it is not. Technical "ineligibility" applies only to persons who by error or fraud receive benefits to which they are not legally entitled. Frequently more important, however, are two other groups that are not among those for whom the program was designed.

One group discovers inadvertently that its circumstances permit it to receive benefits, although the program may not have been intended for it. The early controversy about students' applications for food stamps is a case in point: students meet the income test of eligibility, although the program was, presumably, not designed as an educational subsidy. This situation can be remedied by redefining the eligible population; but each such redefinition is likely to have its own undesired side effects, among them inadvertent inclusion of undesired persons, exclusion of desired persons, or enforcement costs.

The second group involves people who actively alter their behavior—that is, voluntarily redefine their personal characteristics—in order to qualify for benefits. Thus, for example, if a program is designed for the poor, the unemployed, or female heads of families, people may technically qualify as eligible by reducing the number of hours they work or altering their family structure. In general, the availability of a subsidy establishes unintended—and undesired—incentives to alter behavior, which, in turn, heightens public interest in enforcement and consequently affects participation rates. Because subsidies can affect future behavior as well as respond to present needs, the total cost of a program needs to be understood from two viewpoints—the direct budgetary outlay, and the real, but nonbudgetary, indirect costs that arise because of unintended incentive effects. For example, if an income-based program influences some people to work less in order to qualify for the program (even though the program was not intended to have this influence), then the total output of the economy will be reduced, and there will be a transfer of purchasing power from taxpayers to the people coming into the program.

The conflict of entitlement is typically measured by a rate of *under*utilization and a rate of *over*utilization. Rates of under- and overutilization are themselves functions of the level of benefits—that is, the higher the level of benefits, the greater the incentive for eligible persons to apply for, and incur the costs associated with, program participation and, similarly, the greater the incentive for ineligible persons to falsify statements so as to obtain the benefits. Thus, an inherent conflict exists in program selection, since an increase in benefit level is likely to decrease *under*utilization among eligible persons—a change that is presumably regarded as desirable—while simultaneously increasing *over*utilization among noneligibles—a change that is generally regarded as not desirable.

One response to this conflict is to adopt stricter enforcement procedures, to screen out people not in "need" while publicizing entitlement for those who are eligible. Such a "solution," however, presents three other sets of conflicts that help to create the inclusion—exclusion dilemma.

1. The "tighter" the enforcement procedures, the greater the extent to which eligible as well as ineligible persons will be deterred from applying. In general, the greater the "costs" that an applicant must incur—whether involving more elaborate application forms, closer scrutiny of personal behavior, or being subject to demeaning, stigmatizing treatment—the smaller will be the number of persons, eligible or ineligible, who are likely to seek participation. Such behavior simply illustrates the usual negative elasticity of demand with respect to cost.

2. The more successful the efforts to publicize entitlement, the greater will be the extent to which ineligible as well as eligible persons will learn about the program and seek to obtain the available benefits.

3. The more money spent on enforcement and publicity, other things being equal, the greater must be the total budgetary cost of the program,[3] or (if this cost is held constant) the lower must be the level of benefits, or the more narrowly defined must be the eligible group.

In other words, the inclusion—exclusion dilemma arises because as sensitivity (participation rate) increases, specificity (the proportion of users who are eligible) declines. It is the twin goals of a high capture rate and a low error rate that are in conflict.

The sensitivity and specificity indexes derive from an interaction of two attributes: status as a user, and status as an eligible person. From these two attributes it is possible to develop a 2 × 2 table. In the columns of the table we would have users and nonusers, and in the rows of the table, eligibles and noneligibles. The sensitivity ratio deals with the pool of current recipients and expresses the fraction of current users who are eligible for the benefits they receive. By contrast, specificity measures what proportion of eligible people receive the benefits to which they are entitled. This measure deals with the pool of users and expresses the fraction of eligible clients who become users. The fourth cell refers to the group that is neither eligible nor users. This group does not concern us.

In brief, then, I assume that for any given level of need, the more attractive the program is (high benefits and low enforcement), the lower the specificity and the higher the sensitivity will be. The opposite is also true: the less attractive the program (low benefits and high enforcement), the greater the specificity and the lower the sensitivity will be, as it will become increasingly difficult to persuade eligible people to make use of the program.

How can we deal with this dilemma? Let us assume that sensitivity and specificity are determined by only three variables: (1) direct expenditures for families (benefit level), (2) administrative or screening costs (the cost of enforcement and information), (3) the level of "need" in the population (eligible population, assuming that "need" or eligibility can be operationally defined. This can be a very troublesome problem because of the phenomenon of self-made or manufactured eligibility: people alter personal circumstances, e.g., a husband deserts his family so his wife can become eligible for benefits.).

If we change the benefit levels but leave screening processes and qualifying needs unchanged, then sensitivity rises and specificity declines. If we change the screening process, we can affect the levels of both sensitivity and specificity, but still not alter the basic dilemma. If we broaden the definition—for example, by eliminating income as a measure of entitlement (the so-called universal approach versus the selective)—while keeping the screening process and the benefit level unchanged, we increase the cost and thus return to our first dilemma of how to maximize benefits while minimizing costs.

Thomas Willemain examines the problem of the trade-off between sensitivity and specificity in the field of nursing homes.[4] Health planners believe that the greater the number of beds made available in nursing homes, the lower will be the level of specificity. They reach this conclusion because they accept the hypothesis that when the supply of hospital beds becomes inflated, the beds are filled by people who do not need hospital care.[5] According to this hypothesis, if we provide twice as many beds, we do not satisfy twice as much need, but instead have a more wasteful use of beds. This argument that demand responds to available supply has been widely accepted with respect to long-term care. But Willemain believes that the assumption is wrong, that it is plausible that the supply of nursing-home beds is a response to the level of "need" and that the more beds there are, the more possible it is to increase specificity, i.e., to reach those in need.

What, then, is the counterpart argument in the area of income support? In general, we can say that as we extend the reach of a program, we pick up both people who do not need the service (ineligibles) and those who need it (eligibles). There are two views of how the process of ordering, screening, and "gatekeeping" works. One view assumes that the neediest get the service first. Then, as the program expands, the less needy increasingly make use of the available resources. Another view sees the gatekeeping role working in reverse: the most needy are the least likely to receive benefits, because they lack skill in overcoming the administrative obstacles to access. Nevertheless, as the scope of the program increases, they, too, are eventually included.

Willemain's model assumes that, in nursing homes, the first to be admitted are those most in need. But this assumption may be wrong: the screening process may operate perversely, first creaming off those who are relatively the least needy. As suggested above, the condition of the client and the operation of the gatekeeping process may act either to reinforce each other (reaching those most in need first) or to nullify each other (creaming off those least in need). Both theories of the screening process recognize that a program reaches both those it was intended to serve and those it was not intended to serve.

Such value tensions and conflicts exist in every program. The next section will provide a vocabulary for discussing these value issues.

Earlier, I defined a program as a specification of an eligible population and a level of benefits. The addition of two more objectives necessitates redefining an income-support program to include the following elements: (1) an eligible population, (2) a level of benefits, (3) the proportion of those in need served, and (4) the proportion of those not in need served. The inclusion of the last two points suggests that we again redefine and expand the dimensions of an income-support program, adding the following to the previous four elements: (5) total enforcement costs to exclude those not in need, and (6) total information-entitlement costs to include those in need. Specification of these six elements not only identifies a program but also determines the total budgetary outlay for the program (element 7).

The foregoing discussion of how value conflicts arise suggests that any income-support measure can be considered not only as a list of elements but as a system of elements, inasmuch as each element relates to others in some regular way. The elements can also be pictured in a hierarchy of relationships. These are, of course, analytic categories; and policymakers often make their decisions by deliberately or unconsciously concentrating on only a few elements. The decisions as to who gets what, and how, may be called *first-order decisions*. (The term *order* does not imply a decreasing level of importance.) These, in turn, result in *second-order features* of utilization, including: intended eligibles (participation of the original target population); ineligibles (fraudulent cases); unintended eligibles (those inadvertently qualifying for benefits); and self-made eligibles (those changing behavior or circumstances in order to qualify). Together these groups produce underutilization of benefits by eligible people and overutilization by ineligible recipients. Over- and underutilization, which can occur simultaneously, are considered second-order features because they depend on the primary program elements: eligibility, form and level of benefits, and the mix of information, dissemination, and enforcement efforts.[6]

The *third-order effects* can be defined as the total costs of the program expressed in social and dollar terms. Some of the indirect costs will be generated when potential recipients alter their behavior in order to qualify for the program or as a consequence of the program benefits. Their actions, in turn, generate reactions from administrators, from the nonrecipient public, and from others who deal with recipients.

A MODEL OF THE MAIN ELEMENTS IN THE
DESIGN OF AN INCOME-SUPPORT PROGRAM

The three orders contain seven main elements of an income-support program. The pattern of their interrelationship can be specified in more formal terms by means of the following formula:[7]

$$C = B (aP + N) + E + I,$$

in which C = total budgetary cost for the program, including indirect costs such as disincentives to work (cost can be expressed in absolute terms [dollar amounts] and relative terms [as a proportion of total expenditures]; absolute costs can increase while relative costs remain stable or decline[8]); B = the average level of benefits, including income not taken into account in determining benefits (disregards) and earning retention provisions (expressed in dollars per person); a = percentage of eligible persons who participate in the program (the take-up or participation rate); P = number of persons (units) eligible for benefits; N = number of technically ineligible persons who become participants; (aP + N) = the size and composition of those currently receiving benefits; E = total expenditures on enforcement and the structure of its administration; and I = total expenditures on information and the structure of its administration.

The model is *descriptive* (an accounting system in relation to financial cost, and a scheme that identifies the major substantive issues of policy), *simultaneous* (explains the interaction among the variables and how changes in one variable affect changes in the others), and strategic (most of the variables are subject to manipulation).[9] The model is additive; it shows how knowing the magnitude of some variables makes it possible to determine others. It does not show how the functions themselves change over time; the model captures only static contingencies.[10]

The dynamic and strategic uses of the model will be stressed in this analysis. It should be noted that some of the seven program elements in the equation are direct instruments of policy whereas others are not. Elements C, B, P, E, and I are all directly controllable; but a and N depend on the values of the other elements (see discussion below). C may be set initially as an independent element, but it then affects, and in turn is affected by, the values of the other elements. Thus, the potential program choice is varied. For example, a program may be designed broadly for all low-income families or may be confined to families headed by females. Eligibility, benefit levels, enforcement, and informational costs may be such that benefits may be open to many, but reach few, or open to a few, but reach most or all of the more limited group.

As I have indicated above, a number of interactions occur among the six variables on the right-hand side of the equation, but the variable on the left, C, can affect the variables on the right. All these elements of a program are relevant to efforts to cope with the inclusion—exclusion dilemma, but each element can also be treated as proper, the other elements serving as means to its realization. Let us consider four examples.

The first example can be expressed as follows: a = (B, I, E). Higher benefits and higher information, considered apart from other factors, will probably encourage increased participation. Higher benefits make the program more worth acquiring and hence bring increased participation. More information makes the benefits more accessible to claimants, and would probably bring increased participation from both the eligible and the ineligible populations.

Higher benefits may also be accompanied by higher enforcement, and hence the net effect on participation rates will depend on the relative impact of each on the participation decisions of potential claimants. Greater enforcement, by making it more difficult for the applicants to secure benefits, may cause decreased participation by not only the ineligible but also the eligible populations. The concept of stigma is often invoked to explain the process that an individual experiences when enforcement is high.[11]

The second example refers to financing the costs of the program. The structure of financing can influence program administration. For example, in the public assistance program, the federal government makes matching grants to the states. From the beginning of the program, the amounts of the funds were related to the states' fiscal capacity; but more recently they have been used to influence variables such as B, E, and I. Department of Health and Human Services (HHS) regulations calling for a proportionate loss in federal matching grants for states that do not curb their ineligibility rates provide a case in point.

The third example further refines the benefits in the model. The mean level of benefits available to program participants does not distinguish between the programs in which the same benefit is available to all participants and those in which benefits vary with certain characteristics of the participants, such as their "need," or "means," or work effort. A variable benefit level that provides different amounts to individuals according to their circumstances is likely to bring increased costs for enforcement and administration because decisions must be made not only on whether a particular person is eligible but also on the level of benefits for which he or she is eligible. Because a variable benefit tends to lead to greater enforcement costs, it may also be more stigmatizing[12] and thus, in principle, decrease utilization, both among persons for whom the program is not intended and among those for whom it is intended. On the other hand, variable benefits also increase the grant levels that some individuals secure, and this makes the program more attractive to these potential claimants.

In the fourth example we consider how the efforts to alter information costs increase utilization among the target population. For example, extensive efforts were made to inform potential beneficiaries about the new federal Supplemental Security Income (SSI) program for the aged, blind, and disabled.[13] It is interesting to speculate whether enforcement decreases when information efforts increase. Two outcomes seem plausible. First, that a take-up campaign, such as SSI Alert, will attract ineligible as well as eligible people, and that increased attention to screening out the ineligible should, in principle, accompany efforts at recruitment. The second view holds that policy moves in cycles and that when high informational costs are politically acceptable, a liberal orientation prevails. Such a perspective tends also to be accompanied by less concern for enforcement, on the assumption that a preoccupation with enforcement will increase stigma and decrease participation rates. There is some evidence that SSI has adopted the first option; it is obliged by law to pay attention to information, and it is obliged by administrative policy to increase enforcement costs vigorously. Of course, it also matters whether the benefit is to be "permanent" (e.g., SSI) or is meant to be "temporary" (unemployment compensation).

These interactions among variables raise more basic issues about the overall purpose of a particular program. Without attempting to be exhaustive, I shall review some of the value issues that arise when alternative program elements are grouped together.

NORMATIVE OPTIONS

When program elements may be joined, two normative options emerge—one focusing on holding expenditures down to some acceptable level, and the other, on completeness and adequacy of coverage. We can (1) minimize cost, thus minimizing overuse, and also minimize universal categories of eligibility, benefits, and information while maximizing selective categories, conditions, benefits, and enforcement, or (2) maximize adequacy, thus minimizing underuse, maximize coverage and information, and minimize conditions and enforcement stigma.[14]

Both options represent the kind of interrelationship of choices that traditional debates have considered basic in income-support programs: the first is popularly known as the "conservative" approach, and the second, as the "liberal" one. The first option concentrates on variables C, N, P, and E; its main emphasis is on selectivity, efficiency, and stringency. The second option clusters about a different combination of elements, those emphasizing adequacy, coverage, eligibility, and access. Here elements B, a, P, and I are given prominence.

Note that P appears in both options, but in each it is given a quite different role. In the first option, the eligible population is limited to social subgroups whose behavior is associated with negative moral overtones, for example, a program restricted to unwed mothers. In the second case, there is a commitment to morally positive categories. A universal or broad definition of P creates a category of eligibles whose characteristics approach those of the whole population. There are often ways of defining P so as to have wide appeal to users, providers, politicians, and the general public.

These clusters of interactions may create unintended incentive effects on the cost side of the model. For example, the decision to provide a subsidy for persons with low wages (Family Income Supplement in Britain and Family Assistance Plan in the United States) raises questions about the strength of the work-incentive effects. Because the size of these effects is largely unknown, the definition of the eligible group is generally accompanied by much controversy. To some extent these effects show up in utilization rates, but more is involved. For example, as previously noted, if an income-based program influences some people to work less in order to qualify for the program (even though the program was not intended to do this), then, at least theoretically, the total output of the economy will be reduced, and there will be a transfer of purchasing power from taxpayers to the people coming into the program.

The problem of how to reduce disincentives yet increase participation poses a dilemma in the design of income-support programs and, moreover, raises the question whether the task is intractable in the sense that no "satisfactory" trade-offs are stable over time. Dilemmas and intractability may be the essential issues in the design of an income-support program. It therefore seems important to examine systematically what a dilemma is and to identify some of the most common ones that arise in designing a program.

DILEMMAS IN INCOME-SUPPORT PROGRAMS

If program design has to do with strategies of coping with value dilemmas, it is important to specify clearly what a dilemma is. A dilemma arises only when there are multiple aims. With only one aim there may still be an insoluble problem if no means exist to achieve an acceptable degree of satisfaction of that aim, but the problem is not a dilemma until two or more goals or values are pursued and none of the courses of action available can adequately fulfill all the goals. In other words, satisfying one goal or value may inhibit achievement of another at some specified level. Intractability occurs when the second goal cannot be forsaken or the acceptable level redefined; hence, every means for a stable resolution is unacceptable.

A dilemma in logic arises when there is a logical inconsistency between propositions. A program or action dilemma takes a somewhat weaker form because it is about incompatibilities within the ranges of acceptable achievement of each goal. A tacit dilemma can be inferred from major cyclical changes in the value of program elements. An example of this would be a period in which benefits kept up with wages followed by a period in which inflation eroded the value of the benefits and the administrative focus was on stringency, reduction, error, and abuse. Dilemmas are therefore about limits and elasticities among variables in an area of conflicting values.

One way to cope with a dilemma is to specify other ranges of acceptable behavior with regard to the values sought. Redefining limits may enable the conflict of values to disappear. Whether the goals are incompatible within a specified range of acceptable behavior in a given situation is an empirical question.

A concrete example may be useful here. If people's rights to benefits are subject to a minimum of discretion by officials, they are likely to be clearly understood and accurately administered. Take-up rates can rise because more claimants apply, and sensitivity increases. But this precludes more complex systems that might provide help more exactly (and, perhaps, more economically) tailored to people's needs. Important in the minds of many officials who administer income-support programs is the fear that publicity for benefits will attract claimants who have to be turned away because they are ineligible. This happened, for example, in Britain when "Exceptional Circumstances Additions" for heating costs were widely advertised and, as a result, offices were swamped with requests for heating subsidies. The bureaucracy tries to avoid this kind of situation, presumably because it is considered politically damaging.

To convert a conflict into a dilemma requires a specification of limits—the levels set are arbitrary, but they do correspond to implicit standards of political acceptability. Policymakers may want an 85 percent take-up rate (the goal set in Britain for an effective participation rate in its Family Income Supplement Program) and no more than a 3 percent ineligibility rate and a 5 percent level for overpayments to eligible persons (the goals established in the United States for effective quality control of its public assistance programs).[15]

It is now an empirical question whether, with minimizing costs as a goal, progress in achieving the desired take-up rate undermines achievement of the goal of limiting overpayments and the number of those ineligible who receive benefits. Assuming that a conflict in these values at these levels does exist, there is a creative solution to the dilemma; and intractability can be avoided if it is possible to alter the values so as to allow all of them to be realized at an acceptable, but not at an optimum, level. If, however, legislators cannot, or will not, specify the range of acceptable performance with respect to both values, i.e., rates of ineligibility (error) and participation, no design dilemma is evident.

What appears to happen in practice is that when the political and economic context changes, sensitivity or specificity emerges as a program objective. As indicated above, federal regulations in the United States have specified tolerance levels for ineligibility and overpayment, but there is no public policy that declares what are acceptable participation rates. In this situation the dilemma can only be sensed, not identified in any concrete and measurable way. To bring the dilemma to the surface, participation levels must be set along with the ineligibility levels; and to determine how severe the conflict of aims is, it is necessary to measure the effect that a change in one value produces on other values.

The quality-control program initiated in 1973 by the U. S. Department of Health, Education, and Welfare (HEW) to limit error in the welfare program focused almost exclusively on payment errors, defined as receipt of benefits by ineligible persons or recipients' receiving overpayments of benefits, and administrative errors arising from failure to follow a prescribed procedure, such as checking bank accounts or filing Social Security numbers. Underpayment and denial of aid to those who were eligible were not defined as official errors. This policy was inspired by a desire to reduce costs, and justification for it was based on an interpretation of the federal fiscal responsibility for reimbursing states for approximately half of the expenditures made in conformity to the official state plan. "The federal government took the position that it was only concerned with the validity of it payments, not with the quality of the overall program or its adherence to other aspects of state plan or federal regulations."[16]

In 1976, administrative guidelines were developed by HEW to withhold federal financial participation in welfare programs when erroneous payment to recipients exceeded the prescribed tolerance level of 3 percent of overpayments to ineligible and 5 percent of overpayment to eligible recipients. But the legality of the sanctions was challenged in the courts. The U.S. District Court in the District of Columbia ruled that the tolerance levels were invalid because they were arrived at "in an arbitrary and capricious manner" and were therefore "an abuse of discretion."[17] The court decision, however, was concerned only with the procedure for arriving at a nonarbitrary threshold for error rates to be used as the standard for acceptable practice: if HEW had made use of a less arbitrary procedure, the levels set would have been legally valid. The court did not address the design dilemma of how to achieve nonarbitrary procedures for dealing with the trade-off between error and participation rates.

New legislation and regulations were issued following the court ruling. States are expected to reduce error rates to 4 percent by September 1982 or they will lose federal matching funds for errors above this target.[18]

Trade-off relationships cannot be identified when there are no specified acceptable ranges, stable over time, between two goals that are potentially in conflict. In this situation it is necessary to treat the problem as a tacit action dilemma, which is very typical in public welfare policy. When policy swings from one goal to another, or when there are paralysis and inaction, then it can be inferred that a tacit dilemma exists.

Some of the major dilemmas in this model arise between direct costs and adequacy of benefits, adequacy and acceptability (to those who are not program participants), adequacy of work incentives and indirect costs, and participation and ineligibility. The existence of these dilemmas suggests that the difficulties in welfare reform (altering the elements of the program design) are not simply the result of willful politicians' refusing to follow enlightened advice from academics and other experts. Expert advice has usually confirmed the fact that inherent contradictions plague the very subject matter of welfare reform. Seemingly sensible aims that are in themselves accepted as self-evident—to provide adequate subsistence benefits, to encourage work, and to contain total costs—are difficult to reconcile when combined in the designing of a program. And these conflicts of purpose are constant concerns in program design and program change.

Income-support programs and the problems of their design change over time, not just because people, when faced with a real dilemma that they can perceive, disagree about the urgency of the problem or the best way to resolve it but also because no one knows what the "real" relationships are among elements in program design—that is, what the trade offs are among changes in the levels of benefits, enforcement, participation, and cost. I do not wish to imply that changes come only from empirical ignorance: they come from shifts in societal goals as well.

THE INTERPLAY OF ELEMENTS AND CONTEXT

The discussion thus far has focused only on the elements or variables in the model, their interactions, and the dilemmas they pose for the design of an income-support system. But the model is also embedded in a context of forces that influence the values assigned to the elements of design and, indeed, the model as a whole. To avoid a static and mechanical picture of elements, it is important to place them in the context of ideas, in the organizational and policy environment, in the state of technology, and, finally, in the informal social system. These contextual elements have been selected because they are closest to the design model under discussion. It seems clear, however, that these four features of context must be viewed as elements in the broader context of the economy, the policy, the society, and the cultural system. This is simply to say that programs cannot be designed in isolation from the society of which they are a part.

In general, this theory must be acknowledged as a model of "economic man," with the attendant assumptions of individualistic, materialistic, market behavior designed to optimize utility. The dynamic aspects of the model are founded on assumptions such as the presumed effects of changes in benefits on participation rates and behavior (for example, on marital status and the number of children) and the effects of changing enforcement procedures or information requirements on ineligibility. Whether such assumptions are valid depends significantly on the context in which the program and its potential and actual recipients are situated. The contextual dimensions that affect the basic assumptions of the model include: ideas about acceptable behavior; the formal and informal arrangements that produce economic aid (the family and kinship system and the labor market); the level of technology available to carry out enforcement, to acquire information about eligibility, and to distribute benefits; and, finally, the policy environment, in particular how crowded the environment is with other social programs that directly or indirectly affect entitlement to, and the level of, income support.

A full analysis of the interplay between context and elements would require a specification of the ways in which the context gives meaning to the elements of the model or changes their dynamic relationship. Although such an elaboration of the link between the model and the context is beyond the scope of this paper, the accompanying diagram is a preliminary step toward a more systematic analysis.

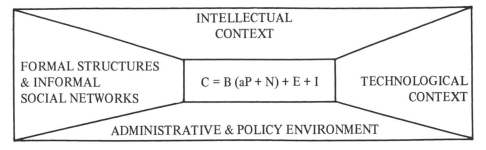

$$C = B \, (aP + N) + E + I$$

FORMAL STRUCTURES & INFORMAL SOCIAL NETWORKS

INTELLECTUAL CONTEXT

TECHNOLOGICAL CONTEXT

ADMINISTRATIVE & POLICY ENVIRONMENT

The intellectual context provides the ideal and the ideologies that become compelling enough to influence both the form and the values that the variables in the model take. Currently accepted ideas can best be understood as a protest against previously accepted points of view. In this sense, ideas in good currency are part of a dialectical process, reactive to views held earlier and proactive to visions of social improvement. In income support we find examples of changing views about how benefit levels and benefit structures can fulfill the aims of adequate support and strong work incentives.

The distinctive feature is not the linear development of these objectives, but the difficulty of abandoning competing views that are in partial conflict. Hence, policy oscillates between competing norms designed to assure that people do not starve in the midst of plenty and that the incentive to work is not eroded by the guarantee of help. Consequently, programs swing between a concern for minimizing work disincentives for the low-paid but employed worker and maximizing work incentives for those in receipt of public aid who are only marginal to the labor force. Income-support programs thus cannot be understood in isolation from the intellectual context of dominant ideas and their dialectical development.

The administrative and policy environment sets the elements of design in a historical and organizational context. The organizational context identifies the pattern of administration and the sources of funding. Although our model considers the cost of a program, it does not specify how the cost is met or the share of funds received from federal, state, and local governments. An income-support program may be administered by the federal government through its regional offices, as in the case of the SSI program, through state governments and the regional offices accountable to them, by local government directly, or by a combination of all these administrations. Income support in the United States is administered through all three of these approaches. The level of administration matters, because the delegation of responsibility also requires an elaborate system of accountability. There is much slippage in the system, leading to periods of stringency in administration, followed by eras of laxity.

It is necessary in understanding the adequacy and latent disincentives of a program not only to take account of the pattern of administration of the income-support program that is the focus of concern but also to pay attention to the other income-tested programs of which it is a part. Thus, a cash assistance program must be understood in relation to other programs, such as food stamps, Medicaid, and public housing. Knowledge of related programs is important in any effort to design or redesign the elements of a single program. The recent interest in income-tested programs arises from two different programmatic preferences. Both views are concerned about severe work disincentives, but one favors a universal program such as children's allowances, whereas the other view holds that work disincentives arise from a proliferation of uncoordinated means testing and that, therefore, a single, unified, means test, such as the negative income tax, is needed.

Technology involves the advance of scientific knowledge and its translation into technological innovations. These can influence the ways in which a program is administered. Computers, for example, make possible a system that can integrate cash grants with the wage and tax system, automatically alter benefits to meet price changes, etc. The existence of this technology increases administrative options. The strategies chosen for coping with problems of ineligibility are shaped partly by the technology available to identify clients. For example, photo-identification cards have been used as a way of reducing fraud.

Informal social networks have to do with the ways in which individuals and families render services similar to those government provides. There is an informal system by which relatives aid their kin and friends help each other in periods of economic distress. The establishment of a public program to provide income support influences this informal pattern of intrafamilial and interneighbor transfers. Income-support policies have been very sensitive to the existence of this informal sector and have only slowly moved to relieve relatives of their customary responsibility for providing financial aid.

These four features of context—the intellectual, the technological, the organizational and policy environment, and the informal social network and formal structures——all affect each other. In addition, each is part of a broader system used to describe our society. The wider questions of context become important as we become sensitive to how changes in them affect the design of social programs. Very little systematic work has been done in explicating this interplay between program elements and contextual elements, despite its obvious importance in program design.

CONCLUSION

One of the main points of this chapter is that the design of a program must be viewed within the context of four "fuzzy" areas (the social, the technological, the administrative, and the intellectual) that are themselves a constant subject of change or controversy. Hence, flexibility and incrementalism must be important elements in the analytical thinking that goes into design.

A "systems analysis" or "math programming" approach sets up the problem in formal terms: selecting E, I, and B levels that lead to minimizing the (weighted) sum of costs, C, subject to the constraints that identify the relationship between E,

I, and B and the a and N results. But this technical approach to design does not address the problem of the changing context in which the problem is viewed.

The formulation of the design problem can be construed as involving such a rich variety of important goals, effects, and behavioral relationships that attempts to structure the problem of choice in a well-defined, simplified model for which there are optimal solutions are misleading. The context is much richer than is suggested by systems analysis attempts to characterize it in an optimal choice context.

Although it is possible to express the descriptive model of value tensions strictly in terms of dollars, this is inherently unsatisfying because we want to treat expenditures on goats differently from expenditures on sheep. At some point we must interpret the total budgetary cost in terms of some set of values. We must envision a weighting of the costs to yield a net social benefit, but it is not clear how concern about "lost sheep" is to be weighted.

The main lesson I want to draw from this review of value tensions is that technical analysis cannot resolve the value dilemmas in program design. I believe a purely technical analysis inadvertently masks these dilemmas by favoring a design focused on either sensitivity or specificity. Both approaches are needed. But broadening the perspective exacerbates the value questions and complicates the analyses.

I have tried to further understanding of why technical solutions remain problematic and how these difficulties can be usefully characterized as a question of how best to formulate the nature of the problem. Problem setting precedes problem solving. By focusing on the nature of value tensions and the lessons from history and practice on how they have been addressed, we can better appreciate the value foundations on which program design rests.

NOTES AND REFERENCES

1. The model used here was developed with the help of Burton Weisbrod, who applied it to the analysis of health issues. See Ralph. L. Andreano and Burton A. Weisbrod, *American Health Policy*. Chicago: Rand McNally, 1974. Pp. 45–46. Hugh Heclo suggested how the model could be further specified. Tom Willemain, Don Schon, and Mike Miller offered critical comments on an earlier draft.
2. These two criteria were first set forth by Burton A. Weisbrod, who termed them, respectively, horizontal and vertical target efficiency. See his "Collective Action and the Distribution of Income: A Conceptual Approach." In Joint Economic Committee, U. S. Congress, *The Analysis and Evaluation of Public Expenditures: the PPB System*. Washington, D.C.: U.S. Government Printing Office, 1969. Vol. I, pp. 177–97. The concepts of target efficiency—vertical and horizontal—are discussed on pp. 184–87.
3. Implicit in the above proposition is the notion that total costs should be as low as possible. But there are factors that also operate to force a program above a minimum budget: the program is a source of employment; and there is a desire to demonstrate, symbolically, charity and compassion to those who are economically worse off.

4. His more optimistic view is discussed in Thomas Willemain, "A Model for Certification of Need for Long-term Care Beds." *Health Services Research*, 1977, *12*(4), 296–406.
5. Martin S. Feldstein, *Economic Analysis for Health Service Efficiency*. Chicago: Markham, 1968. Chap. 7.
6. This point raises conceptual problems. Should the process of carrying out the program, i.e., second-order aspects that deal with questions of implementation, be treated as ancillary, conceptually and analytically, to the first-order decisions, which define the program in terms of who gets what? Perhaps the issue is one of whether processes and outcome are considered more important than structure.
7. This was developed with Burton Weisbrod, as was the understanding of interrelationships among the variables that are discussed above and are discussed further in the following pages.
8. For a fuller discussion, see Martin Rein and Hugh Heclo, "Which Welfare Crisis?" *Public Interest*, 1973, No. 33.
9. Many administrative issues, such as vertical relations between levels of government, horizontal relations with other programs, public–private auspices, etc., are not explicitly dealt with in the model, however.
10. A trend analysis can be introduced by placing the subscript (t) under each of the variables, so that comparisons among different time periods can be integrated in the model. To keep the model simple, however, the time dimension has been omitted.
11. For a discussion of the economics of stigma, see Burton Weisbrod, "On the Stigma Effect and the Demand for Welfare Programs: A Theoretical Note." Unpublished paper, Institute for Research on Poverty, University of Wisconsin–Madison, DP82-70, November 1970.
12. Weisbrod, Ibid.
13. "Getting the SSI Program Underway." *Commission Bulletin* (Social Security Administration), No. 136, August 14, 1973, p. 4.
14. These clusters are only suggestive; there are other options. For example, we can set out to maximize adequacy without maximizing coverage by focusing on improving the position of present recipients.
15. For a discussion and critique, see: Comptroller General of the United States, *Better Management Information Can Be Obtained from the Quality Control System Used in the Aid to Families with Dependent Children Program* (HRD-80-80). Washington, D.C.: U.S. Government Printing Office, July 18, 1980. P. 4.
16. Michael Lipsky, "Prospectus for a Paper on Quality Control and Social Policies." Cambridge, Mass.: MIT, July 15, 1980 (mimeographed). P. 6.
17. State of Maryland v. F. David Mathew. United States District Court, District of Columbia. May 14, 1976. *415 Federal Supplement*. P. 1214.
18. Comptroller General of the United States, Op. cit.

Chapter 7

Implementation: A Theoretical Perspective

BETWEEN INTENT AND ACTION

In the past, social scientists interested in public policy directed their attention to the ways in which policies develop. More recently, they have concentrated on determining whether policies actually accomplish what they are intended to accomplish. They are therefore investing a good deal of intellectual capital in the problem of how to evaluate the outcomes of governmental actions. But between the inputs and the outputs there lies a terrain that is still fairly unexplored: the question of how policies change as they are translated from administrative guidelines into practice. This chapter is about that process, what I call "the politics of implementation."

I do not intend to propose a theory, but to develop a perspective. Practitioners—those who carry out policy—have accumulated whatever wisdom on implementation exists; but the advice they offer and receive is incomplete and often inconsistent. Thus, "Implementers are often faced, on crucial matters, with principles leading to divergent alternatives and inadequate information (and understanding) to choose among them."[1]

In my perspective on the processes of implementation I intend not only to sum up existing experience but to provide a framework for understanding such departures from legislative intent as became apparent to the people who were charged with evaluating the social legislation of the 1960s. The "nothing works" interpretation of governmental intervention that arose from such evaluations led many observers to conclude that the scope of government should be reduced because government lacks the capacity to translate its lofty ideas into effective programs of action. Such an indictment may be too sweeping; indeed, the liberal response to this assault is that some programs judged to have failed may never have been tried at all.[2] Attending to the implementation process permits us to consider the point at which intent gets translated into action and where and why slippage and reformulation occur. Our purposes for doing this are both practical and theoretical: we hope to delineate the imperatives of the implementation process in such a way that they can be taken into account during the formulation of new policies. Then, perhaps, we can avoid the appearance of impotence that seems now to haunt us.

IMPLEMENTATION AND DEMOCRATIC THEORY

Some of the ways in which we can approach an inquiry about implementation involve a theory about democracy. Central to this theory is the question "Which actor dominates in the relationship among those who shape and implement governmental policies?" The traditional approach takes as its starting point the need to develop ways to assure that the activities of subordinates in a hierarchically organized institution comply with directives from their leaders. Herbert Kaufman, for example, writes, "Democracy . . . presupposes that changing a handful of officials in high places will ultimately change the action of thousands of employees throughout the system . . . subordinate compliance is a pillar of democratic government."[3]

Kaufman's anxiety about the problem of compliance is so fundamental to the development of an implementation perspective that we need to explicate further the normative principles on which it rests. For example, the citizen as voter is assumed to provide the ultimate authority over the production of public goods, the priorities for expenditure, and the principles according to which this largesse is distributed. Just as the individual controls the political system, he also controls the economic system through the principle of consumer sovereignty: "These economic and political theories are basic to a larger image of a democratic . . . society which is comprehensively subordinate to the ultimate power of the individual. The individual being in charge, he cannot be in conflict with the economic or political system. He cannot be in conflict with what he commands."[4] Because laws are best understood as an expression of citizen will, bureaucratic compliance with legislative intent is morally justified and deemed necessary. Accordingly, when subordinates fail to follow a legislative mandate, the foundations of democracy are seen to be threatened.

If, however, the political system and the economy do not rest securely on citizens' preferences, as expressed democratically through voting or through preferences in an open market, then a different perspective about implementation emerges. Here we find competing interests at play, within an atmosphere of give-and-take and conciliation. In fact, this view holds that the public never really plays a primary role in implementation even when the society is democratic. The public lacks the single, unified interest that can be translated directly into voting power or policy directives. Organized interest groups do function; but they, too, take positions that do not wholly correspond to the views of their aggregated constituents. Moreover, interest leaders themselves tend to become self-serving over time; they begin to maximize survival and organizational expansion. (This problem of noncompliance is the opposite of that posited by Kaufman: how to get elected leaders to comply with what their members wish, rather than how to get subordinates to comply with the rules their leaders set.) This implementation context then becomes a sort of arena in which the contending views of different interest groups are engaged. But again, the differences are worked out in the course of a dialogue that represents the positions of the legislators, administrators, and managers. They, in turn, do not precisely represent the contending views of the different interest groups for which they supposedly speak.

Yet another view incorporates the notion of competing interests, but it assigns a more prominent role to executive initiative. An executive (president, governor, or mayor) responds to both constituent public opinion and the management and resource problems he encounters in the performance of his job. His role in management is the most important game he plays, for in playing it he raises issues that are not in the public view. This forces the executive to generate new policies; he can no longer merely respond to what the public prefers. In this context public opinion assumes a different role: the public can either permit or prohibit, but it cannot direct. According to this interpretation, administrative practice does not simply follow policy initiatives set by leaders in response to public opinion mediated by pressure or interest groups.

I posit a different view about implementation, one that emphasizes the interrelationship between the process and the product rather than the roles of the different actors who dominate in a competitive field. Policy and administration, by their nature, are continuously comingled. Purposes are redefined at each stage of the implementation process.

In this view, implementation is a continuation of the political process in another arena. This continuity enables the contending views held by different interest groups to be worked out at each stage on the policy–practice continuum. Interest groups responsible for the development of policy may differ quite substantially from those that enter the process at the stage of implementation. Thus, administrators and interest groups distill from legislation and express in the official process different interpretations of the legislative intent. Implementation is interpreted as an expression of an accommodation to institutional realities. The imperatives in the law are redefined to take account of the problems faced in practice. Implementation viewed as learning about feasibility seems especially appropriate in arenas in which there are little practical experience and little cognitive understanding about how best to achieve the goals of legislation. Implementation involves administrative accountability to Congress to assure that a program works, not merely that the program was faithful to the letter of the law. Accordingly, the management role assumes a prominent position. An executive at the federal level responds to a piece of legislation not only in terms of what it directs but also in terms of constituent opinions and the demands of administration in a world of scarce resources. It is his or her job to turn legislation into workable practice by balancing the claims of legislative intent, public opinion, and administrative effectiveness.

If we consider the politics of program administration a continuation of the legislative-political bargaining process rather than an altogether different and apolitical process, then we want primarily to understand more about the conflicting imperatives in the politics of administration and how they can be managed. Guideline developers, interest groups, and program administrators continue the process of reaching accord in the postlegislative phase. Implementation becomes an attempt to reconcile three potentially conflicting imperatives: what is legally required, what is rationally defensible in the minds of the administrators, and what is politically feasible in striving for agreement among the contending parties with a stake in the outcome. The concern for political workability has apparently led some to take the view that increased participation of the affected parties is needed in the writing of government regulation. For example, Secretary of Labor John Dunlop, in arguing for increasing such participation, declared: "The rule-making and adjudicatory procedures do not include a mechanism for the development of mutual accommodation among conflicting interests."[5] To sanction interest-group participation formally might, of course, pose problems for the other imperatives of statutory compliance and administrative rationality—and thus exacerbate the dilemma of the guideline development process. It is evident that there is no obvious way to combine these imperatives or to select among them.

Accommodation during implementation may be viewed not only as political bargaining but also as administrative learning. Anthony Downs, for example, formulates the problems of programs designed in the 1960s by explaining that they arose because the issues under consideration were complex and multifaceted whereas the institutional structures and the practices of government were narrow and fragmented.[6] The inability of the key actors to coordinate their efforts, combined with their narrowly specialized skills, caused them to perceive problems and to respond to them by means of narrowly defined, highly specialized tools and behaviors. Although the result was a discrepancy between the apparent goals of legislation aimed at coping with very complex problems and the actual results achieved by that legislation, the process was justified on the grounds of institutional learning. Downs's ultimate view is that the discrepancy is inevitable: action instruments are always going to be more specialized than the problems themselves. Hence, implementation is always going to uncover new and unanticipated problems. Then, at best, we can learn from experience; we modify the instruments and make new attempts to deal with the problems.

Ideals do tend to drift in this context; and, whether or not this is a serious concern, it is unavoidable. We want, therefore, to structure the implementation process so that it encourages cumulative learning. It is not difficult to find evidence that supporting principles often do follow administrative practice and rationalize what is administratively or politically necessary. We can learn by observing the noncompliant action of subordinates. Hugh Heclo has pointed out that:

> ... if policy is understood not simply as intended action but as what actually occurs consequent to intentions, then the place of civil servants in the development of modern social policy has been crucial ... Social policy ... has most frequently evolved as a corrective, less to social conditions as such, and more to the perceived failings of a previous policy. It is to officials that has fallen the task of gathering, coding, storing and interpreting policy experiences. ...

It would follow that policy implementation is a matter not only of power but of puzzlement, of "men collectively wondering what to do."[7]

This perspective derives from an interpretation of the nature of policy different from the other views. Subordinates may fail to comply with their leaders' directives because they do not know what is required of them (since they are asked either to pursue uncertain or evolving goals or to reconcile incompatible requirements), because the resources at hand are insufficient for the task, or because they lack the knowledge and skill to take action. When the purposes of policy are unclear and incompatible, each successive stage in the process of implementation provides a new context for seeking further clarification. One of the consequences of passing ambiguous and inconsistent legislation is that the arena of decision making shifts to a lower level. The everyday practitioners become the ones who resolve the lack of consensus through their concrete actions. When many key groups and individuals are excluded from the arena in which policy is formulated, it is typical that "the implementation phase of the political process [is where] policies can be modified to suit individual or group interest."[8] This situation is particularly evident in developing countries.

A similar process, in which interest-group pressures are brought to bear largely after legislation is passed, is beginning to occur in such types of legislation as revenue-sharing, in which the federal or the state governments act only as bankers and substantive policy decisions are, in principle, made at a lower level. Some observers have speculated that when interest-group politics enters later in the process, its force is felt in more oblique ways than when it enters at the legislative stage. But, on whatever level or whenever disagreements are masked by ambiguities, implementation becomes the strategic stage for the resolution of problems.

The effect of this process on the capacity to learn collectively and cumulatively from experience is unclear. The current argument holds that the capacity to learn is greater when participants have a more intimate knowledge of a local situation. There are cases in which, to the extent that the implementation process is not structured to redesign public policy, the intrusion of interest-group politics into the implementation phase raises unanswerable questions for bureaucrats who have few criteria for translating citizen pressure into professional practice. In this environment the chances for learning are likely to be remote.

There are other reasons why policy is often justified at the implementation level.

Consider the situation in which "a subordinate has no doubts about what his superiors would like him to do in a given situation (and when all superiors agree). Even if he would sincerely like to do what he is told, he will occasionally find it impossible to comply."[9] In these circumstances a subordinate must do what he can with the knowledge or resources at his command. If he does not, he will shift the decision making still lower down or, by indecision, create paralysis and inaction. Assuming the level of commitment to the purposes of the legislation holds true, such difficulties in compliance should create pressures for a better solution. Administrators may, for example, use their influence to secure more time, manpower, or funds. Or perhaps they may look for a more flexible method for doing what they have to do. Administrators must be aware, however, that whenever they give flexibility and discretion to the practitioner, though the situation may provide opportunities for organizational learning, they risk creating inequitable treatments.

Theodore Lowi, a primary proponent of the compliance view, argues that legislation in the decade of the 1960s derogated democracy because interest-group politics was applied to implementation. Liberal leaders did not wield the authority of democratic government with the resoluteness of men certain of the legitimacy of their positions. They were thus rendered impotent: government could not plan and did not have standards, and this erosion of authority weakened the capacity to live by democratic rules. Formal procedures became meaningless; it was impossible to "play it by the book."

Lowi's prescription is to restore the rule of law, to declare invalid and unconstitutional any delegation of power by a legislature that is not accompanied by a clear standard of implementation.[10] I believe Lowi's injunction is incomplete. In a government of laws the scope of learning is restricted for the very reason that all participants must accommodate to previously developed principles. Lowi restricts governance to legal imperatives when, in fact, rational and consensual imperatives also must operate in the implementing process. It is to these imperatives that I now turn.

THE IMPERATIVES OF IMPLEMENTATION

If implementation is understood as (1) a declaration of government preferences, (2) mediated by a number of actors, who (3) create a circular process characterized by reciprocal power relations and negotiations, then the actors must take into account three potentially conflicting imperatives: the legal imperative to do what is legally required, the rational-bureaucratic imperative to do what is rationally defensible, and the consensual imperative to do what can help to establish agreement among contending influential parties who have a stake in the outcome.

There is a striking relationship between each imperative and one of the interpretations of democratic theory. The legal imperative corresponds to the first view of implementation, which stresses the importance of subordinate compliance to rules that derive from, and are presumed to be consistent with, legislative mandates.[11] The law itself becomes the reference for all the actors in the process. The rational imperative corresponds to the process by which the executive and his bureaucracy engage in problem solving. The criteria for an acceptable solution encompass what, from a bureaucratic point of view, is morally correct, administratively feasible, and an intellectually defensible course of action. The consensual imperative expresses concern for reaching agreement among contending interest groups, legislators, and administrators.

I argue that implementation involves drift from declared purposes in which all three imperatives operate together in translating policy into practice. However offensive this may seem to those who prefer an orderly division of labor among politicians, interest groups, and bureaucrats, we need to accept the reality that the implementation process exists precisely because no acceptable trade-off rules can be formulated in advance of practice and because we cannot assume that the legal imperative will always dominate. In other words, in order to understand how legislation is implemented, we need to appreciate how the legal, rational, and consensual principles manage trade-offs, first, by considering the underlying logic of each imperative, and then by examining implementation as a process during which the conflicts among the three imperatives are resolved.

The Legal Imperative

Policies embody the results of barter, compromise, accommodation, and the judgment of what is politically desirable after most of the interests affected by the policy have had their say. But politically desirable policies may be unjust if politically weak groups are systematically ignored, if small interest groups are better organized than large ones, if preferences are aggregated in money rather than in votes, or if some citizens cannot vote. Thus, administrators may seek to redress injustices by policies. The more lawyers dominate the implementation process, the greater may be the effort to adhere faithfully to the policymakers' intent. In contrast, when scientists are responsible for implementing legislation (as they do at the Atomic Energy Commission), they may be more inclined to challenge the legislative will when it conflicts with their interpretation of how best to protect the community. However, such simple generalizations are really not adequate. We know, for example, that some lawyers are more preoccupied with changing rules than complying with them. What the circumstances are that lead bureaucracies to recruit one type of lawyer or another is an intriguing but neglected question.

The interplay between the legislative process and the legal imperative as a guide to implementation is not well understood. A number of factors are relevant to understanding when legal compliance is strict, but their importance in relation to one another has not been studied systematically. The following list provides a beginning: (1) the strength and prestige of the legislative committee in which a bill orginates; (2) the expertise of the committee's members, hence the presumption that the bill is technically sound; (3) the extent to which areas of disagreement are squarely faced and clarified during legislative debate; and (4) the level of support for the law, among both lawmakers and the local communities where the legislation is implemented. In a case such as tax legislation, when all these factors are positive, those who are responsible for implementation will try faithfully to reflect the intent revealed in the bill's legislative history. This process is facilitated by the fact that, as Stanley Surrey explains, "Government personnel . . . involved in the drafting of the tax legislation are also involved in the preparation of Regulations . . . it is understood that explanatory material contained in the Committee Reports on the floor debates will usually be included in the Regulations. . . ."[12] In large part the same persons and interests (whether inside or outside government) involved in the legislative process are equally involved in the implementation process.

The fact is, however, that explicit, tightly organized legislation also limits political maneuverability in the legislative arena and makes building a coalition difficult. Thus, we may at the outset assume that when clarity, consensus, prestige, and expertise reinforce each other, the legal imperative will be most binding during implementation. It is not possible most of the time to resolve disagreements fully early in the legislative process so that clear statutory guidelines will follow. Controversial issues are often left open and ambiguous in order to avoid confrontations that could threaten support for and successful passage of a bill. When this happens, guideline writing becomes most important, and implementation is only partially controlled by legal redress through the courts.

Legislation is frequently left very vague when time for passing it is short and the means to a particular end are poorly understood. The Economic Stabilization Act, for example, authorized the President "to issue such rules and regulations as he may deem appropriate to stabilize prices, rents, wages and salaries. . . ." Former President Nixon passed the authority delegated him by this act to the Cost of Living Council and the Pay Board. Kenneth Davis[13] points out in a discussion of this situation that Congress was forced to provide a law simply stating that the administrators responsible to the President should "as rapidly as feasible supply the standards," because no one had a clear idea of what particular measures should be taken to achieve stabilization.

The Rational-Bureaucratic Imperative

Even when all the conditions demanded by the legal imperative have been satisfied, the law still will be put into effect only if it does not violate the civil servants' sense of what is reasonable or just. Bureaucratic rationality embraces a number of different perspectives, the first of which includes "consistency of principles." Consider a concrete case. In 1968 Congress included statutory guidelines in the Economic Development Act (EDA) that are internally contradictory. The bill authorized loans only to businesses in sound financial condition. It also required that loans be granted only when firms were unable to secure money from any source other than the EDA and when there was clear need in the local areas for the firms' products. A business applying for the loan could not hope to advance its position if by doing so it created a possible loss of business for someone else. However difficult it may have been logically to reconcile these principles, we can surely appreciate the motives that inspired businessmen eager to protect local firms from unwanted competition to insist that they be included in the legislation.

The head of the Business Loan Division in Washington had little recourse but to ignore the legislation as it was written. But how did he reconcile the contradictions? He sought principles that he thought were based on reasonable bureaucratic criteria for disbursing loans. He developed a new set of goals inspired by a variety of purposes that were not in the original legislation: speed in approving projects, which not only made administration easier but also avoided a large unexpended budget for the division at the end of the year; the desire to build a local constituency, which would lend political support to EDA if ever this became necessary; and the wish to protect himself against the charge of fiscal irresponsibility in supporting businesses that were likely to fail. This strategy specifically called for loans to businesses that could immediately create jobs, encourage entrepreneurship (at a time when the concept of black capitalism was much in vogue), and demonstrate their economic viability (thus protecting EDA's investment).[14]

A second aspect of bureaucratic rationality is "workability." In the legislation that created Health Maintenance Organizations (HMOs), the statute clearly required that employers in certain firms offer their employees the choice between an HMO and some other form of health care. The law also required doctors who participated in the HMO program to practice in a group, not alone, and to be reimbursed on a capitation basis. These stipulations had the perverse effect of alienating both consumers and providers. The unions felt that the "dual choice" requirement weakened their position as sole collective bargaining agent, and doctors opposed the narrow insistence on group practice as the only form of providing care, and capitation as the exclusive system of reimbursement. Without the cooperation of the unions and the doctors, the program was unworkable. Because the legal and the bureaucratic imperatives conflicted, those responsible for implementing the legislation were confronted with a dilemma. Ultimately they ignored the legal imperative and designed new regulations that would minimize the opposition of the two major interest groups.[15]

Another case in which workability was an issue arose in legislation on education. The Federal Bureau of Elementary and Secondary Education felt it had a clear mandate to disburse automatically funds allocated by a formula prescribed in Title I of the Elementary and Secondary Education Act. Instead of monitoring the funds directly to see whether they actually reached their targets, those at the bureau decided to rely only on the original applications to judge whether the applicants' intent was to conform to the requirements. They made this decision in light of the stormy debate about federal control of education that surrounded the legislation. Moreover, as in the health case, the recipients of funds comprised the fledgling bureau's major constituency. Thus, bureaucratic rationality dictated that directly confronting the major source of support should be avoided whenever possible if the program was to be workable.[16]

A concern for institutional maintenance, protection, and growth is the primary inspiration for bureaucratic rationality. But such a rationale is more complicated than the simple posture of self-regard by which members of an organization defend their domain. It is also a sense of what professionals and managers who administer the program believe is correct policy; a judgment about what is administratively feasible, which draws on experience accumulated in the collective memory of the bureaucracy; and the determination of the forces that make legislation operationally untenable.

The Consensual Imperative

Finally, one must take into account the interest groups affected by the legislation. Under the consensual imperative, implementation is governed entirely by the preferences of these groups at the same time as the legal and the bureaucratic imperatives are both subordinated.

When a bureaucratic agency is new, weak, and under pressure to produce visible results, the outside interest groups it is supposed to affect actually manage implementation almost by themselves. The Office of New Communities, part of the Department of Housing and Urban Development (HUD), provides an extreme case in point. The office was supposed to develop guidelines for determining what constituted new communities and how they should be distributed across the nation. Inexperienced, understaffed, faced with 200 inquiries by applicants, it came under congressional criticism because no grants had been made a year after funds became available. In its desire to respond quickly, the office had developed guidelines by generalizing principles from material in applications already in for review. Then, once the office had sent the guidelines out to client constituent industries for comment, it adjusted and published them. From the $240 million in loan guarantees controlled by these guidelines, the office awarded grants to the large private companies whose priorities and definitions had themselves already set the standards for judging the qualities desirable in new towns.

When an agency owes its existence to outside interests that also control the legislative process through which its programs develop, it has to pay substantial obeisance to these groups. For example, the environmental policy and its administration through the Environmental Protection Agency (EPA) developed out of the very political movement that made environmental quality a public issue. The agency, as a result, faced activist, informed, educated constituencies whose pressures accounted for its very being. Therefore, any opposition to existing regulations has come from outside interests attached to oil and energy industries that are in competition with the EPA.

When the consensual imperative dominates, a power shift among the different outside interest groups produces a corresponding shift in the implementation process. Consider the case of regulating the radiation from power plants. About 1971, at a time when the environmental lobby enjoyed a position of maximum influence and power, the authority to set standards was assigned to the Environmental Protection Agency. The agency, in turn, set strict standards for individual plants and tried to intervene at each step in the radiation cycle in order to ensure that nuclear power plants were guarding against the potential dangers of radiation. When the energy crisis later shifted the source of power to the producers of energy, the Nixon administration, without a change in legislation, reassigned the responsibility for radiation control to the Atomic Energy Commission, which, presumably, had a more relaxed attitude toward radiation protection.[17]

In this situation, when the environmentalists lost control of implementation, they turned to seeking change through the initiative process (a procedure by which citizen groups can petition for legislation).

When Imperatives Conflict

Tension among legal, bureaucratic, and consensual imperatives can, and often does, surface. This is hardly surprising, since the power of government is, after all, cooperatively exercised. When tension occurs, different government bodies have different ways of dealing with it. For example, Congress can sometimes pass laws based on executive policies with which it substantially disagrees. Its usual device for dealing with such a problem is the attachment of riders.

We used to believe that this conflict among imperatives was our protection against the arbitrary exercise of government power. As Paul Appleby wrote in 1949, "The very complexity . . . the often unclear intermingling of responsibility, the fact that various roles in government compete, intervene and engage in conflict, is assurance of the existence of checks and balances more pervasive than those formally defined by the Constitution. . . ."[18] When the demand for action is high and the effects of influence on the results of that action are obscured, the general result is not a sense of protection against arbitrary behavior, but primarily a widespread sense of frustration.

THE STAGES OF IMPLEMENTATION

Thus far we have treated implementation as if it were a unified process. But in fact implementation proceeds through three major stages—guideline development, resource distribution, and oversight—with the legal, rational, and consensual imperatives operating at each stage along the way.

First, guidelines are developed at the point where legislative intent is translated into administrative prescriptions for action. Once developed, guidelines are promulgated to those individuals in departments who must ultimately administer the program. In the case of federal legislation, the new regulations and their guidelines are printed in the *Federal Register*, and these are often modified after interested parties get a chance to challenge them.

Second, resources are allotted to the administrative agencies responsible for carrying out the legislation. However, the amount of resources available is not en-

tirely set beforehand, because there are usually discrepancies between appropriation and authorization. Furthermore, the time when resources will become available
is crucial for implementation.

Third, some process of oversight must be started as a way of promoting accountability at the lower levels of the bureaucracy. This procedure follows Herbert Kaufman's interpretation of how noncompliance threatens democratic principles: if
guideline evasion is rampant, the legitmacy of legislation is threatened. The three
most commonly used forms of oversight are monitoring, auditing, and evaluation.
(Monitoring how legislation is put into practice is different from evaluating its
outcomes: the former is concerned with whether practice complies with guidelines;
the latter, with whether practice produces results.)

It should be noted that discussing these three stages of implementation separately
is only a heuristic device, since the process is not linear, but circular. Thus, the
legislature monitors the guidelines developed by the administration; those who
must implement the guidelines monitor and attempt to influence that administration; and those who develop guidelines must determine whether the lower reaches
of the bureaucracy comply with them.

Guideline Development

Guideline development—normally the responsibility of an administrative agency
—is the first stage in the process of implementation. Administrators, by demonstrat-
ing the conformity of guidelines to legislation, often try to reassure the legislature
that their programs are neutral in terms of their legislative intent. In testifying on
the administration of the revenue-sharing program, John Ehrlichman, then chief
counsel to the President of the United States, said that "in developing revenue sharing guidelines we merely converted the requirement of the law into administrative
regulations."[19] Nevertheless, this is the stage in making legislation consistent with
the bureaucracy's interpretation of what is reasonable at which the scope for administrative initiative is actually enormous. For example, the legislative committee
investigating the California Welfare Department's implementation of the 1971 reform act criticized the former director for issuing regulations that "in general conflicted with legislative intent and . . . specifically conflicted with understandings
reached in executive—legislative negotiatons on the bill." The director of the State
Welfare failed, according to the report, to implement *all* the provisions of the act
particularly favored by the legislature.[20] Or consider the conflict between the
U. S. Congress and the then Department of Health, Education, and Welfare over
guidelines for social services: Congress had intended that social services be available to a broad clientele, including those who might potentially become welfare
recipients in the future, but the existing guidelines restricted social services primarily to those who were already receiving welfare. By concentrating on those in
severest need, the guidelines prohibited the broader spectrum of the lower- to
middle-income population from receiving welfare and made access to services very

highly selective. This conflict between the administration and Congress was bitter and acrimonious, with the Senate Finance Committee threatening at one stage to overturn the regulations and to report out of committee a program that had no federal regulations on how the states should spend social service funds.[21]

Some states' governments have recognized explicitly in their own procedures that guidelines have the power to modify legislative intent. Michigan, for example, has a standing joint committee that regularly reviews administrative regulations and can bring them before the entire legislature for new action.[22] In the national government, on the other hand, there is no mechanism other than Congress itself for resolving disparities between legislation and guidelines. The Office of Management and Budget (OMB) is mandated to act as arbiter when conflicts among regulations by administrative agencies become rampant.

There is more to the guidelines process than the mere reinterpretation of legislation. Buried in guidelines are numerous decisions about how to make a program work. For example, an agency often must decide whether it should prescribe specific requirements or simply indicate the type of result it favors. The Model Cities administration commissioned studies of citizen participation and concluded that it preferred "maximum expression," which involved citizens at eight different parts of the decision-making process. Although some bureaucrats within Model Cities' local agencies argued that such citizen activity should be prescribed at each stage along the way, the central agency considered that it had issued this study finding as information only and had set broad standards for participation.

Decisions also have to be made at this stage on whether new policies should be retro- or proactive. The standards for building density and height under the 1961 revisions of the New York zoning ordinance embodied choices as to whether existing industrial establishments should conform to the new standards and whether there should be a year of delay to allow buildings in progress to be completed under the old standards.

Despite its substantive impact, the guidelines-development process rarely has been analyzed by students of policy and administration. Perhaps they have neglected this stage because it seems at first glance so simple and so technical: Congress passes a law, and then administrators write rules that provide detailed instructions for carrying out that law. But if the whole process is examined in detail, such an interpretation is hard to sustain. In fact, once I had recognized that policy was first defined as legislation, and then translated into guidelines, my colleagues and I decided to commission a set of detailed cases on guideline development, in order to understand that process better.[23]

Resource Distribution

The second stage in the implementation process is characterized by negotiations about the amount of resources and the timing of their availability as the process moves from appropriation through authorization to the ultimate release (or possible impounding) of funds. In the American federal system the congressional committees alone do not actually control the flow of resources, with one exception: the administration of formula-grant programs such as welfare. In these cases, funds are awarded through an open-ended grant formula and then disbursed by the Office of Management and Budget, an arm of the executive branch. In 1970, only about 65 percent of the funds authorized were appropriated, in contrast with a rate of 80 percent in 1966. The divergence that had developed between authorization and appropriations was particularly dramatic in the then Department of Health, Education, and Welfare (HEW), where appropriations as a percentage of authorizations fell from 80 to 50 percent.[24] Roy Ash, former OMB director, indicated in response to questions about an impounded item that "it was never intended that all authorized funds could be spent."[25]

The authorization-appropriation-disbursement split can affect the implementation process itself. This can happen when there are time delays in making authorized funds finally available. One outcome is the well-known end-of-the-year fund dumping—a common feature in the operation of many programs. Why should scarce resources be casually dumped to prevent their reverting back to the government? One explanation is the fear that spending less than was requested will be interpreted as having overestimated what was needed, and that this could threaten the next year's appropriations. The only time appropriations committees, which are by nature anxious about the cost of programs, actually become directly involved in their implementation, however, is when, for example, they commission special investigations to ferret out possible abuse.

Timing—that is, when the resources really become available to an administrative agency—may be as crucial for implementation as their actual amount. The fact that the legislative and executive branches reckon time differently—one by the fiscal, the other by the calendar, year—creates problems. In the interim between presidential budgeting and congressional action, agencies with routine programs do better than new programs. New programs, "subject to sudden shifts in workloads or demands for speedy action, are condemned to inauspicious starts, so that their managers are seen to be failures before they have a chance to act. More energy in Washington is consumed, more frustrations are generated, and more constraints are placed on effective management by apparent conflicts in legislative and executive calendars than by any other single condition."[26]

Timing arrangements for financing also provide enormous bureaucratic leeway, as HUD's experience indicates. When it was first organized, HUD set aside millions of dollars of its program funds for cities to cover their projects from inception to completion. Angered by the inflexibility this created within cities, the next administration's officials asked cities to plan on a short-term basis, a year at a time, but still on the basis of funds from the committed long-term allotments. Impounding stopped the shell game—and left most cities with half-finished projects and no future funds.

Normal OMB procedure permits the program's office to dole out the appropriated funds by standards it sets itself. In one instance this power led to very rapid spending, without debate, of money set aside for the Highway Trust Fund. Owing to such occurrences, Congress has now reserved for itself the privilege of "reserving" or "apportioning" the money for the fund; but the effect of this move on policy is still not clear. Of course, not all programs have the degree of flexibility allowed the Highway Trust Fund. Many operate with a time constraint that by law controls the flow of funds; and when fiscal time schedules are rigidly routinized, implementation naturally has a different history.

The Oversight Process

Oversight takes three forms: monitoring, auditing, and evaluating. Of the three, monitoring is the least publicized. The American government has always had procedures for monitoring departmental compliance, and the agency responsible for it is the OMB. Normally the OMB issues numbered circulars that establish what the monitoring process will be for particular departments, but agencies often do not conform to a circular's directions for setting up the communications systems needed for continuous monitoring.

Auditing traditionally refers to the inspecting of financial accounts. In most countries many agencies perform this service; for example, there are special internal units that audit the agencies' programs, and there are independent auditing agencies, such as the General Accounting Office (GAO). Either way, unlike the monitoring procedure, auditing is kept organizationally separate from the implementing departments of the agency being audited. This practice was established to assure disinterested review. Even so, one might speculate that the internal audits are undertaken as a way of warding off or dealing with the external audits. As such, they are not devices for learning, but a defense of established practice.

Of course, both kinds of audits may languish for want of subsequent action. For information acquired in audit to be used, it may be necessary to leak the findings to persons outside the process so they can feed it back as pressure on those within. The audit, through such indirect routes, may serve as the handmaiden to guideline development. This gives rise to one very intriguing question: Under what conditions does the audit function in the political game of attack and defense, and when does it serve as a mechanism for collective learning?

A certain program may call for a highly standardized auditing procedure, in which each audit, internal or external, is expected to conform to the same rules. On the other hand, there may be room in an audit for considerable discretion. When allowed discretion in their review, some auditors probe the relationship between operations and legislative intent. When this is the case, audits fulfill functions similar to those fulfilled by evaluations.

Evaluation traditionally refers to the assessment of a program's achievements. The recent emphasis on evaluation has emerged from the discovery that even when monitoring confirms that proper procedures are being adhered to, there is still no guarantee that they will achieve the desired outcome. Evaluation is in principle a logical and appealing idea, because the emphasis on results allows Congress to assess whether its policies are working. In practice, however, evaluations are often not precise enough instruments to determine whether a program has failed and should be ended.[27]

The distinctions among these three types of oversight processes are becoming quite blurred. This is evident, for example, from the way in which the General Accounting Office, the government's principal auditor, conducts its audit programs. GAO's own figures provide an idea of the scope of its activities. The Office estimates that about 30 percent of its professional staff evaluates federal programs under the authority granted it by the Legislative Reorganization Act of 1970. Under this act, the GAO has considerable scope and can initiate evaluations (aside from audits) on its own as well as respond to congressional requests for evaluations.

No matter how well oversight mechanisms such as these work at the outset, they all tend to wear down with time. Usually, the overseer starts taking into account mitigating circumstances that could endanger performance or required procedures. Eventually, the laxity he perceives becomes the object of criticism. The old procedures for oversight are nonetheless retained, but now the overseer creates a new institution to check on those who do the checking.[28] Thus, the process of oversight is just as subject to criticism as the guidelines-development process. When during the sixties government relied chiefly on the guidelines process for control, administrators complained that procedures were unrelated to results. In the seventies they complained that the achievement was thwarted by the preoccupation with measuring progress!

THE PRINCIPLE OF CIRCULARITY

I have pointed out that all the stages of implementation are interdependent. The process is not one of a graceful, one-dimensional transition from legislation to guidelines and then to auditing and evaluation. Instead it is circular or looping. For example, in the tax arena we find that civil servants affect legislation even before it is drafted. They take account of the law's potential for implementation by trying to anticipate the reactions and preferences of those for whom the program is designed. Guidelines are not simply imposed on new tax legislation. The law requires that they be drafted and published in the *Federal Register* to give interested parties a chance to react to the new proposals. Then interest groups and the bureaucracy responsible for implementation have an opportunity to intervene. Obviously, the more negotiation with and accommodation to the groups that are to be affected by federal guidelines, the greater the disparity between legislation and practice.

The postwar American experience with gasoline rationing provides a good example of the circulatory process at work in legislation initiated from the bottom up. Local boards, out of a sense of moral obligation, began on their own to give returning veterans extra gas allotments. This maneuver became popular with the public, though it was not within the legislation or the national guidelines for gas rationing. Regional boards then requested the national board to legitimize the policy.

The national board ultimately changed its guidelines, bowing in part to the preferences of local subunits and in part to the fear of the regional boards that they would lose control over the local boards through these ad hoc decisions.[29] The politics of accommodation, in this case, did not cease after the legislation had been developed.

Again, no one participant in the process ever really is willing to stop intervening in the other parts of the process just because his stage has been passed. For instance, Congress sometimes insists on participating in the implementation process. Recognizing that different agencies have characteristically different approaches to programs in the same subject area, Congress also frequently attempts to influence implementation at the outset by specifying which department will administer a new program.[30] But Congress's choosing a unit does not ensure the kind of implementation Congress wants. A case in point is Section 7 of the enabling legislation for the Department of Transportation (DOT). Initially Congress asked that the department develop its own standards for federal investment in transportation. Dissatisfied, it later decided on stricter controls. It modified the bill so that the department had to submit its proposed guidelines to Congress for ultimate approval. There have been times when Congress has gone even further in certain fields by expressly prohibiting various departments from researching their own implementation standards.[31]

Congress has sometimes demonstrated that it does not understand that it operates under the principle of circularity. It has tended to resist proposals for simplifying implementation, such as the OMB-backed idea of combining joint funding for categorical grants into single packages, or the proposal of the Advisory Commission on Intergovernmental Relations for consolidating certain grants. Its argument has been that legislative prerogatives should not be confused with executive initiative, although in fact such mixtures are a regular occurrence.

Oversight and Circularity

Programs have both an exchange value and a use value. Some scholars have argued that new programs are valued primarily as a medium of exchange for politicians, bureaucrats, and interest groups.[32] Their very existence provides legislators with an activities list to justify getting elected again, bureaucrats with similar rationales for continuing their appointments, and groups outside the executive arena with tangible evidence of service to particular interests. But for the overseers of social programs it is the use value that is of primary importance. Therefore, the result of monitoring, auditing, and evaluating should be to stimulate the process of circularity by altering legislative intent and administrative practice.

When oversight is taken seriously, it generates pressure to develop indicators of program performance, which are not only in-process measures of service activities but also outcome measures of program achievement. Surprisingly, the most complex arguments have developed over the meaning of specific performance measures as outcome indicators: Are police arrest figures useful as measures of officer performance, or must arrest-conviction rates be computed? Do complaint clearance rates tell us about the efficiency of fraud prosecution offices, or do the rates need to be weighed for types of consumer crime? These questions may be complex, but they are clearly relevant. There is a danger, however, that the search for objective outcome measures may obscure the initial assumptions about the program and pre-empt the legislative function. The very assumption that programs are designed to achieve measurable ends may itself be unwarranted.

In order to elucidate how the oversight process stimulates the principle of circularity, I think that it is necessary to establish a somewhat broader list of potential program outcomes than currently exists. Let us concede that legislation is designed to bring about some level of change, once implemented. In the case of social legislation, however, there is often no clear consensus about the overall social goals the legislature is aiming toward. This is where a broader set of possible outcomes would be helpful. Limiting my comments to the evaluation process, I propose three different ways in which evaluation may influence legislation and administration: it can produce changes in program activities, changes in purpose, and changes in the climate of opinion.

By a change in program activity I mean a shift in something like the volume of resources available, the character of the program in question, or the distribution of beneficiaries or costs. When those shifts occur, as they often do, a program evaluation can detect them and thus provide clues for understanding how purpose evolves from practice.

For example, there are programs that have more than one ultimate goal. Often the success of one part of the program may not mean that another has succeeded as well. A medical care program such as Medicaid was designed to improve the access of low-income groups to medical resources and hence the health of the population. Evaluation has demonstrated that Medicaid did, in fact, improve access to good care; but to date it has not demonstrably improved the health of our low-income citizens. There are other programs that have not only multiple but also ambiguous, uncertain, and evolving goals. Confronted with these circumstances, evaluators find it difficult to ferret out purpose without imposing their own interpretation.

By a change in purpose, I mean simply that a program has accomplished its critical mission, even though somewhere along the way its content has changed. Consider the case of manpower programs. By the late sixties a marked change of purpose in the programs emerged, in which priority was given to disadvantaged groups rather than to middle-income workers, as before. Consequently, the volume, programmatic character, and clientele of these programs changed dramatically. An evaluator typically might ask if a manpower program provided its graduates with jobs that represented an economic improvement over their past circumstances and if they had been able to hold onto those jobs, thus improving their net position over time. He or she would find that despite the changes that did occur, the program's central aim of securing stable and adequate jobs had not changed.

A change in the climate of opinion is one in which a program contributes to altering the context or atmosphere in which policies are developed. A program may fail to capture substantial resources or achieve its mission but nevertheless contribute to altering the political climate in which issues are discussed. For example, some voter registration programs have failed to achieve their objectives because they ran into stubborn opposition from local political parties that feared that the inclusion of new groups in local politics would threaten their established position. Nevertheless, their actions created a climate of opinion that made government more willing to experiment with other forms of participation less threatening to established institutions. The idea of community control of schools and medical care may also be understood in this context. In other words, a program may fail in the short run but nonetheless influence the trend of future developments.

ENVIRONMENTAL CONDITIONS

I have sketched out a broad framework within which to consider the imperatives, stages, dynamics, and outcomes of the process of implementation. It seems clear that the way legislation is actually implemented also depends on environmental conditions. There are three such conditions that crucially influence implementation: goals saliency, the complexity of the process itself, and the nature and level of available resources. These conditions have different impacts on the various levels of government that exist within our system.

Goals Saliency

Policies differ in how clearly they state what aims should be accomplished, whether these aims should be accomplished immediately, and whether they are more symbolic or more realistic. For example, the U.S. Congress has sought to bolster the economy of depressed areas by making the economic goal a secondary consideration and assigning this mission to agencies that have other primary purposes. Following the same principle, the Defense Department has always resisted paying the cost premiums that the use of suppliers in depressed areas would require because it is under *greater* pressure to keep costs down and to sustain the plants created by its captive suppliers than to encourage suppliers to move to depressed areas.[33] And in the New Communities Program, HUD argued that the slow pace of its work was not caused principally by vague and conflicting goals but by the fact that "most of the original provisions of the Act designed to achieve these goals have not been funded." Administrative action terminated all of those provisions, a good indication of unwillingness to incur the costs of reaching a program's original goals.

Ambiguous, symbolic, low-saliency programs are characteristically implemented in a very complex, circular fashion. Programs whose goals are clear, instrumental, and urgent are generally more centrally and hierarchically implemented.

Implementers of newly created programs who have little past precedent may try to deal with uncertainty in goals by developing weak and general guidelines. Alternatively, they may rely on blue-ribbon panel reviews designed to observe the program and guide it through its formative years. Older programs that have benefited from institutional learning about what their goals are may rely more on solid guidelines and less on monitoring and review.

I think that a comparison of some aspects of foreign policy with similar aspects of domestic policy would show that the process of implementation in the former is much more straightforward and that interest groups are much more limited in their ability to intrude their preferences. I therefore conclude, as common sense would dictate, that purpose should, and does, affect process. But under what conditions is it possible to enjoy clear purposes that have been agreed upon and in this way to limit the complexity of the implementation process? John Kenneth Galbraith explains the phenomenon in terms of the decline in power of the legislature: Just as public bodies can become the captives of the firms they seek to regulate, so too have the armed services and appropriations committees become the allies of public bureaucracies that enjoy substantial amounts of power because of the influence of the constituencies supporting them. The members of these committees "derive power in Congress, patronage, and prestige in the community at large by identifying themselves fully with the interests of the military bureaucracies of which nominally they are the watchdogs."[34]

When analyzing the question of clarity of intent and priority of purpose, we need to ask, "Clear to whom?" If a bill has clarity and saliency for a particular sponsor in Congress who heads an important committee, he or she can influence the size of the program's resources, as well as the peace of mind of the civil servants who administer it. It is anticipated that a bill that has a close and influential guardian will have a different history of implementation from a piece of legislation that has no such overseer.

Moreover, each new administration selects legislation to symbolize the main philosophy of the newly elected government. We should therefore expect that some programs will have greater urgency and enjoy higher priority than others. Under these circumstances the executive office will review the regulations, set down clear deadlines for developing the guidelines, and assign loyal and able civil servants the task of implementation, all the while bypassing the established bureaucracy if necessary. Clarity, consistency, sincerity, and saliency of goals should lead to greater centralization of the process of implementation. The fewer the loops among legislation, guidelines, and practice, the more will be done, and the less urgent will be the need to monitor and review the process.

Complexity

Implementation is also a function of the number of levels, the number of agencies, and the number of participants who have a say in the process or are able to veto any stage along the way. A study by Amos Hawley illustrates this point.[35] From an analysis of urban renewal decisions he concluded that the wider the range of participation, the less likely were urban renewal programs to be implemented in the community. Similarly, J. D. Greenstone and P. E. Peterson concluded that more poverty funds were received and distributed in cities where community participation was low than in areas where maximum feasible participation was emphasized.[36]

Participation, according to this latter study, inhibits decision making. The idea is that the more open the system is and the greater the number of actors with decisions and veto power, the less likely are decisions to be made. An open and complex decision process that functions at many levels is always in danger of eroding consensus and distorting its initial priorities.

One can also argue, however, that complexity itself is a protection. For example, urban renewal generally takes quite a long time. A HUD management study conducted in 1969 reported that the process for approving an urban renewal project had come to contain some 4,000 steps. Saying no at any point was impossible because the several thousand preceding steps locked the reviewer in.

Another aspect of complexity is the nature of the policy environment in which particular programs are to be carried out. In the absence of uniform, coherent objectives and overriding principles, an environment overcrowded with various legislative mandates may create a situation in which the multiplicity of programs may cancel each other out.

Consider an example in housing policy that is not atypical in many countries. The value of tax relief to aid home purchases rises in proportion to the individual's tax rate and hence income. But construction subsidies for rented units bear no relation to the income of tenants. Rent controls do provide a way for low-income families to find accommodations at prices they can afford, but at the same time they may provide disincentives for building privately constructed housing. Subsidized public housing offers high housing standards and relatively low rents that the poor can afford. All these programs in combination represent a substantial expenditure for public aid to home-owners and tenants. Nevertheless, because they have no clear rationale for distribution behind them, they not only distort housing markets considerably but also create a situation in which mandates may come into open conflict and undo each other.

Resources

Implementation is also a function of the type and level of resources required for action. Not all legislation requires that resources take the shape of a direct outlay of expenditures. For example, if a law is passed that requires all utilities to use coal for 25 percent of their energy, no new spending is required by government. (There are obvious beneficiaries of such a policy, although it may not be clear who pays the final costs.) Removing the legal obstacles to clinical abortions or requiring that all applications for airports and sewers by cities be approved by an areawide planning agency are other examples of laws that do not need direct outlays of funds. Still another example is legislation that makes it worthwhile for middle-income families to own their own homes in order to take advantage of tax concessions. Although intermediaries may be necessary to notify people of their rights and their potential eligibility for such benefits, such legislation should not require elaborate machinery for monitoring and review.

The pattern of implementation is expected to vary according to the nature of the resources required. Therefore, it may be useful, in line with the examples just cited, to distinguish among types of legislation by resource requirements: some are designed to regulate the standards of products or the performance of individuals, firms, or agencies; others provide incentives or distribute public largesse in the form of services or cash.

When he studied administrative feedback, Herbert Kaufman[37] tried to identify agencies in which he expected feedback to be well developed because the functions they performed required accountability and control. Accordingly, he classified agencies by function—whether they administered programs, disbursed funds, or regulated behavior; whether they served clienteles or administration; and whether they administered their own or intergovernmental programs. He found widely different feedback within the same classes. For example, his classification of service agencies administering their own programs included the Forest Service, which had tight feedback, and the Bureau of Elementary and Secondary Education, which had lax feedback. Consequently, Kaufman's classification has little explanatory value; no better classification exists, however. Perhaps it would be more rewarding to associate administrative activities with classes of policies instead of with agencies.

The level of resources to be distributed also influences the way implementation takes place. When the stakes are high, pressure for a piece of the pie will accordingly be strong. For example, every consultant to EDA recommended that projects be concentrated in a single growth center in each district; but because congressmen had to gain support from constituents all over their districts, the resources were spread out. Similarly, the original Model Cities program was to be limited to just a few towns. Congress eventually halved the appropriation for this program, but not before it had doubled the number of cities receiving grants from the original 75 to 150. Of course, the effect of these new pressures diluted the amount of resources available to perform the functions of monitoring, review, audit, and evaluation and thus reduced oversight and vigilance.

Implications

Many societies operate with paradigms of pluralism. Pluralistic theory asserts that governments respond mainly to demands that are exerted through organized interest groups. Because of the great numbers of interest groups, some competing against with each other, the power to make policy is quite dispersed. Policy, then, results from compromises among these interest groups. Every contender gets some benefits, for no interest is altogether forsaken.[38] Overlaps in membership among groups and general socialization toward overriding societal values help to reduce polarization. Governments reconcile whatever conflicting demands remain or assign priorities among them.

Such a conception is incomplete. Groups and governments both act not simply in terms of demands and pressure, but in terms of their own perceptions of future requirements. Governmental agencies not only respond to external pressures but vigorously attempt to create constituencies. Efforts to impose standards of behavior on reluctant or indifferent citizens demonstrate that governments themselves generate agendas for reform.

Incrementalist theories were designed to correct for this defect in pluralistic theory. Incrementalism captures the separate importance of managerial initiative, but incrementalism is oriented toward the past. It encourages the view that what happens is, and ought to be, pretty much determined by what happened earlier, because administrators should, and do, rarely depart abruptly from what they have been doing. They muddle through as best they can, making only marginal changes in activities.[39]

Marginal increments can describe the actions of implementers, but policies and programs vary greatly in longevity and resources, and some represent rather abrupt innovations. Indeed, some administrators take pleasure in bringing about dramatic, abrupt innovations.[40]

One critique states that bureaucracy works, all right, but to its own purposes only. Robert Wood, for example, has noted: "The real difficulty is that public agencies often achieve goals and carry out objectives that political observers or the public have come to feel are out of date, inadequate in scope or plain wrong. (Alternatively we feel that the objectives are in fact set internally by the public organizations themselves; hence, they are self serving, not serving us)."[41] The radical critique disagrees: it argues that governmental agencies are instruments of one or another organized interest group. Both critiques oversimplify, however, because both are partly correct.

Implementation may be best understood as attempts to resolve conflicts among authoritative, rational, and consensual imperatives. How these conflicts are resolved depends on the saliency of policies, their resource requirements, and the complexity of the implementation process itself. In general, clear, salient, and realistic goals that can be implemented simply and that are supported by adequate, but not plentiful, resources will lead to programs in which there is minimum discretion, little deviation from the policymakers' intent, and maximum consensus among implementers. In some instances clear goals emerge from initially ambiguous policies. For that to happen, consensus must develop among the competing interests. But clarity does not always increase. Some policies remain forever mired in uncertainty, ambivalence, and contradiction. Under these circumstances, consensus is always fragile, for interest groups cannot reach stable agreement about unclear policies. Moreover, clear goals may not be realistic.

NOTES AND REFERENCES

1. Paul Berman and M.W. McLaughlin, "Implementing Innovations: Revisions for an Agenda for a Study of Change Agent Programs in Education." Working

Note WN 8450-1-HEW. Santa Monica, Calif.: Rand Corporation, November 1973.

2. Robert Weiss and Martin Rein, "Input Analysis in Program Evaluation." Cambridge, Mass.: MIT Department of Urban Studies and Planning, 1978 (mimeographed).

3. Herbert Kaufman, *Administrative Feedback.* Washington, D.C.: The Brookings Institution, 1973.

4. John Kenneth Galbraith, *Economics and the Public Purpose.* Boston: Houghton Mifflin, 1973. P. 15.

5. "Dunlop Asks Policy Shift on Regulatory Agencies." *The New York Times,* 9 November 1975.

6. Anthony Downs, personal communication to the author.

7. Hugh Heclo, *Modern Social Politics in Britain and Sweden.* New Haven: Yale University Press, 1974.

8. Thomas Smith, "The Study of Policy Making in the Developing Nations." *Policy Studies Journal,* 1973, *1,* 247.

9. Kaufman, Op. cit. P. 3.

10. Theodore Lowi, *The End of Liberalism.* New York: Norton, 1969.

11. Stanley Surrey, "Treasury Department Regulatory Material under the Tax Code." In J. Pressman, F. Rabinovitz, and M. Rein, eds., "Policy Implementation: Guidelines." *Policy Sciences,* 1976, *7* (4–Special issue).

12. Ibid.

13. Kenneth Davis, *Discretionary Justice.* Baton Rouge: Louisiana State University Press, 1969.

14. Jeffrey Pressman and A. Wildavsky, *Implementation.* Berkeley: University of California Press, 1973. Chap. 4.

15. Drew Altman and H. Sapolsky. In Pressman, Rabinovitz, and Rein, eds., Op. cit. Pp. 417-39.

16. Jerome T. Murphy, "Title I of ESEA: The Politics of Implementing Federal Education Reform." *Harvard Educational Review,* 1971, *41,* 35–64.

17. Richard D. Lyonds, "ESP Loses Its Authority to Limit Plant Radiation." *The New York Times,* 12 December 1973.

18. Paul Appleby, *Policy and Administration.* Birmingham, Ala.: University of Alabama Press, 1949.

19. Juergen Haber, "Revenue Sharing Report: Ehrlichman Promises Audits and Strict Evaluation of Local Programs." *National Journal Reports,* 1973, *5,* 274.

20. Senate-Assembly Subcommittee on Implementation of Welfare Reform, California, *Report to the Legislature.* Sacramento, Calif.: State of California, 17 March 1972.

21. Judith Turner, "Welfare Reform: HEW Sidesteps Showdown with Congress over Revamping Social Service Regulations." *National Journal Reports,* 1973, *5,* 1132–38.

22. Malcolm E. Jewell and S.C. Patterson, *The Legislative Process in the U.S.* New York: Random House, 1966. Chap. 19.

23. See Pressman, Rabinovitz, and Rein, eds., Op. cit.

24. Advisory Commission on Intergovernmental Relations, *The Gap between Federal Aid Authorization and Appropriations: Fiscal Years 1966–1970.* Report

M-52 (in cooperation with the Council of State Governments). Washington, D.C.: Government Printing Office, 1970.
25. *The New York Times,* 19 January 1974.
26. Robert Wood, "When Government Works." *The Public Interest,* 1970, *18,* 39—51.
27. Genevieve J. Kelezo, "Program Evaluation: Emerging Issues of Possible Legislative Concern Relating to the Conduct and Use of Evaluation in the Congress and the Executive Branch." Library of Congress Publication No. 74-78SS. Washington, D.C.: Congressional Research Service, 1974.
28. H. L. LaFramboise, "Administrative Inspection and Method Analysis in the Department of Veterans' Affairs." *Canadian Public Administration,* 1959, *2,* 195—201.
29. William H. Riker, "The Veterans' Gas Ration." In H. Stein, ed., *Public Administration and Policy Development.* New York: Harcourt Brace, 1952. Pp. 744—59.
30. James A. Noone, "New Federal Programs Seek to Aid State in Control of Coastal Area Exploitation." *National Journal Reports,* 1973, *4,* 1889.
31. Richard W. Bamess, "Policy, Challenges and Objectives of the Department of Transportation." *Quarterly Review of Economics and Business,* 1969, *9,* 63—76.
32. Robert R. Alford, "The Political Economy and Health Care: Dynamics without Change." *Politics and Society,* 1972, *2,* 127—65.
33. Anthony Downs, "Testimony on National Public Works Investment Policy." U.S. House of Representatives, *Congressional Record,* 1 November 1973.
34. Galbraith, Op. cit. P. 174; see also Harvey M. Sapolsky, *The Polaris System Development: Bureaucratic and Programmatic Success in Government.* Cambridge, Mass.: Harvard University Press, 1972.
35. Amos Hawley, "Community Power and Urban Renewal Success." *American Journal of Sociology,* 1963, *68,* 422—31.
36. J.D. Greenstone and P.E. Peterson, "Reformers, Machines and the War on Poverty." In James Q. Wilson, ed., *City Politics and Public Policy.* New York: Wiley, 1966. Pp. 267—93.
37. Kaufman, Op. cit.
38. For a criticism of this view based on survey data, see R. F. Hamilton, *Class and Politics in the United States.* New York: Wiley, 1972. Pp. 34—36.
39. Otto A. Davis, M. Dempster, and A. Wildavsky, "A Theory of the Budgetary Process." *American Political Science Review,* 1966, *60,* 529—47; C. Lindblom, "The Science of Muddling Through." *Public Administration Review,* 1959, *29,* 79—88.
40. Peter B. Natchez and I.C. Bupp, "Policy and Priority in the Budgetary Process." *American Political Science Review,* 1973, *67,* 951—64.
41. Wood, Op. cit.

Chapter 8

Practice Worries

The minor professions (teaching, social work, and planning, for example), their sciences, and their policies all hover on the margins of credibility and tolerance among the governmental structures of the more developed and affluent Western societies. Yet the human services, the domain of these professions, are well established within the framework of modern government. The resources we devote to them are extensive and expensive, and are becoming more so. We know they are needed, but are not quite sure why, where, or by whom. We are deeply uncertain about how they ought to be performed. We are ambivalent about the moral bases for entrusting to some people the destiny and life chances of others. Thus, millions of people now work in human service professions that rest on debatable purposes, moral uncertainties, weak theories, and few or no established techniques. As a result, practitioners must live with chronic professional anxiety.

We shall deal here with the new, variegated, and free-floating concerns of the minor professional, with new practices requiring new ideas. Most of the very old occupational roles on this planet—farming, mining, manufacturing, crafts—have to do with things. Roles that have required people to deal with people have been either management work, directing people toward the more efficient manipulation and use of things, or religious or women's work, these last two not being regarded as completely "serious." Before 1880, most of the positions that involved dealing with matters of the human spirit, human welfare, or human development were in one way or another associated with religious management. Governments did concern themselves with people in trouble, but largely in the interest of keeping the public peace through the provision of devices such as the poorhouse, the almshouse, the workhouse, or subsidized relocation; they helped people keep body and soul together and subdued those who threatened to disrupt the community. In the latter half of the nineteenth century, governments began to get into the business of saving souls through the rise of secular professions dedicated to furthering human education, rehabilitation, psychotherapy, mental hygiene, personal development, and social welfare. These new secular professions, moving in where formerly there had only been clerical professions, were all concerned in one way or another with human salvation or perfection.

This development of secular roles occurred at just about the time the philosophers began actively worrying about *geisteswissenschaft* [knowledge of the spirit] versus *naturwissenschaft* [knowledge of nature], the social sciences began their modern rise to prominence, the Marxists and Social Darwinists began trying to construe the growth and changes of the human spirit as expressions of historical and natural forces, and the social and political apperception of the managerial welfare state unfolded. Hence, with the flourishing of the social sciences, there arose the concept of a professional skill rooted in a knowledge base and intent on serving people.

Not all of this professional growth came from philosophy or from academic movements of the social sciences. As societies enlarged and urbanized, the needs for education, child guidance, social work, and provisions for social security became increasingly apparent. Private and public charities arose to address such needs; and as the resources of voluntary, private efforts proved inadequate, structures of government at city, county, state, and federal levels were developed.

As awareness of these social concerns developed in Western societies, there emerged from the intelligentsia and the universities an impetus to increase and codify knowledge: to take the individual and the society as objects, to organize knowledge-gathering groups, and to build rational bases for social action. The informal and voluntary efforts of private individuals merged with the knowledge base to form the social service professions of the twentieth century.

People appeared whose main business was to help other people develop and adapt to the complexities of modern society. Labor could no longer be expected to come onto the market "raw"; it had to be "finished" and made to fit the requirements of a more demanding system of production. The teacher helped children acquire the intellectual equipment to survive in society and, in later years, the specific skills necessary to take an honorable place in the occupational role system. Teachers of teachers prepared them to do this on the authority of educational psychologists and educational researchers who provided the knowledge base. Social workers encountering an individual, family, or local community in trouble used the knowledge of sociology, psychology, and psychiatry to facilitate constructive adaptation. Physicians served human health and, in the twentieth century, extended medical practice to well-baby care and treatment of the myriad modern forms of mental disorders.

But all these were activities of a new kind, and problematic. One of the persistent problems of the twentieth century has been an effort to come to terms with the possibilities and limitations of these activities. The human services are grounded in the human sciences; and these are, as everyone knows, weak in stipulating those conditions and regularities upon which successful engineering depends. The human service professional deals with people in grief or pain, with such problems as abused or neglected children, with the crises of the human spirit that attack not only the weak, the infirm, and the aged of any society but all of us.

No matter how large the social establishment of a profession, how moral or ideal its purposes, how certain its basic knowledge and command of theory, ultimately the practice of that profession comes down to one person in real time living with other people. It is in that lived experience that practice worries are rooted and, from time to time, intrude upon the consciousness and disturb the settled pattern of meaning by which the minor professional lives.

OPPOSITIONS, WORRIES, AND PROBLEMS
IN THE PERFECTIONIST PROFESSIONS

Practice worries arise in the actions of an individual—not in words or ideas, but in murky psychological events that are registered as oppositions, resistances, feelings of awe, or moments of malaise. Any task a person performs day after day is marked by a normal flow of activities and a sense of being intellectually in charge of one's actions. But there are times when *oppositions* appear in practice. The practice resists the practitioner's efforts. Untoward and/or unpleasant things happen that have not occurred before. The practitioner is by no means clear about what is going on. The oppositions manifest themselves at first as inchoate sensations of felt difficulty. They are quite common in any routine practice, and they exert a pressure on the person to cognize them, to recognize that they are there, and to associate them with a "reason" or a "situation." This pressure to cognize the oppositions of practice is felt by the person as a *worry*. The person experiences an ill-defined emotion of the kind usually characterized as anxiety or tension or concern. In the end, the practitioner tries to achieve cognitive resolutions. He or she construes the worry, sees it as the expression of a *problem*.

The experience of oppositions is transformed into practice problems. Such a transformation provides the professional with a cognitive construction of the experience. It suggests a form that action might take. Ideally, practice problems constitute the intellectual basis of a plan to reduce the felt oppositions of practice. Ideally, as well, they embody an ethical commitment, not only declaring what is good and bad about the experience of oppositions—construing them within a framework of moral judgment—but also offering a good way to act. A practice problem is, by its very nature, a good thing to try to solve.[1]

The individual finds problems in his or her practice through what we envisage as a three-step process. In the first step, oppositions and emotional experiences of the practitioner register themselves on his or her thought and memory as *declarative moments.* In the second step, the practitioner forms practice worries out of the experience of unease and frustration that signal a deep sense of doubt about the meaning of his or her professional life. These troubling experiences we call *declarative moments.* The practitioner seeks to interpret the elusive forms of thought and emotion registered by such moments. Eventually, a propositional and/or operational form is found for the worries. A *practice problem* then evolves that may or may not be solvable, but at least is definite. A cognitive problem has been addressed.

In the limits of action lie the seeds of knowledge. In the life of any professional there come declarative moments, oppositional experiences that are remembered and reflected upon that come, in time, to shape the self-definition and self-concept of the practitioner.

——A policy analyst, trained to view his or her role as one of disinterested objectivity, has a friendly discussion with "the chief" about a new project. Something about the conversation sticks in his or her mind. He or she has a vague sensation of having been gently told that his or her findings must reflect agency interests.

——A therapist confronts a patient who has been in psychotherapy for a year and a half. The patient does not seem to have improved. The patient, because he or she has run out of money, bids the therapist good-bye.

——A legal service lawyer opens a file on a new client with an intake discussion that lasts an hour and a half. The client never shows up for his or her second appointment. Waiting for the client, the lawyer is uncomfortably aware that he or she did not listen to the client during the first meeting. Had he or she lapsed into "slotting" the client into a definition of need that fit the purposes of the agency? "Slotting" is a practice that he or she actively and publicly dislikes.

——Once more with feeling, an eighth-grade teacher faces this year's class of urban slum children whom he or she is to lead up the down staircase. For the dozenth time the teacher reflects on the slim possibility that there might be some more encouraging way for a middle-aged teacher to make a living.

——A welfare worker begins to suspect that he or she is dealing with clients who have an active culture of perjury and deception. One client is concealing a well-paying job; another has a husband with a fine income. There are even, he or she finds, clients in collusion with one another to create false eligibility for welfare dispensations.

There appear to be episodes in the taken-for-granted ceremonial and dancelike interchanges between professional and client when felt experience so arranges itself as to create the *possibility* of an articulate declaration. A declarative moment is latent with declaration; it says *something* only if one knows what it is. How does the possibility offered in declarative moments become an actuality?

The declarative moment in professional experience is, so to speak, a moment that cries for meaning. We feel that something in the world is resisting or eluding us, and we are in some sense intellectually forced to construe and symbolize what has gone awry. The experience of this elongated time of unsettlement we speak of as "practice worries." The worries that flow forward in time from declarative moments are always worries about self in relation to self's experience and self's role.

Who am I in relation to these clients? What is my personal and moral responsibility toward this practice in the midst of which I try to act?

The heightened experiences of declarative moments are sooner or later cognized. "Cold knowledge" is fashioned from "hot knowledge." Cold knowledge consists in the expression of aspects of pure experience in a symbolic and communicative discourse. It is characteristic of all modern professional practices that people within such practices are bound together with strings of prose—the prose of textbooks, journals, professional charters, government enactments and regulations, conventions, conferences, gossip, conversations with clients, etc. The hot knowledge of people in a profession becomes expressed in communicative discourse, offered either as a narrative account of experience or as models, hypotheses, or rules directed toward the issues that hot knowledge is construed as offering. Hot knowledge is like poetry, containing and expressing emotion, but not usually terribly instructive or directive for action. Cold knowledge is a prosaic reinterpretation of hot knowledge that can be shared and that can be used artfully in the organization of cooperative action and problem solving. Part of professional experience becomes describable; another part lingers forever outside as "something one just can't put into words." But the describable portion can be used to fashion practice problems that, as we see it, are "construals"* and theories that seem to the practitioner to explain and settle practice worries.

The rendering of social services in general, however, is first and foremost a passionate affair. To say that dealing with people arouses passion is not to convey the full force of the experience. Talk to a teacher; listen to that teacher discussing both the joy and the pathos of teaching. Talk to a social worker; listen to that social worker describe the complexities and the difficulties of the human grief encountered in social work, the feeling of empathy and of pain for humans who are in trouble and trying to find ways out of that trouble. Talk to a pediatrician about an abused child or a child one suspects is neglected. The encounter with such children is the everyday life of the professional, and it is neither simple nor emotionally neutral.

The public advocacy that stems from such primary encounters with joy, pathos, and grief is a notoriously unruly affair. Those who appear before governments and legislatures as advocates for the interests of service providers and clients do not always speak in measured ways and do not always show either restraint or a judicious respect for cost-benefit ratios. If inflated and powerful demands on behalf of human services seem self-serving—professionals asking for support of their status—this is only part of the story.

Here we encounter a paradox. Hot knowledge, which arises immediately in connection with the experiences of the practitioner, administrator, or planner, is emotionally charged. In cold knowledge, the primary experience no longer plays an es-

---

*A coined term to suggest an invention that gives meaning to experiences one cannot grasp.—M.R.

sential role. Yet in both cases we want to speak of knowledge, on the assumption that propositions bearing an emotional load versus a neutral load still contain knowledge. To be productive cognitively and practically, we need to cool the hot experience and the rage that accompanies it, because if we are compassionate and angry all the time, we lose our ability to think clearly, and we therefore limit our ability to be helpful.

Practice problems appear as theories about why we are worried, about the meaning of the declarative moments we have experienced. As symbolic "construals" are set forth, articulate formulations of the shortcomings of practice emerge. These can be discussed with others; they can be used to communicate and to teach; they may serve as a basis for planned action. Yet the very process of cognizing gives to the flux of professional experience a form and definiteness that it does not have. The practicality of cold knowledge is a trade-off for the authenticity of hot knowledge.

Some Specific Practice Worries

In recent years a series of careful studies has been made of the problems experienced by professionals in their everyday practice.[2] These studies identify the confrontations and confusions that appear as leitmotifs running through all accounts of the work of the minor professions. How does the practice of the minor professional oppose him or her? What constitutes a confrontation sufficient to create a declarative moment? Momentary experiences of dismay, such as those discussed above, seem to draw their force from what they seem to point to. They seem to be a symbol or index of certain critical configurations of practice, among them the following.

Signs of inefficacy. The legitimation of all professions rests on the presumption of efficacy, and the rhetoric of all professions is a paean to efficacy. Yet the experience of all professionals is riddled with declarative moments in which things happen that should not happen to a fully competent, knowing, and benevolent professional. The professional repeatedly encounters situations in which he or she does not have what it takes to assist the client, and the question of cause or fault floats free in the air. Is the weakness in him or her as a person, in his or her professional tools, in the client, in the agency or the system?

Routinization of practice. People who become professionals invest time and money in the achievement of their certification. They do so on the presumption that professional life offers certain rewards: freedom to act spontaneously and creatively in their work, the opportunity to take responsibility, avenues for personal growth, and a chance to do something that makes a difference for clients. Professionals, by and large, believe in people and in personal growth. But the pressure and the bureaucratization of professional life are such that the professional repeatedly finds himself or herself in encounters with clients that are distant, cold, formal, and full of suspicion and maneuver.

The infliction of damage. Sooner or later, professionals encounter situations in which their well-meant efforts do more harm than good. The practitioner experiences his or her power as a destructive force. The canons of all professional practices emphasize *primum non nocere*, the obligation to avoid harm as a precondition for any attempt to do good. But a teacher can accidentally demoralize a child; a lawyer can bungle away five years of a client's life; a social worker can lose a child's growing years in the gray void of the foster-care system. Sooner or later all professionals face what appears to be incontestable evidence that their work is part of a system that creates as well as reduces human happiness.

The experience of betrayal. The human service professions rest on ancient Enlightenment doctrines that hold that people are inherently good, although their circumstances or environment may frustrate or distort the expression of that goodness. Professionals tend to believe this in a deeply personal way; their very choice of a human service profession is often a testimonial to this kind of faith. Evil has no place in their professional doctrine, and yet a regular and dismaying fact of professional life is meeting clients who deliberately lie, cheat, distort, swindle, and/or connive. Wrongdoing arises not as inadvertence, error, or pathology, but as willful acts inspired by perverse notions.

Coping

All professionals, I believe, "know" the kinds of confrontational moments just described—lack of efficiency, routinization, the experience of inflicting damage, the experience of betrayal. The social forms by which people harmonize their activities—bureaucracy, rules, professionalism—are leaky vessels. The journey from experience to worry to the formulation of professional problems is experienced by professionals at all levels in all agencies in the human services.

The worries are tricky to handle, in both a private and a public sense. How much attention should one give to the declarative moments and free-floating worries with which practice abounds? What is at stake in the private recognition and articulation of practice worries is often nothing less than an assault on meaning. All live in a web of mythic statement that expresses goals and values, some sense of the agency involved (i.e., personal power), and the past and the future. This webbing is more than private rationalization and cognitive structure and mapping. It offers crucial emotional and ethical equilibrium. The intact webbing holds back guilt; it diffuses responsibility for what one does or does not do with a client or colleague into the powers and meanings of the professional system of which one is a part. The intact webbing supplies rituals and ceremonials by which one may respond to, and share, the pains and injustices encountered in everyday practice. In facing practice worries, the professional approach very often tears at the webbing.

There are standard human ways of handling threatening worries. First, one can create a gap between experience and the self-articulation of experience. One can refuse to recognize and deal with worries. One can displace them, or project them, or dissipate them in busywork. The often passionate nature of the engagement of the human services professional with his clientele makes these quasi-Freudian devices difficult, but by no means impossible. A second major approach to threatening worries is to try to "cool down" the experience of dealing with clients, to re-treat to a colder, more formal, more "businesslike" engagement with people. In self-defense the professional hardens himself or herself against the degrading effects of constant association with human problems.

SHARING WORRIES IN A BUREAUCRATIC SYSTEM

An ideal solution for practice worries would arise if one could, somehow, recon-stitute the webbing of social meaning and make it more robust for the individuals contained within it. But now we must face directly the anguish of achieving human cooperation through the channels of a bureaucratic network.

The declarative moments and practice worries so far described are part of the hot knowledge of the professional; but hot knowledge must be considerably re-duced, recoded, and transformed in order to be shared by others. The nerves of bureaucracy carry symbols, narrative discourse, and numbers back and forth among individuals who hold different positions of power and influence. Like all languages or art, these communicative media reduce, select, and organize experience in the act of transmitting it. The nerves of bureaucracy transmit facts, propositions, ideo-logical statements, arguments, invocations, stories, rules, declarations, testimonials. They are faithfully high-fidelity communicators of the formal, the argumenta-tive, and the propositional. What they will transmit to only a very minor extent— one must "read between the lines" to find these messages—is worry, uneasiness, guilt, anguish, nervousness, desperation, insecurity. Most hot knowledge stays with its receptor; the little that enters the nerves of bureaucracy signals weakly and is rapidly degraded as it travels.

We have, then, a group of individuals organized within an institutional structure that we may, for the moment, represent by the table of organization of a bureau-cracy. Some are "near" to one another: a line runs directly from the occupational slot of the one to the other. Some are "far." There may be ten or twenty junctions to be crossed in moving from one person's box to another's. What this is most likely to mean, in the everyday world, is that the "near" people will see each other rela-tively frequently, will see the same or similar people, will participate in the same or similar scenes and playlets, and will talk about similar kinds of practical issues. The "far" people will know of one another, but they will know of one another's activi-ties and experiences only as they are transmitted in the paperwork of the system, or as they briefly encounter one another in very selected committee experiences. Near people can, to a limited extent and subject to the very general problem of human communication, share hot knowledge. They can address together, to a limited extent, declarative moments and practice worries. But "far" people can only share the cold knowledge that is transmitted by the nerves of bureaucracy. They can "read between the lines," and they do—always. But there is very low-fidelity communication of practice worries among people in a bureaucratic net-work. How do people distributed at a distance pool their efforts in order to address, and try to alleviate, the worries they all share?

In general, they create a *problem*. A problem is a rational package for worries. Embedded in its necessary vehicle—a set of facts, and a story that integrates them—the declaration of a problem has for professionals the force of the declaration of a motive, goals, and direction in the near future.

The Intelligent Network*

Professional practice is constituted by more than a set of individuals with distinct skills.[3] Professionals function in an *institutional setting* that provides a framework of group purposes, power arrangements, and myths so disposed as to maintain a stable network of legitimated social arrangements. Let us consider the disposition of knowledge arrangements in a social network of practitioners.

The fact that hot knowledge must remain local and that propositional and formal knowledge travels rather well means, in the end, that the "collective mind" of the professional group will address most clearly and firmly the highly codified and the formalized. What can a group of professionals agree about? They can agree about the exact wording of a piece of legislation, the text of a governor's speech, the unemployment figures for last year, the number of people hired and fired "downtown" last year, the budget figures proposed by the Senate and the alternative figures proposed by the House—all these can be precisely formulated in symbols in one place and transmitted, without significant degradation, by paper or wire to all other places in the bureaucratic network. When a group of professionals begins to fall apart, when the "collective mind" begins to look hazy or woozy, is when one asks something about the *meaning* of the collectively shared knowledge. Then one inquires about feelings, attitudes, hope, despair, frustration. The collectivity does not know how it "feels" about the facts; individuals know how *they* feel. Only political leadership in building the professional group toward a consensus can develop a semblance of a group's shared meaning of experience.

If one could surgically separate knowledge from emotions, then perhaps this limited collectivization of human feelings in a professional group would be all right. Group members would share and agree on objective meanings, "the facts." The dross of sentimentality and emotionality would be left behind with the individual as a kind of superfluous "waste product" of professional activity. Alas, the best psychology and philosophy we have today maintain that there is emotion in cognition and cognition in emotion. When we transmit throughout the professional network only the "propositionalized" and the formalized, we leave vast amounts of vital information and knowledge out of the group's ken. The professional group cannot know collectively what its members know individually. Furthermore, what gets left behind with the individual in the communicative processes of the system is

---

*An "intelligent network" is the system of institutional arrangements that gives meaning to our action. These arrangements have a kind of intelligence that comes from their history and provides an account of why they function as they do.—M.R.

something more than a few little puddles of smiles and tears. The hot knowledge experienced in professional practice may take the form of intense frustration, despair, ethical quandaries, and/or guilt.

The teacher, the social worker, and the mental health practitioner must deal both with the genuine problems and pains of their clients and with their own feelings of incompetence and frustration. Administrators, higher up in the delivery system, do not directly feel the problems of the on-line practitioner, though most of them have "been there," since, more often than not, administrators supervising professionals have risen from the ranks. But the day-to-day experience of administrators involves encounters and hot knowledge of a kind that line professionals do not share, and perhaps may not suspect is there. Most of the time, administrators must make do with limited authority and resources. While they are held responsible for making the system work, they must compete with other administrators for resources and authority. Obviously, there are pains and joys in the experiential field of the administrator, but he or she cannot share with the line professional the full knowledge and meaning of these experiences.

How, then, do we conceive of the professional collectivity as a whole? How do we see its unity? How do we provide shared meaning so that all the individuals in the group can work with some degree of unity toward a common goal? It is here that we come to the historic function of planners and theorists. Today, high-level planners and academic social scientists play a critical role in the professional service structures of modern societies. Working sometimes with government, sometimes against it, and sometimes in the service of contract houses, corporations, labor unions, or professional advocacy organizations, the expert and the planner offer myths and formulations that serve to unite and justify experience for individuals in professional networks.

But the planner or the expert, no less than the functioning bureaucrat, has his or her share of painful hot knowledge. Nobody has ever communicated the delicate anguish of the expert better than Voltaire, who wrote, "The necessity of saying something, the embarrassment produced by the consciousness of having nothing to say, and the desire to exhibit ability, are three things sufficient to render even a great man ridiculous."

The expert—who, after all, must live outside the nerves of bureaucracy and whose knowledge of life-in-practice must often be very cold—has the uncomfortable task of asserting his or her relevance for a world that hardly anyone fully understands. The expert may comfort himself or herself with the thought that he or she is standing back, "unbiased," and in the best social science tradition providing a critical interpretation of why things are as they are. The expert sees himself or herself as a knight of purity and power, riding in to slay the dragons of error. But a highly experienced modern expert with a wealth of practical experience and a disdain for abstract theory has summarized his hot knowledge in the following insightful quotation:

Lord Keynes wrote at the end of a *General Theory*: "Practical men who believe themselves to be quite exempt from any intellectual influences, are usually the slaves of some defunct economist. Mad men in authority, who hear voices in the air, are distilling their frenzy from some academic scribbler of a few years back. In my experience the opposite is more often true in our times. Academic scribblers are the slaves to politicians; they seek to bring elegance and rationalization and sometimes a modicum of respectability to directions already chosen by practical men confronted by hard and immediate problems. Decisions rarely flow from the ideas of intellectuals, their voices in the air or from their memoranda. And interest groups are far too pragmatic to be the puppets of intellectuals."[4]

The Limits of Intelligent Networks for the Perfectionist Professions

The metaphor of an intelligent network implies a managerial approach to dealing with the problems that exist within the network. As problems arise, there is the almost instinctive impulse to tighten up system operations. Favored devices are schemes of accountability, tightened evaluation, more planning, and other techniques intended to make the system more coordinated and coherent. In the context of modern societies and governments, the overwhelming source of "intelligence" for service networks is knowledge and wisdom derived from the management of things. We know a lot about creating complex structures for a product-oriented system. A large corporation that manufactures automobiles will productively harness the activities of thousands of people around the world, producing an integration and synergy of disparate human activities toward the maintenance of one overarching, corporate goal. What we know about the making and marketing of things we try to apply, reasonably enough, to the management of people. The perfectionist professions live awkwardly in corporate houses that were not really designed for them, because the "product" of the perfectionist professions is people in the process of becoming.

There are inherent limits in the use of a product-oriented approach to dealing with matters of the human spirit. These limits are felt by every worker in the system of the intelligent network. They are felt stresses and strains emerging, psychologically, as practice worries.

The power of an intelligent network to absorb, rationalize, articulate, and offer absolution for the experiences of people living in its web is very limited. The limitation is inherent. In the first place, any intelligent network must be founded on the human being's limited capacity to put his or her experience into symbols. In the second place, the day-to-day functioning of the network introduces noisiness, gaps, and drift into the flow of messages that give it life and coherence as a system. Bureaucracies, as we all know, have limited efficiency. Because hot knowledge and values are at the heart of their practice, perfectionist practitioners are particularly apt to suffer discomfort. The intelligent network covers practice like an ill-fitting glove. Stresses, strains, and doubt are felt.

1. The on-line practitioner senses, from time to time, that his or her practice slips toward chaos and absurdity.

2. The researcher or expert planner senses, from time to time, that his or her wisdom slips toward impotence and irrelevance.

3. A drift of guilt and ethical concern afflicts individuals at all levels of the system.

4. Problems of "low morale," "alienation," and "burnout" reduce or terminate the commitment of practitioners to one another and to the system. Practice worries are chronic in professional practice, and potentially lethal to it.

Practice in the context of ill-fitting theory. Any intelligent network contains a codification or image of the practice "known" to it and managed by it. Managers operate on the basis of expectations about what practitioners can be expected to accomplish on a day-to-day basis. Various rules, prescribed procedures, deadlines, pay scales, specifications, and organizational forms all embody further expectations of what practitioners can do. A network can hardly be intelligent unless this kind of knowledge exists at its higher levels. A network is, among other things, a theory of practice. Unfortunately, this theory must be, by the very nature of things, highly inaccurate. It embodies stylized, standardized, normative expectations of what any practitioner can and should be expected to accomplish; but since people, situations, and momentary possibilities are not all alike, the lived experience of the practitioner repeatedly clashes with the typical and the expected as it is portrayed to him or her by the theory of his or her network. Inevitably, the practitioner must sometimes feel subversive, lost, futile, disconnected, wrong, incompetent, or maligned. The incoherence of declarative moments is not fully resolved in the codes and accounts of his shared professional world, nor can it be. The accounts, like the social structure, offered by the collectivity are standardized. So the practitioner feels, from time to time, that he or she works in a chaotic and absurd position.

Limitations of knowledge and wisdom. The intelligent networks of the perfectionist professions—the educational, social service, mental health, and health care bureaucracies—are not simply human inventions, nor are they fully known or understood by anyone. They appear to be products of a rather prolonged evolutionary process during which institutions, buildings, professional structures, research facilities, laws, regulations, coordinating bodies, etc., have slowly been established and interlinked with one another at local, state, federal, and international levels. The "intelligence" of the intelligent network is not fully known to anyone, but there are people whose role it is to try to "see" large segments of its operation, to articulate what they see, and to offer suggestive or prescriptive ideas for its management. These people are the high-level managers, planners, researchers, and experts who form what might be considered the intelligentsia of the intelligent network. They are held responsible, within the network by those throughout the system, and without the network by those concerned about its function, for declaring the means, methods, goals, and issues that pervade the intelligent functioning of the professional system.

However, living at the furthest outposts of cold knowledge and having intimate acquaintance only with the symbolic messages that run through the communicative channels of the system, these theorists can and do feel out of touch with the realities of practice. Complicating the intellectual problem is an inherent power problem. For an intellectual, being listened to is the equivalent of being treated as a person. Being listened to certifies one's activities and opens the way to power and influence. Hence, theorists do not lightly entertain the idea that their disconnection from practice gives them limited authority or relevance for it. A reasonable presumption may be that practitioners are too conservative, or limited, or fearful to acquiesce to new ideas. (All the folk tales of intellectuals repeat those wonderful moments of the past when the pen proved mightier than the sword, when ideas conquered power.) So the intelligentsia of the intelligent network struggle against the one-line operatives, though from time to time they recognize the severity of the problem of distance and disconnectedness.

The recrudescence of moral issues. An intelligent network of professional practice is a moral enterprise. Any slippage in the efficacy of the network releases deeply troublesome moral questions that are a plague to individuals and the collectivity. Problems of value are stirred up, and these are seen as problems in the ethical standing of the professional enterprise. Are we helping or hurting people by what we do? Are we part of the answer or part of the problem? But even more is involved in the historical drift of ideology away from the action it once presumed to cover and justify: questions of individual guilt and culpability arise; inquirers, practitioners, sponsors, and managers have to confront their basic responsibilities as decent human beings.

Why do moral questions inevitably arise when the ideology of a bureaucratic network is no longer functional? Any significant action that one human being undertakes for another has implications for the other's welfare, motives, or values. That statement is essentially tautologous. Human service professionals are given a special set of privileges and exemptions in their activities on behalf of other human beings. They are permitted invasions of the privacy, freedom, dignity, and civil protections not normally accorded any human being by another. They are allowed to act toward other people in ways that signal harm or sometimes actually harm, because the rationalization for their professional acts is that their overall activity will bring some greater good for those people.

Ethical questions are embedded in the fabric of professional practice with clients and treated in the intelligent network that provides ideology and meaning for the professional. It is characteristic of modern bureaucratic management to try to convert moral and ethical problems to technical and administrative problems. Either a value-laden practical question is completely transformed, so that it presents itself as an ostensibly scientific question (e.g., questions about equality of educational opportunity are obliquely addressed by the presentation of ostensibly technical arguments about hereditary variance in IQ tests, or questions of welfare compensation and eligibility are addressed within the framework of a cost-benefit analysis) or, more commonly, ethical and technical questions are juxtaposed when social and bureaucratic problems are dealt with.

The growing governmental use of formal scientific evaluations involves a subtle transfer of questions of value from the hands of politicians to the hands of scientists and experts.[5] Pretty much the same thing might be said for the various kinds of formal and informal policy analyses now widely used by governmental program planning and budgeting agencies. Policy involves the adjustment of actions and values. Technical questions about the practical consequences of various courses of action have to be combined with questions about the short- or long-term acceptability of envisioned consequences of those actions. The action pattern of an intelligent network, its policy of the moment, inevitably involves practical and ethical considerations. When practice worries become increasingly great, ethical concerns are inevitably involved. Practitioners worry about whether they can justify their actions to others, or to themselves.

The loss of solidarity. A fourth consequence of a slippage of covering ideology in the intelligent network is a kind of entropy of the system as a system. Individuals lose their commitment to the system, or systematically reduce their commitment, to protect themselves. Thus, we find that teachers reduce their commitment to espoused goals of teaching; social workers, to the ideals of rehabilitation; lawyers, to the protection of clients in an adversary position; etc. At the level of individuals or of institutional units, we find routinization and loss of efficacy. Sometimes all this is referred to at the individual level as "burnout." Accepting the proposition that burnout may be a real psychological event in the lives of individual human services professionals, I should argue that it is part of a pattern of individual and group adjustments whose overall effect is to reduce the functioning of the intelligent network.

When we try to decipher the generally loose usage of the concept of burnout, we find five reasonably concrete expressions of the problem. Burnout seems to occur when:

1. There is low morale, expressed as deep dissatisfaction with the professional's work, its auspices, the sincerity of the organization's commitment, etc.

2. There is turnover. People leave their jobs in any one of several ways. They change jobs in the hope of finding a better bureaucratic home, back away from direct practice into "off-line" positions, or retreat to academe, expressing the belief that more education will make things or themselves better.

3. People join radical movements. Staying where they are, they join groups dedicated in one way or another to the radical transformation of the intelligent network. Through affiliations, political action, and journals, they establish secondary alliances that may be dedicated to change in the network by evolution or resolution. They may directly address the organization of the network, as in social reform movements. They may dedicate themselves to reforms that are marginal to the profession itself, as in movements dedicated to various kinds of personal liberation—e.g., gay rights, feminist rights. (See Chapter 10.)

4. Professional work is modified. A continuum of change may occur, ranging from retreat in the interest of bureaucratic safety to a perversion of practice that may include indifference, hardening, or callous exploitation.[6] The minor and most common modification is "protective practice," in which the discretion of the worker is cautiously exercised so as not to rock the boat. The professional's actions are

best understood in terms of the motto "Protect your position." Extreme cases occur in institutional settings in which professionals lose their ethical moorings. Compassion gives way to sadism, and salvationist ideals are converted to the dehumanization of organizational routine.

5. Exhaustion, expressing itself psychosomatically in various odd expressions of physical and mental disease, is evident. People are haunted by work stress. Signs of personal exhaustion are apparent in all of the complex emotional and physiological problems that are manifestations of a kind of bodily "aura" surrounding practice worries. This shows up in collective statistics as occupationally specific rates of morbidity for disease, suicide, and personal disorganization.[7]

Normal Crises of Everyday Practice

The four stresses and strains discussed above are, in effect, four expressions of a problem Peter Marris has insightfully described as the separation of meaning and action.[8] The stories, slogans, maxims, principles, and myths by which many individuals in a bureaucracy feel themselves welded together and harmonized, many people sharing one overarching rational and ethical purpose, all "slip" a little. There is still orderly action. The buildings, paperwork, procedures, clients, authorizations, regulations, resources, and chains of communication remain constant, and the day-by-day routine goes on. But this complex structure of actions is partly unshielded and unjustified in an ideological and emotional sense. There is a split between meaning and action. People keep on doing their jobs, but they are no longer sure they know what they are doing. What they are able to do cannot achieve what they take to be meaningful, because there is no concordance between their sense of the way the world is and their sense of the good.[9]

We may call this kind of slippage a "crisis," and in a real sense it is; but we must recognize that in the domain we are discussing, a sense of crisis may be a normal and unavoidable fact of life. We are talking about Michael Lipsky's[10] street-level bureaucrats: teachers, policemen, social workers, judges, public-interest lawyers, mental health workers, unemployment counselors, and related social service workers. All live in systems that are chronically subject to pronouncements of crisis. The schools are perennially in crisis, and have been so ever since common schooling became a reality near the turn of the century. Crime nearly always hovers near a critical level; and, as Lincoln Steffens demonstrated in his autobiography many years ago, newspapers can virtually initiate a "crime wave" any day simply by printing a complete report of what passes through the police courts on a particular day. For that matter, a series of newspaper articles on plea-bargaining will inexorably reveal a crisis in the courts, and an examination of conditions in mental health facilities will often uncover severe shortcomings. What can one make of a social service system for which newspapers, politicians, and social service workers can variously, each for their own purposes, manufacture crises at will (and, often enough, provide a plentitude of data to "prove" that a crisis exists)?

A certain amount of crisis-mongering and calls for reform seems to be normal to the operation of social service systems. What "crisis" usually means is that someone else within the system rediscovers the leaks in the plumbing and the threadbare state of the ideological fabric. The response of the individual may be good or bad. It is a form of "growing up," of facing reality. It is also, at the same time, a slight loss of motivation and purpose. But probably the pronouncement of crisis in the service delivery system is routine and not fully meaningful in most historic periods. Practice worries of a kind that are endemic eventuate fairly often in calls of crisis. But there are times, of course, when the perception of crisis signals a condition more serious than growing pains. When should the call of crisis be considered a critical event? How do we act on a large, loosely coupled system of practice whose work and whose meaning we do not understand very well?

MANAGING PRACTICE WORRIES BY
RECOMMITMENT AND RECONSTITUTION

The art of maintaining a viable organizational structure for the minor professions involves a delicate balancing, which has been well characterized by Whitehead:

> It is the first step in sociological wisdom to recognize that the major advances in civilization are processes which all but wreck the societies in which they occur: like unto an arrow in the hand of a child. The art of free society consists first in the maintenance of the symbolic code; and secondly in fearlessness of revision, to secure that the code serves those purposes which satisfy an enlightened reason. Those societies which cannot combine reverence to their symbols with freedom of revision, must ultimately decay either from anarchy, or from the slow atrophy of a life stifled by useless shadows.[11]

Generally speaking, intelligent networks of social service descend to a critical condition as they slowly and inevitably move out of harmony with surrounding economic and political conditions. Economic, political, and demographic changes gradually alter the public's need for service, its willingness to commit resources to it, or its tolerance of the traditional efficacy and efficiency of the system. There is a gradual decline in birthrate. Sooner or later, this trend triggers a reconsideration of the organization of school services. For one thing, there is a rising number of superfluous schools and teachers; for another, the delicate political balance between resource allocations directed at different age groups—the very young versus the very old, for example—has to be renegotiated. So changes appear in the organization of schooling.

What triggers the search for a new alignment of consideration and revision is the fact that the intelligent network of the system ceases to adapt to its milieu. There must be a reestablishment of adaptation. There are two levels of problems, to be handled in two different ways. Problems of crisis in the system are always handled by combinations of private and professional activities. In a private solution, frameworks of conventional action are maintained, but the professional takes personal steps to maintain himself as a human being by allowing himself a partial divorce and distancing from the system. In a public solution, the profession as a whole seeks to perfect itself, *within its current stated and normatively accepted standards of what constitutes perfection.*

When the problems of social and political adaptation become larger—as they regularly do every one or two decades for most social service delivery systems—then the system seeks to make a larger adjustment. The system seeks and finds a new myth; it reconstitutes "policy," meaning, and shared purpose. A "glove" is refashioned to fit the hand of practice. Although it is never perfect, it provides for a revival of group solidarity, for community and a sense of shared purpose, and it reinvigorates the individual practitioner. In the enthusiasm of recommitment to the system, the private and public solutions of practice worries tend to merge. A "crusade" develops.

The Approach through Reconstitution

Normal problems arising within a system of practice tend to be approached by the devices already available to the system. This is essentially a bureaucratic tautology. The normal flow of information and communication in schools, service agencies, courts, and clinics regularly brings messages that here and there proper services are not being provided. The almost automatic response to such messages in an intelligent network of practice is to call for more effective coordination.

When a routine response is not immediately obvious, a slightly more complex, but still thoroughly "physiological," response is to search for a point of application of a potentially routine response. Declarative moments and practice worries endemic in the perfectionist professions often enough come to rest on visions of ultimate reconstitution: some superimplementation of the normal will put things to right. So we have fervent appeals for coordination of services, better training, and/or massive new funding, presented with the spirit of salvation entailed in the argument.

The Approach through Recommitment

But the most common approach to large-scale solution, and to crusades, is not through enhancement of normal reconstitutive processes. Great changes in a social service agency take place through recommitment. Indeed, the mythic and policy structures of social service agencies are essentially designed to permit such recommitment to take place as a way of keeping practice worries within bounds.

We have experienced a quarter of a century of consensuality around the ideas summarized by the slogan "the welfare state." The functioning of the economy was not treated as problematic. Indeed, the whole idea of fiscal drag required that resources be spent by government lest that drag undermine the viability of the economy itself. Thus, economic growth and the welfare state reinforced each other. It was in this environment that the service professions could address the question of reconstitution. But now we have entered a period in which the economic institutions are unsettled, productivity is in decline, inflation and unemployment mount restlessly together, the balance of payments is threatened, and large public deficits appear on the horizon. In this new graying of the economy, bold assertive action is called for by a conservative administration, which seeks a "radical" solution—namely, one that "gets to the root" of the malaise. It does so by reopening those once-settled questions about the role of the state that make up the sacred symbols under which the perfectionist professions have sought to create an ever-expanding practice.

The new economic realities will provide the context for the new era we have entered. There are shrinking resources. The society appears to be yearning for the restoration of the old sense of order and stability. The restoration of economic growth would provide the resources that could lead to restoration of the social programs of the welfare state. But in a new global context, as we experience the limits of economic growth, restoration of productivity may not be feasible.

What is unsettled in this period is whether there is a deep transformation in the values of society or whether we can assume that, under the surface, there is continuity of commitment to the prevailing values. If we cannot restore economic growth, then the commitment to the welfare state may be thrown into question, and a new set of values may be evolving. All that can be said with certainty is that the situation is in flux, and the perfectionist professions are practicing in an uncertain and changing environment.

Some observers are very critical of these new developments on the American scene; others view them as an opportunity to realize neglected values. Questions about the rightness or wrongness of current political developments are not, however, relevant for my analysis.

If we take seriously the above quotation from Whitehead, then we, as a society, have to balance reverence for symbols with fearlessness in revision. Generally, movements toward the Right recommit the system to reverence for symbols, and movements toward the Left move the system toward reconstitution and liberal reform. An intelligent network has to be able to move both Left and Right if it is to function in a changing political environment. Perhaps practice worries are the very "feedback signals" that signal momentary strains on the system and permit a continuing flow of reregulation and readjustment. Practitioners of the minor professions seem destined always to be beset by doubt.

NOTES AND REFERENCES

1. The turning of worries into problems represents a *pragmatic* approach to experience. The pragmatic approach is regarded as simplistic (the American primitive addicted to a "quick fix"), but it is actually more complex than it appears to be on the surface. Pragmatic approaches to experience provide not only for

operational declarations—what it is possible to do—but also for ethical declarations—what it is good to try to do.

Isaiah Berlin has remarked that it is rather characteristic of the twentieth-century person to try to turn moral, ethical, and religious questions into technical and administrative ones. This is undoubtedly true. In fact, they are not two classes of question. Neither kind of question has primacy, and each class of question is an expression of the other. But there has been very little analysis to date of how the operationalization of thought, the turning of experience into plans, *instantly and automatically*, also creates an ethical calculus of action. Isaiah Berlin, *Against the Current: Essays in the Literacy of Ideas* (edited by H. Hardy). New York: Viking, 1980.

2. Michael Lipsky, *Street-level Bureaucracy: Dilemmas of the Individual in Public Services.* New York: Russell Sage Foundation, 1980; Eliot Mishler, "Discourses in Medicine." Harvard School of Medicine, 1981 (mimeographed); Carole Joffe, "What Abortion Counselors Want from Their Clients." *Social Problems*, 1982, *26* (October), 112–21; Carole Joffe, *Friendly Intruders.* Berkeley: University of California Press, 1971; Cary Cherniss, *Professional Burnout in Human Service Organizations.* New York: Praeger, 1980.

3. Martin Rein and Sheldon H. White, "Knowledge for Practice." *Social Services Review*, 1981, *55*, 1-41.

4. John T. Dunlop, "Industrial Relations, Labor Economics and Policy Decisions." Presidential Address, International Industrial Relations Association, Geneva, Switzerland, September 1970. P. 5. For a somewhat different interpretation of the policy/research alliance, see Chapter 11 of the present work.

5. See Chapter 11 of the present work.

6. It may be of some interest to speculate about what happens when the pains and worries ("frustrations," "tensions," "disappointments," and the like) that the professional experiences continue unrelieved, when the search for relief through legitimate reform fails. The ordinary human answer is that people "harden." They "get used to it," they "get inured." Recently, Richard Solomon and John D. Corbit have published an opponent-process theory of emotional organization and addiction. They present an argument to the effect that an emotion repeatedly experienced sets up in an organism an internal process "a." This process is subdued, and the organism is restored to equilibrium by an opponent process "null a." The opponent process "null a" may become independently conditioned to arousing conditions, so that it may be aroused in the individual without the original presence of "a." Faced with a disturbance in the form of "null a," the individual may paradoxically seek to reconstitute the "a" emotional experience in order to restore equilibrium. The mechanism is interesting in that it can account for such things as psychological addiction, some of the psychoanalytic hypotheses proposing that individuals reconstitute the traumatizing conditions of their infancy. In the case we are addressing here, it could account for cases of institutional sadism on the part of professionals who regularly deal with human grief. The argument implies that people not only become hardened to the experience of human sorrow: they may actually experience an ultimately perverse desire to establish it. The analogy would be

to the fireman who begins to set fires himself in order to "seek thrills." The mechanism of "institutional sadism" could represent a similar "inversion" of the emotion of sympathy. Richard L. Solomon and J. D. Corbit, "An Opponent-process Theory of Motivation: I. Temporal Dynamics of Affect." *Psychological Review*, 1974, *81*, 119–45.

7. J. W. Eaton, "Stress in Social Work Practice." In C. L. Cooper and J. Marshall, eds., *White Collar and Professional Stress*. New York: Wiley, 1980.
8. Peter Marris, "The Meaning of Life and the Distribution of Uncertainty." Report No. 54, School of Architecture and Urban Planning, University of California. Los Angeles: UCLA, 1980.
9. David Burrel and Stanley Hauerwas, "From System to Story: An Alternative Pattern for Rationality in Ethics." In H. Tristram Engelhardt, Jr., and Dan Callahan, eds., *Knowledge, Value and Belief*. Hastings-on-the-Hudson, N.Y: The Hastings Center, 1977. Pp 111–52.
10. Lipsky, Op. cit.
11. Alfred North Whitehead, *Symbolism: Its Meaning and Effect*. New York: Putnam, 1959. P. 88.

Chapter 9

Comprehensive Program Evaluation

THE CONTEXT OF PROGRAM EVALUATION

Most evaluations focus on program outcome as their primary task. The critical aim of an evaluation study is the specification of whether the original intent is being, or has been, realized.

I think this "reading" is not correct. There is more to evaluation than the study of effects or analysis of the extent to which intent is realized. The latter makes clarity of intent critical; yet, a decade of experience with evaluations makes it clear that programs change in midstream. Even if programs did not adjust to changes in the environment as they evolved and rigidly conformed to the prespecified set of legislative intents, over time the users themselves would change their ideas about the results preferred.

Experience in implementing a program often leads to a change of mind about what the program can or should do. A review of outcomes helps in understanding intentions. In this sense, the beginning and the summative review of a program are parts of the same process. The meaning of the outcome is different after the effort of getting there because, at a later point in time, a new context of events has emerged. Having discovered what the outcome looks like, one can then reassess whether that objective seems either more or less important than when the program began.

A recent General Accounting Office (GAO) report, "Finding Out How Programs Are Working: Suggestions for Congressional Oversight,"[1] cites some difficulties involved in attempting to make a one-time, or summative, assessment of a program's achievements. The report observes that "what is desirable is often altered with the passage of time by circumstance or the availability of additional information. . . . Early overspecification of program goals or measures for oversight questions may lead to questions being asked that are simply unanswerable from inspection of the program as it actually operates."

The idea that we cannot specify in advance the destination of the chosen journey may seem counterintuitive. As Joseph Wholey states, "If you don't know or care where you get to, then it doesn't matter which way you go."[2] These insights naturally draw us to the further specification of our goals.

The United States Senate resolved to work on the problem of goal clarification. A Senate resolution required the specification of legislative intent so that Congress could judge program effectiveness during appropriation or reauthorization decisions. The GAO was asked to assist, which it did by testing the feasibility of goal specifications in an intensive examination of two cases. It concluded that "the results of the dry run did not produce an optimistic forecast that the resolution could do what it intended." Why can't govenment be clear about what it is trying to do? The GAO report explains, "People in groups [that is, interest groups] are often interested in and will accept only certain measures of outcomes. These may be of no interest and/or completely unacceptable to other people and groups." A wide range of oversight questions seems plausible "depending on whose interests are accepted by the analyst."[3] In summary, then, the GAO found that different groups of people wanted different things; and much depended not on intent, but on the way the program was in fact implemented. Because of these considerations, programs can be evaluated from a variety of perspectives.

What is the scope of evaluation of effects? This question assumes special urgency because specifying aims depends on a variety of factors, ranging from the source of knowledge about the subject to the micropolitics of legislative committees. The constructive message of the GAO report appears to be that a useful evaluation essentially requires learning about the experience of a program from two perspectives: why the program did what it did, and what outcomes it achieved by taking account of a broad range of measures that reflect different interests. The report somewhat optimistically recommends that learning can effectively occur through improved communication among the responsible legislative committees and agencies. The GAO puts its faith in Congress's potential for learning from what might be called the "doctrine of the three Cs": communication, clarification, and consensus. Presumably, in a spirit of open and trustful communication, the intent of the various competing groups will become increasingly clarified, and this clarification will eventually lead to an agreement on purposes. "More frequent communication will not only provide more assurance that the objectives and effectiveness measures are agreed upon but that policy makers have realistic expectations as to what information will be forthcoming from the evaluation."

I accept the insights of the GAO appraisal of the problem, but I doubt that the "three Cs" strategy will work in practice except in unusual circumstances in which the commitment to consequence overrides partisan interests. But what are the implications of the GAO diagnosis for those who carry out the evaluations? In order to be able to learn from experience, we must be able to look at the experience as a whole. Studies of intent, implementation, and the measurement of outcome are parts of the experience. Hence, a perspective broader than outcomes, yet including outcomes, is essential.

The difficulty of achieving agreement on detailed aims that can be operationalized in the legislative process rather than at a later stage by evaluators is now widely acknowledged. This difficulty arises partly because of conflicts of interest and the requirement of smoothing over such conflicts in the effort to reach consensus. We can also pose a new and less familiar question: In whose interests are evaluations carried out? Once stated, the question seems obvious. However little systematic attention has been given to an analysis of the interests in evaluation, I believe that the way in which inputs, process, and outcomes are evaluated depends on what we want to do with the evaluation. That interests dominate inquiry is not surprising.

The interests relevant to evaluation are positional interests in the policy-development process. We can usefully identify four of the main interests based on different positions in the process: overseers, administrators, advocates, and policy evaluators. The list is obviously not exhaustive.

Most evaluation studies arise from an interest in oversight. Congress and other legislative bodies want to know if public funds are spent for the program for which they were intended and are not being used as a substitute for locally financed programs; therefore, they request audits. They also want to know about the costs for a given program rather than for some alternative. These studies are carried out by the Congressional Budget Office. Finally, they want to know if they are getting their money's worth—whether the program is doing what it is supposed to be doing. The type of study used in this case is program evaluation mandated by legislation. The oversight interests in accountability are common to the different kinds of evaluations. Is the claim made against scarce governmental resources legitimate?

To appreciate how selective the oversight interest is we need only identify another type of interest, that of the administration of a program or an interest in getting something done. In this setting, political and administrative feasibility dominate. An administrator is interested in ways to achieve compliance without sacrificing morale. For some administrators, the critical question is how to acquire resources to assure the growth and vitality of their bureaucracies. The interests of the practitioners are not the same as those of the administrator; the kinds of evaluation they would undertake would be informed by a different set of questions, including how to protect themselves against intrusive systems of accountability that reduce their scope for the use of professional discretion.

An evaluation to satisfy consumer interests would be different from ones that satisfy the administrative and oversight interests. The critical evaluation of public policy on behalf of consumer advocate groups illustrates the point. Client satisfaction, safety, and investment dominate their interests.

Can we posit a harmony of interests in which all interests are in pursuit of the public interest? It seems more likely that people view the world from their special position in it. Where they stand determines or strongly shapes what they see and what they want to know to increase effectiveness.

Evaluators also have interests. Basically, they want to carry out evaluations with the tools they have. The evaluator imposes order on the world in the context of his or her disciplinary interest so that he or she may study it with the techniques and concepts at his or her command. One celebrated example is the evaluation of the Head Start Program. Evaluators knew something about the measurement of cognitive competence but much less about social competence. As a result, they imposed the objective of the development of intelligence on the program to enable them to evaluate the program with the tools they had on hand.

Briefly, there is no way to achieve understanding without the bias of interest from which an inquiry begins. This does not mean that there is no objective reality. Rather, it means that programmatic posture and disciplinary interests shape the questions that are asked and the methods used to find the answers.

In summary, then, evaluation cannot separate the programmatic interests that commission the study from the disciplinary interests that organize the inquiry. To appreciate the role of the separate interests, we need only consider a given institution, such as a university, and imagine the kind of evaluation studies that would be useful to the boards of overseers, the deans of the schools, the heads of departments, the faculty, and the students. Although there are some topics on which all might agree, each interest would raise quite different questions that they would like to have answered by the evaluator. But each question raised by the various interests would be answered differently, depending on the disciplinary interest of the evaluator. Economic, sociological, and psychological studies would yield different insights. In the analyses that follow, I shall try to give examples of how interest affects the process of evaluation. My main objective, however, is to make a case for comprehensive evaluation. In particular, I want to comment on the assumption in most evaluations that the programmatic unit to be evaluated is self-evident.

I suggest that four elements are necessary in evaluation: we must examine what the program is, what it does, what results these inputs yield, and through what processes these outcomes are realized. I shall cite some examples to illustrate each approach and offer some preliminary suggestions about the research design appropriate for each.

WHAT IS THE PROGRAM?

We assign names to the activities we evaluate, and these names help to specify what we are evaluating. These names comprise the definition of what evaluators call "the program." But the social definition of a program is only the starting point for analysis. We cannot assume that a program is what it is socially defined to be. A program such as manpower training may be defined as an investment in human capital, but in practice it may also come to function as a transfer program, replacing lost wages.

An important aspect of an evaluation, then, is examination of what the program is. Finding out a program's intent begins with the program's rhetoric. Getting beneath the rhetoric to the realities of intent and interest is another question. Defining a program is difficult when there is little agreement on the activities to be included or on the intent that unifies those activities into a coherent purpose. Since the "activity" to be evaluated is not self-evident, it must be treated as problematic, rather than established.

To begin with, we must determine how interests contribute to bounding the unity of activity into budgetary categories. To do so, let us briefly review the different intellectual approaches to the problem of budget classification proposed by the General Accounting Office, which represents the legislative interest in auditing, and the Office of Management and Budget (OMB), which represents the executive interests in the preparation of the federal budget.

Budget classification is essentially an evaluation procedure in which governmental activities are sorted into a set of categories. The underlying logic for this procedure is that similar activities should be grouped together, and the positional interests shape the selection. I should like to illustrate this point with some specific examples.

An early discussion of the question of budgetary classification was published by Murray Weidenbaum,[4] drawn from his experiences working with the federal budget. He summarized the statistics reported in the budget that specify the distribution of the same activity across different administrative agencies. Thus, the answer to the question "How much money is spent on student aid for university students?" cannot be found simply by examining the budget of the Department of Health, Education, and Welfare (HEW) (renamed Health and Human Services [HHS]), which was responsible for the administration of educational programs. In fact, the bulk of the money for student aid is distributed by the Social Security Administration as part of the dependents' allowance for children of aged, disabled, and deceased workers covered by the program. Weidenbaum's generalization led to the development of a table in which function (health, education, income support, training and employment, and so on) was cross-tabulated by department (HEW, Veterans, Labor, Military, Agriculture, Housing and Urban Development). Inspired by Weidenbaum's insight, OMB introduced this kind of analysis in the *Special Analysis of the Budget*.[5]

When income support is cross-classified by function, we find that in 1977, 65 percent of income support was spent by HEW and 35 percent by other agencies (that is, almost $60 billion).[6] In the example above, a grid was constructed of different administrative groups classified by the same activity. This approach has a more general application. The same activity can be assumed to have multiple purposes, and overlapping rather than mutually exclusive categories. For example, a manpower-training program can be classified both as income support and as investment. Other functional goals such as health (psychological well-being) might also be added. From these functions and purposes one could construct a social policy grid based on function by purposes, on the assumption that the same function serves multiple aims. Of course, carelessly adding across the totals would lead to double counting, but adding the rows and columns separately could yield considerable new insights.

The Office of Management and Budget approach to budget classification stems from a different interest and, hence, embodies a very different analytical scheme. OMB approaches the budget classification task by developing mutually exclusive categories. If a program has multiple goals, only the primary goal is used in the classification; the secondary goals are ignored. If a program has ambiguous or conflicting goals, the classifier must make a judgment or inference about intent. OMB describes the logic of this procedure as follows: "The functional classification focuses on the end of ultimate purposes of governmental activity. The stress is on what the federal govenment seeks to accomplish rather than on the means of accomplishment, what the government purchases, or the clientele, or geographic area served."[7]

The skeletal framework on which the budget classification system is based is a set of appropriation accounts and the variety of programmatic activities that are associated with these accounts. The accounts are grouped under a set of functions and subfunctions.

There are only 17 functional categories and about 80 to 90 subfunctions. To be classified as a function, an activity must have a common end purpose, be of national interest, and be of significant size and represent at least 2 percent of total budget outlays over several years. To illustrate the system of classification, consider the specific example of income security. This activity is a function (the functional number is 600) with four subfunctions: general retirement and disability insurance (601); federal employees' retirement and disability (602); unemployment compensation (603); and public assistance and other income supplements (604).[8]

It is the Appropriation Account that provides the building block of the federal budget. It is the smallest level of aggregation for which expenditures are consistently reported in the federal government; it is based on "the *single* best or predominant purpose served." But despite the best efforts at coherence, an account can include quite disparate activities. For example, the Human Development Services Account combines basic grants for rehabilitation services and facilities, Head Start, and nutrition programs for the elderly. Identifying the predominant purpose underlying these activities can be achieved only at a very high level of abstraction.

Clearly, for some purposes, some of the activities in the Human Development Services Account could reasonably be classified in another account. However, moving an activity across accounts is very difficult, because the classification system is tied to organizational structure and moving it would require a departmental reorganization. Thus, the analytic task of classification cannot easily be separated from the bureaucratic turf.

When we take a disciplinary interest in budget classification, we find, surprisingly, that the concept of "program" is not a key analytical concept. In fact, it is never defined in the budget, though accounts do distinguish between direct and reimbursable programs. This is a very special use of the term *program*. Its meaning derives from the budgetary context of its use. The concept of "activity" is closer to the common meaning of the term *program*, but "activity" should not be confused with the concept of a program, because a single activity may contain several programs. For example, under the appropriation account Elementary and Secondary Education, there is an activity called "grants for the handicapped, migrants, the educationally deprived, and grants to the states for administrative purposes."

But what methodology can be used to infer the true intent of an activity that is not self-evident or obvious after a review of the legislative history? The GAO, in its report "Finding Out How Programs Are Working,"[9] offers this advice: "The evaluators must determine from the rhetoric of policy exactly what was intended." Guided by such advice, the evaluators may be able to show, only after much effort, time, and measurement, that the world is quite different from what it was thought to be. In the public arena, evaluators will have difficulty distinguishing a program failure from a misdesigned evaluation that accurately measures programmatic effects if they naively accept the legislative rhetoric as the program's "true" aims.

The same issues arise in budget classification, in which efforts to identify the "ultimate purposes of governmental activity" must address the difficult question of how to infer "true intent" from rhetoric. A specific example might help to illustrate this point. The Basic Educational Opportunity Grant activity is classified under the subfunction "higher education," and the activity "comprehensive education and training (CETA)" is classified under the subfunction "training and employment." The logic of the classification depends upon the assumption that these activities are sorted by their ultimate purposes—education and employment. We could also argue, however, that it would be useful to separate distal and proximal purposes. The most immediate purpose of student aid and training is to provide individuals with cash income. Tuition and training costs should be reclassified under the function "income security." A thoroughgoing reclassification of activities organized according to different conceptual categories would lead to a very different distribution of expenditures by function and by account, and therefore to a very different understanding of existing public priorities. It would also mean a functional reorganization of the agency's organizational structure.

If we further extend our disciplinary interest to understanding not only the activities of the direct federal budget but also the allocation of resources, we are led to a different system of classification. Perhaps the best example of such an effort is the work of the late Richard Titmuss, the "father" of critical British social policy. Titmuss's seminal essay on the classification of activities is based on the argument that activities having similar effects, regardless of their formal intent, should be grouped together. He suggested that occupational welfare, fiscal welfare, and social welfare should be grouped together.[10] His purpose in this recategorization of the activities of the welfare state was to show that, with a broader definition of welfare, society would recognize that income redistribution had not been achieved and that a substantial amount of reverse redistribution had developed—that is, that more welfare outlays had been spent on the middle- and upper-income groups than on the poor.

Budgetary classification is a useful place to begin an examination of what constitutes the meaning of "program." This is an extraordinarily important step in evaluation that has not received the attention it deserves. A first step in advancing understanding in this area would be a systematic effort to reclassify accounts from different intellectual perspectives. As OMB explains, "There is no single best way to classify Federal activities. The functional structure chosen for the budget is the classification deemed most useful for the specific purpose of budgetary exposition." [11]

"WHAT DOES IT DO?"

Let us turn from a discussion of the nature of intention (how it might be understood and classified) to a discussion of the evaluation of the activity as put into place or implemented. Here I distinguish between the program as intended and the program as carried out. Each requires a different evaluation procedure.

In a discussion of programmatic inputs, a primary concern is how a program is put into operation in the field. Evaluators are led to undertake input studies when they are not certain that the program's conception has in some measure been realized in practice. Obviously, there is a continuum between full realization (compliance) and complete failure at realization (nonprogram). The case for a rigorous study of input rests on the assumption that most programs are seldom, if ever, fully realized as conceived.

The study of "nonevents," programs never realized in practice, was identified in the mid-sixties by Herbert Hyman and Charles Wright. Drawing their examples from programs carried out in developing countries and during World War II, the authors offer the following perceptive observation:

> All too often a program is simply a statement on paper of what planners in an agency hope to do that has never been fully translated into action by the field staff. Taking the word for the deed, an evaluator may try to observe the effects of the non-existent treatment. By contrast, no experimenter could ever deceive himself so greatly as to make observations of the effect of a non-existent stimulus, since he would know that he had not yet initiated the procedure. [12]

As an example of a program that was never realized, Hyman and Wright cite a study of the relationship between motivational appeals and mass action during World War II. Persuasion was to take the form of a series of posters that were to be distributed by a national voluntary organization. Thousands of posters were printed. However, although these posters had been printed and shipped all over the country, they remained in local depots for lack of volunteers to distribute them. In this case, the investigators did not proceed with the planned evaluation because they discovered the failure of an input.

The typical situation is not the "nonevent," but the partial event. There is reason to believe that a fragmented government system encourages the substitution of resources. An increase in federal resources to provide a new program initiative may lead to a reduction in expenditures of local resources available from ongoing programs. The result, then, is no additional outlays and expenditures, but only a substitution of federal for local money. In the United States, many social programs are financed by the federal government and carried out at the local level, which provides a great incentive for substitution. If we believe that substitution is a serious problem, we need to develop a methodology appropriate for its study, or to make use of the methodology developed in the traditional audits carried out by the GAO. If the audit becomes an important technique for evaluation, then the traditional distinctions among auditing, monitoring, and evaluating must also be sharply redefined. Since social bookkeeping is an essential element in any program evaluation, we can fruitfully turn to the discipline of accounting for methodological guidance.

In addition to compliance, input studies must address the more subtle problem of progressive transformation of broad aims into concrete practice. Four different types of input can be distinguished: inputs as conceived, inputs as distributed, inputs as received, and inputs as experienced.[13]

The study of *inputs as conceived* assesses the relationships among the theory underlying the program, its programmatic design, and the translation of the design into program inputs, as conceived by the designers. An implicit assumption in this formulation is that a program is an intervention designed to address a problematic situation. "Delinquency" is a problematic situation accompanied by the theory that frustrated opportunity is its cause and that opening pathways of opportunity for those so deprived will reduce its occurrence. The theory must be translated into a concrete method for opening opportunities, which include the design of a program for manpower training or community action. In practice, budgetary, political, administrative, and conceptual constraints influence the conception and design of specific kinds of training and educational programs that could relieve the frustrations that theoretically produce delinquent behavior. A study of inputs as conceived traces the "fit" of problems, theory, design, and projected resources needed to realize the design. At the conceptual level we are dealing with inputs thought necessary for achieving a transition from our understanding of the problem to a strategy for addressing it.

Underlying the intervention, then, is a theory concerning the kind of activities most likely to reduce or eliminate the problem. A program is like a scientific theory, and an evaluation is an empirical test designed to see if the theory can resist falsification. At the empirical level, an evaluator must attempt to discover whether the theory, the design, or the implementation led to the outcomes that he or she observes. An input study addresses only one of these questions—the movement from design to practice. It tries to understand the extent to which the design as conceived was realized or frustrated because of the difficulties in implementation.

The study of *inputs as distributed* focuses on the dissemination of resources in the aggregate administrative units. The Brookings Institution performed the classic study of the distribution of inputs. This study was to monitor whether the distribution of public-sector-financed jobs led to the displacement of local public jobs (displacement meaning the use of federal money to pay for local public employees' salaries, which local government would have paid had there been no federal program). This kind of study does not evaluate outputs, in that it does not inquire into the effects of public service employment or unemployment. It is an impact study of federally financed jobs.

The Brookings project made use of two approaches to the study of inputs: existing statistical analysis from published data, and a new monitoring survey carried out by Brookings. It first used previously published regression analysis that estimated the extent of displacement by comparing actual and predicted displacement. These studies concluded that two-thirds of the jobs were displaced.

The monitoring study estimated the extent of displacement by fieldwork. It used techniques such as direct observation, review of budget and employment conditions, and assessment of demand for services. The monitoring study reached a conclusion different from that of the statistical study. It found that only one-fifth of positions were displaced and concluded that the public service employment program "was significantly more stimulative than substitutive." They concluded that "funds are not fully absorbed over time into general funds of state and local government."[14]

Of course, the task of input studies is made difficult by the complexities of organizational life. We know that inputs can be distributed differently in different settings. Even in the same setting the flow of resources can vary at different times. These variations in the input over time and across space pose difficult problems for a systematic input evaluation.

The study of *inputs as experienced* focuses on the meaning of the program for those who use it. Most of us who teach in universities know that some of the most distinguished professors listed in the catalogue never teach courses because they are preoccupied with their own research, or they act as program administrators and are not available to students. The student may experience this gap between potential and actual realization as disinterest.

It may not always be necessary to study inputs as experienced; however, in certain programs they are important. For example, it may be necessary to study them if we are to understand how clients experience their assignment to an experimental group and what meaning the program's stimulus has for them. Did clients in the Negative Income Tax experiments fully understand the practical implications of different marginal tax rates and guarantee levels? The experiment may have assumed that the subjects rationally responded to different inputs, but they may not have experienced these inputs as the program had intended. In this situation the subjective understanding of the experience by those who receive it is an important input of the program itself.

A study of *inputs as received* is a logical extension of a study of inputs as distributed, but the focus is shifted from aggregate inputs to individual inputs. An Urban Institute study of a national program for Women, Infants, and Children (WIC) is a good example. The political decision to replace direct distributional nutritional programs with food stamps was at issue. Output studies showed that infants enrolled in the program displayed increases in weight, height, and hemoglobin concentration and a decline in anemia. The Urban Institute report cast doubt on the outcome studies by finding that the foods were used by all members of the family—80 percent of the households used WIC foods for family diets. The study also found that although two-thirds of the health clinics surveyed provided nutritional counseling, only 12 percent of the participants indicated that they learned anything about improving their nutritional intake.[15] The study contributed to the repudiation of the medical evaluation of the output inquiry.The Urban Institute findings that targeting food was ineffective because the family pooled food and that nutritional instruction failed to change the pattern of family sharing showed that the inputs as distributed were not the same as the inputs as received. Hence, analysis of results based on such problematic inputs must be questioned.

In summary, each type of input study required a somewhat different methodology. Inputs as conceived call for a conceptual analysis. The study of inputs as distributed requires an institutional analysis of the flow of resources between the funding and the receiving body. An analysis of inputs as received monitors the resources individuals actually received. The study of inputs as experienced entails subjective study of service users designed to elicit the impact of meaning on behavior.

LINKING INPUT STUDIES TO OUTCOME STUDIES

To illustrate how input and outcome studies are linked, I review an outcome evaluation, by Mary Cunningham, that failed to take account of inputs.[16] The study tried to evaluate the impact of two different theories on how to determine eligibility for an income-support program—a new system of declaration, and the traditional comprehensive investigation. The declaration system had been modeled after the income tax system and consisted of simple eligibility forms to be filled out by the clients. No routine verification was made of what the clients claimed was the situation; but a percentage of welfare cases was checked for error and fraud, much as the Internal Revenue Service audits taxpayers' accounts. By contrast, the full investigation approach required expensive interviews with clients, home visits, and independent verification of the clients' situation. Birth certifications were used to confirm the age and number of children; cross-checking with the Social Security Administration and the Internal Revenue Service was employed to determine whether a client was earning money in the labor market. On the assumption that these two distinct program models were implemented in practice, Cunningham proceeded to study how the different eligibility determination procedures affected outcomes such as error, fraud, and acceptance rates. She discovered a significant correlation between eligibility procedure and error.

Cunningham assumed that eligibility procedures represented two distinct inputs into administrative practice. This assumption is questionable. An input study by the GAO revealed that, in fact, there was very little difference in practice between the two procedures for determining eligibility. This was largely because the procedure for full verification was time-consuming and workers took shortcuts and developed a simplified procedure in order to cope with the heavy demands on their work schedule. By contrast, workers were reluctant to accept the simplified eligibility procedures, because they did not trust the clients. They periodically subjected many cases to a full investigation. The net result of these two different processes was that the two types of program were practically indistinguishable. A program that looked different in principle was much the same in practice.[17]

In retrospect, we can now appreciate that the Cunningham study used a crude scale in ranking agencies by their procedures for determining eligibility. Moreover, a weak correlation existed between error and eligibility procedure, which led the author to reach the unsupported inference that the two were related to each other. An input study would have warned the investigator that the instrument developed to rank the degree of stringency and leniency of eligibility determination procedures was of doubtful validity.

PROCESS STUDIES

Initiative for process studies arises when ambiguities appear between the theory of intervention and the sequence of events following from the program to its effects. A process study tries to lay out the process as it developed. An outcome study shows, for example, a strong correlation between income guarantees and labor force participation rates; a process study documents the process of events and motives that led the one event to produce the other.

Process studies, which seek to understand the way thing go together, contribute to a theory of "fit." The vocabulary of fitting and congruence, however, has not been fully developed. We typically make unwarranted inferences, moving from empirical observation to conclusions about congruence.

For example, many observers have noted that school classes function differently among different social classes. In a class of black youngsters from the lowest social stratum, there is a considerable amount of "horsing around." In a class of middle-class blacks, the children are performance oriented, and the teaching style is authoritarian. A white class is organized like a corporation, with committee work and reports. One might infer from these findings that school classes conform to the social stratification in society—that is to say, the class activity "fits" the group for which it was designed.

I want to distinguish the empirical study of process from the theoretical interpretation of function, which asserts that schools "fit" the class structure—that is, they are functional for the prevailing stratification system. Why, one might ask, do schools "fit" the outcome of class structure? What are the processes by which this accommodation takes place? Perhaps the school administrators cue themselves to parental demand. Perhaps teachers preselect themselves for certain schools. Some teachers cannot function in the way they consider appropriate in ghetto schools.

They want to teach youngsters autonomy, and they are unable to adapt to an environment in which this way of teaching is inappropriate.

A process study commits the investigator to learn about the intent of the actors. Documenting the disparity between the intended and the realized is very much at the heart of the sociological imagination. There are many ways in which this could be done. For example, a study could show that a reception center designed for new migrants does not serve them, but serves permanent residents. A housing program designed for self-help for the poor ends up being used by others as a way to find housing to rent. An institutionalized program designed to be a halfway house for mental patients en route to the community in fact accommodates community residents who cannot function in the local community. These examples can be multiplied, but they illustrate how analysis can expose incongruities.

LINKING OUTPUT STUDIES TO PROCESS STUDIES

The 1970s was a decade for large-scale experimentation. The largest and perhaps the most sophisticated were the income-maintenance experiments. The findings of the Seattle-Denver experiment, the last of four experiments in income maintenance, has caused a storm of controversy because of its provocative finding that income support contributes not only to a reduction of work effort but also to marital instability.

The primary goal of the income-maintenance experiment was to obtain information on the costs of alternative designs of income-support programs. Controlled experiments were assumed to provide the most reliable information about cost. Findings about the reduction of work effort were important because they could significantly influence the cost of the experiment. For example, it is not so impressive that male heads of two-parent families reduced work hours between 1 and 11 percent, that female heads reduced work hours by about 15 percent, and that women in two-parent families reduced their work between zero and 31 percent. When the findings are linked to program costs, however, the meaning of the work reduction becomes dramatic. The results show that when a program's benefits are set at three-quarters of the poverty line with a 70 percent benefit reduction rate, the loss of work effort accounts for 58 percent of the total cost of the program. By contrast, in an experimental program that paid benefits at the poverty level with a 70 percent benefit reduction rate, reduced work accounted for only 17 percent of the cost.

Over time, the question of comparative cost has receded from the political agenda because of the difficulty of winning political support for a negative income tax that would provide unrestricted cash grants to able-bodied males in poverty. But although the type of welfare reform proposed in the experiments has passed from the center of political attention—at least for the moment—the findings of the study remain of great interest to evaluators.

Commenting on the findings, Henry Aaron observed, "the less generous program would usually cover lower-income people who worked less to begin with. A decrease in their work effort would be proportionately greater than a similar decrease in the work effort of a group that initially worked more."[18] But Aaron's comments do not help us understand how work effort declines. After all, many blue-collar jobs do not permit a full-time worker to work four or five hours a week less than a full work week. Nor do Aaron's comments help us to understand why the participants in the experiment decided to work less. We need to understand the subjects' point of view compared with that of control groups. How did the subjects in the experiment interpret the payments they received? How much did they understand about these experiments; what conclusions did they draw from their understanding; and how did these conclusions influence their work efforts? A combined input-process study could contribute to answering these questions. It is extremely useful to begin with a known effect against which to measure these processes, because this provides a firm idea about what kinds of processes need to be explained.

The need for a process study becomes even more pressing when the findings are counterintuitive. The experimental finding that income guarantees lead to marital instability is especially puzzling. The experiment showed that

> rates of family instability were about 60 percent higher among blacks and whites who received assistance than among those who did not . . . However, during the third year of the experiment, the effect from white families declined causing white families in the experimental group to be actually more stable than their counterparts in control groups, although by a statistically insignificant amount.[19]

In addition, the rate of family instability apparently increased more in plans with lower benefits than in plans with higher benefits.

Several theories but very little data have been advanced to interpret the findings from the income-maintenance experiment. Researchers distinguish between an income and an independence effect. They believe that a greater income helps families to achieve their aspirations more fully. The independence effect works in the other direction: the guarantee provides a source of support and induces one or the other parent to separate. The independence effect also seems to dominate the action of some groups, but only at certain times in the experiment and not at others. We know almost nothing, however, about how the independence effect works. Does it promote irresponsibility on the part of the father who decides to leave and let the government meet his family obligations? Or perhaps it is the wife who decides that income support provides a viable alternative to a frustrating and inadequate marriage.

Several other theories about the income-maintenance experiment have been advanced. To determine why low benefit produces more marital disruption, Aaron proposed a welfare discount effect. He suggested "that families do not value a dollar of income from welfare as highly as they value a dollar of income from any other source . . . because of the stigma or administration associated with regular welfare programs."

Lee Rainwater proposes two other effects: an anomie effect, in which destabilization arises because family members do not know how to use the additional money allotted to them, and a role-definition effect, in which destabilization occurs because the husband's role as main breadwinner is redefined. To select among these competing explanations, we need to link process and output studies:

> An understanding of the process by which the experimental effect comes about is crucial for any sensible interpretation or debate about what the effect means for policy. Even a clear understanding of the processes certainly will lead people with different values to have a different valuation of the effect. (Some persons have argued that the independence effect is a desirable policy goal.) But at least at that point the value issue becomes clear, whereas as long as there is no understanding of the process it is likely to be confounded by a different interpretation of what really went on in the experimental families.[20]

A process study can help us move from speculation to a more grounded interpretation.

NOTES AND REFERENCES

1. U.S. Comptroller General, "Finding Out How Programs Are Working: Suggestions for Congressional Oversight." Report to Congress. Washington, D.C., 1977; see also Harry Havens, "Program Evaluation in Support of Public Policy." Paper presented at the International Conference on the Future of Public Administration. Quebec, Canada, May 1979 (mimeographed).
2. Joseph S. Wholey, "Using Evaluation to Improve Program Performance." In Robert A. Levine et al., eds., *Evaluation Research and Practice: Comparative and International Perspective.* Beverly Hills, Calif.: Sage Publications, 1981. P. 92.
3. U.S. Comptroller General, Op. cit., 1977.
4. Murray Weidenbaum, *The Modern Public Sector.* New York: Basic Books, 1969.
5. Office of Management and Budget, *Special Analysis Budget of the U.S. Government Fiscal Year 1978.* Washington, D.C., 1978.
6. Ibid.
7. Office of Management and Budget, "The Functional Classification of the Budget." Technical staff paper. Washington, D.C., 1975.
8. Office of Management and Budget. *The Functional Classification in the Budget.* Executive Office of the President, Technical Paper Series BRD/FAB 79—1. Washington, D.C.: U.S. Government Printing Office, 1979.
9. U.S. Comptroller General, Op. cit., 1977.
10. Richard Titmuss, "The Social Division of Welfare." In *Essays on "The Welfare State."* Boston: Beacon Press, 1969.
11. Office of Management and Budget, Op. cit., 1975. A—4.
12. Herbert H. Hyman and C. R. Wright, "Evaluating Social Action Programs." In P. Z. Lazarsfeld, W. H. Sewell, and H. L. Wilensky, eds., *The Uses of Sociology.* New York: Basic Books, 1967. P. 744.

13. This formulation on the nature of input studies is an extension of the concept developed in an unpublished essay by Robert S. Weiss, "Input Studies and Process Studies as Alternatives and Complements throughout Evaluation." Boston: The Laboratory for Community Psychiatry, 1979 (mimeographed).
14. Richard P. Nathan et al., *Monitoring the Public Service Employment: The Second Round*. Washington, D.C.: Brookings Institution, 1979.
15. John R. Nelson, "The Special Supplemental Food Program for Women, Infants, and Children (WIC): A Case Study of Policy Making." Washington, D.C.: National Academy of Science, 1979 (mimeographed).
16. Mary Cunningham, "Eligibility Procedures for AFDC." *Social Work*, 1977, *21*, 21–26.
17. U.S. Comptroller General, "The Comparison of the Simplified and Traditional Methods of Determining Eligibility for and to Families with Dependent Children." Report to the Committee on Finance, U.S. Senate. Washington, D.C., 1971.
18. Henry Aaron, "Welfare Research and Experimentation." Hearing before the Subcommittee on Public Assistance of the Committee on Finance, U.S. Senate, 95th Congress, 2nd session, November 15, 16, 17, 1978.
19. Ibid. P. 38.
20. Lee Rainwater, "Observations of Marital Instability in the Seattle and Denver Income-maintenance Experiment." Cambridge, Mass.: Harvard University Sociology Department (undated) (mimeographed).

Chapter 10

Knowledge for Practice

In an age of science we make a distinction between acting and knowing and between the active person and the knowing person. One ramification of this distinction is a separation of acting or political institutions, such as social service agencies, and government departments, from knowing institutions, such as universities and research centers.

In this essay I explore the assumption that social work knowledge and skills can be value free and exist apart from their practice setting, and I attempt to point the way toward an alternative conceptual framework.

Typically, we distinguish factual knowledge from practical suggestions. When someone asks, "What is the situation?" we look to factual knowledge on various levels for the answer. For example, we explore a single case or pursue the question as it applies to broad classes of situations. What is essential about the process is that value issues and questions of purpose are supposed to be kept out of the arena as we seek "unbiased" knowledge. In contrast, when practitioners ask what is to be done, facts are of interest not only insofar as they are ascertainable and "true" but also as they have relevance for human values and goals.

How do these two modes come together? According to the dominant view, knowledge must be transported into the practical center through applied science. This presupposition leads us to envisage the progressive elaboration of theories in the research community, followed by an orderly, secondary application of theoretical knowledge in the professional community.

Theory generates the idea for a "widget." The "widget" is invented, tried out in the real world, progressively debugged, and widely distributed.

The argument is seductive. If we substitute the term *transistor* for *widget*, it works reasonably well. But this conception of the linkage between knowing and acting is wrong and mischievous when it is applied to practice with humans. Statements of physical relations hold true within boundary conditions and frames that are, for practical purposes, context free. A transistor will function according to its laboratory-determined laws of operation in a white room, a red room, a capitalist society, a socialist society, in the hands of a rejected child, an overprotected child, and so on. However, let us take statements of psychological relationship, duly observed and recorded in one behavior setting, whether a laboratory or the community. For example, take the statements "Humans work for money. Humans tend to shape their judgments to conform to the perceived consensus." These may be replicable and explainable observations in their settings of origin, but all the evidence says that these propositions do not travel very well. Statements about human behavior are closely bound by contexts of observation in a way that statements of physical relationships are not. (This is *not* to say that knowledge about humans never "travels" across contexts or that there never is a useful generalization or maxim about human behavior.)

I suspect that much of the knowledge that determines practice today originates in the context of practice. This view of the restricted domain of social science knowledge can be found in the writings of critical analysts throughout this century. In 1899 John Dewey, addressing the American Psychological Association, stated:

> ... the completer the control of conditions, with the resulting greater accuracy of determination, demands an isolation, a ruling out of the usual media of thought and action, which leads to a certain remoteness, and easily to a certain artificiality.[1]

Some eighty years later, we find the same argument being presented by a prominent social scientist, Elliot Mishler:

> Context-stripping is a key feature of our standard methods of experimental design, measurement, and statistical analysis ... Our procedures are aimed at isolating variables from their functioning personal and social contexts. We try to find pure variables, measures of unitary dimensions that will be uncontaminated by other variables ... It is clear from the history of psychometrics that it is possible to do this, or at least to create the illusion that there are variables that are both independent and pure. It is much less evident that such variables have brought us any closer to the general laws they were intended to serve or to a deeper understanding of human actions ... There is a crisis of confidence among investigators in the social and psychological sciences ... A prominent theme in these recent critiques is the discovery that research findings appear to be context-dependent. For this reason, the search for lawful generalizations that would be cross-contextually valid has proved to be more difficult than expected, and, some of the critics argue, may be a misdirection.[2]

Both Dewey and Mishler argue that the creation of highly controlled experimental situations invalidates research findings when they are applied to a natural human context. Chris Argyris goes a step further.[3] He argues that the experimental situation is itself a special kind of natural situation in which the values and purposes of the participants are subordinated to a unique human relationship. Subjects are told what to do. Their time perspective is restricted, and their behavior is confined to formally restricted alternatives that allow for objective measurement and predict exact specification and replicability. The scientist "distances" himself or herself from the experiment so as not to contaminate the results. However, the very effort to increase validity is self-defeating because the experimental situation creates a dependency relationship in which the experimenter sets all the terms of the human encounter.

I am critical of the view that knowledge and action are split and then reunited by a process in which one first accumulates knowledge that is based on general principles and that acting people passively receive objective principles handed to them by men or women of knowledge. Before examining how knowledge and action are related, we need a richer and more detailed understanding of what we mean by "practice." Only then will we be in a position to ask what we need to know in order to practice.

THE NATURE OF PRACTICE: AN OVERVIEW

Let us make a distinction between *praxis* and *practice*. *Praxis* is what everybody knows how to do and does in a society. *Practice* consists of a special system of actions unique to, and institutionally vested in, a professional role. It occurs when certain social behavior is drawn from the general behavior of the society and segregated in a special professional preserve.

"Conventional thought has practitioners inhabiting a world of action; they are doers, people who apply skills and knowledge to the solution of practical problems."[4] What we usually mean by social work practice is best described as action in an institutional setting that involves the commitment of a group of individuals to a special set of *skills, purposes, power relationships,* and *myths.* Let us examine each of these aspects in turn.

Skill

Skill is a special ability peculiar to the professional—possession of an effective way of realizing purposes. The professional has "know-how," i.e., *means* that can be utilized in the pursuit of ends. Social workers typically have specialized knowledge about psychological processes, institutional service systems, structures of government, enabling legislation, and psychoanalytic techniques. In this sense, social work is something other than ordinary human social behavior concentrated in a profession. Professional schools of social work are generally regarded as places that teach the required skills to the practitioner.

Since I have already suggested that social workers share purposes, power relationships, and myths as well as a set of skills, I shall examine the curiously complex reasons why public discussion of the professional's role centers on the skill aspect of that role.

In fact, a mass of interlocking assumptions dictate this special view, and they appear to be embedded not simply in our conception of the minor professional. Indeed, they form a broad base for general social conceptions of knowledge, education, and action. Let us consider what some of these assumptions are.

1. *A professional is much like a "social mechanic" and must be dealt with in similar terms.* A mechanic has the ability to fix a machine when it breaks down, a salable skill that we buy at his or her price. His or her human qualities of judgment, knowledge, and faith are largely irrevelant to our relationship, which remains largely formal. We assume that professionals are like mechanics in this special way and that the skills are the interesting and socially valid part of the professional that must be dealt with in treating social breakdown.

2. *Skills are "know-how"—that is, instrumental or operational abilities.* Looked at more closely, what we generally mean by the "skill" of the practitioner is assumed to consist of a set of trainable, teachable subskills. A strongly behavioristic set of assumptions runs through the literature on professional training and practice. John Dewey described the approach elegantly at the turn of the century as the ability to take the living personality as an objective mechanism for the time being.[5] The attributes of human personalities are *functions,* that is, discrete abilities to get things done. A professional, in this view, is a human being with a special set of such abilities.

However, the traditions of social work are complex. The ruling philosophy of pragmatism in social work is also preoccupied with an antibehaviorist "revolt against formalism" that calls attention to the importance of context and resists rigid classification; it emphasizes process rather than formal structure and the reciprocity of means and ends. In a perceptive discussion of the philosophical assumptions underlying Mary Richmond's classic statement about social work method in 1917, Charles Gilbert notes that in her words she

> stressed "individualization" rather than classification of cases, a creative relationship between case worker and "client," the practical indistinguishability of the investigation—diagnosis—treatment stages of the casework process, inquiry into the client's total social situation and penetration of the several "social selves" that shaped his dependence, and the absence of objective tests for the solution of clients' problems.[6]

Without abandoning the tension of its earlier philosophy, social work ambivalently focuses on both discrete abilities and total personality.

3. *People learn professional skills through training.* This view of the professional's skills leads immediately to a peculiar paradox in the case of social work education. The ideological commitment of the social worker is to view human activities as part of a process in which means and ends, subject and object, are blurred. Yet

this view of the substance of social work activity conflicts with the contexts of training offered in schools of social work.

Professional schools of social work share the general perspective of the larger ideology of higher education of which they form a part. They add skills and functions to the individual whose core, in some deep sense, is assumed to remain constant through the process. A person's essential political and moral beliefs and values are considered to be of no concern in the context of professional training and practice.

Of course, it is not possible simply to "add" professional competence or skill on to anyone. It is manifestly clear that a person's human qualities and moral and political commitments make a vast and crucial difference in social work practice. These issues of value can be, and have been, dealt with under the label "mental health." A social work practitioner must be a mature and healthy person with "interpersonal skills."

The culmination of the assumptions I have so far discussed is the ultimate treatment of the knowledge and skills of the professional as a kind of commodity. This commodity, "know-how," may be added to people, who can offer it to others in the spirit of a mechanic, as pure expertise without undue coercion. This valuable commodity, "know-how," is acquired in training institutions that participate in a kind of upgrading of the commodity. The commodity is itself a product of the technology of research, which is the source of its knowledge. Progressive increases in knowledge augment and transform the corpus of "know-how." Conflict, purpose, and power are underplayed in discussion and ignored as much as possible as issues. When they must be dealt with, they are treated in an essentially *ad hominem* style that regards conflict as an expression of the mental health problems of individuals.

Finally, the structure I have discussed mistakenly assumes that clients always come voluntarily to the professional relationship seeking help. The help that is offered is not coercive and does not get into questions of private faith, morals, or politics. The treatment is technological, and it is added on to clients whose problems stem from the fact that they are deficient in their own human skills.

Purpose

Up to this point I have taken a somewhat satirical approach to discussion of the grounds of the skills-oriented approach to professional training and practice and the peculiarities of the assumptions on which that orientation is based. My intent, however, has not been either to denigrate the skills-oriented approach or to deny its utility,; rather, it has been to raise for discussion the latent issues of purposes, power, and myth on which the skills-oriented approach to training rests.

What do social workers like to believe about their purposes? They assume that their allegiance is to society as a whole, not to any segmented solidarity group as represented, say, by social-class, ethnic, or business interests; they legitimate their goals in universalistic terms. The purpose of social work, as stated by one of its outstanding scholar-practitioners, is: "The general aim of the social caseworker, the social agency, and the society that supports them is to restore, reinforce, or to enhance people's personally satisfying and socially satisfactory daily functioning."[7] Note that not only social work but society shares the stated aim; in the statement there is, subtly, but definitely, commitment to see no conflict between individual and social needs.

There is, however, not simply one grand purpose to the social welfare enterprise. Social workers are bound to the realm of the scientifically legitimate; they are committed to self-determination and compassionate service to humanity, as they follow the medical model of diagnosis and treatment. In addition, they are committed, in a secondary way, to such diverse ends as, on the one hand, the maintenance of their profession and, on the other hand, advocacy of more employment and better housing for their clients. We state this array of purposes without asking whether they form a consistent whole. The purposes of a profession do not have to be logically consistent any more than, say, the purposes of an individual human being. The point is that commitment to a profession implies commitment to a set of primary and secondary purposes that are as characteristic of the profession as the skills embodied in it.

Within the rules of legitimate function, social workers have power over others, and they exercise it in both an assertive and a submissive sense. There are formal conditions for entry into client status that define the legitimated reach of the social worker's ability to come into contact with others. People do not always come within the scope of social work willingly; they may be sent by other agencies, such as courts and hospitals, under threat of legal action. Whether willing or unwilling, the client negotiating with the social worker is, to some extent,[8] "in the hands" of the social worker. The social worker is, in turn, "in the hands" of other administrations and authorities. Although the practice of social work includes acceptance of several kinds of power relationships, the quintessential ideal remains self-determination on the part of the client, in which the social worker helps people realize their own purposes as they define them. The worker represents no interests other than universalism, reciprocity, humanitarianism, and individualism in helping the client to achieve self-fulfillment.

In fact, however, these values gloss over the reality of the purposes embodied in social work, because every professional action of a social worker is affected by a network of solidarities and a set of political purposes.

One of the great fantasies of modern bureaucracy is the premise that human beings can form a truly universalistic relationship with other human beings. A universalistic relationship is one in which everyone is treated in exactly the same way no matter who he or she is. The example that comes closest to fulfilling this ideal might be a completely rule-bound game—bridge, chess, checkers—although even this is not completely apt because human behavior may be determined by factors such as degree of trust or liking of the other player as well as by rational calculation.

Because social work can never be a universalistic practice governed completely by rational rules, *we approximate these ideas by maintaining multiple and conflicting solidarities.* A social worker is (1) a member by origin of some distinctive social group (say a big-city resident, Italian); (2) part of the fellowship of social workers; (3) an employee of an agency; (4) a citizen of city, state, and federal government; and (5) a taxpayer. When others come to social workers and place pressure on them in their interests, they are appealing to interests that both they and the social workers have in common. A social worker moved by competing solidarities may approximate the ideal of universalism, but only at some personal cost. The cost is a felt vacillation, a conflict of purposes, and a constant, vague sense of dilemma; these are the feelings of all who try to play universalistic roles in a bureaucracy.

When the social worker is subject to conflicting solidarity relationships, only one of those solidarities is with the client. The social worker and the client share a meaningful human relationship embodying elements of trust and respect for one another's dignity. Within the framework of a professional relationship based on trust and respect, social workers can state with utter sincerity that they want clients to determine their own individual values. This, however, is false. If the client states that his ultimate salvation rests on becoming a successful pimp, a chorus of Jungian *personae* arises inside the social worker to oppose this in outraged terms. So the client who seeks self-determination in discussions with a social worker is, in effect, negotiating with various groups in society incorporated within and expressed by the social worker.

These observations lead to the view that the relationship between practitioners and clients is fundamentally ambiguous. The former must play by the rules in order to channel advantages to their clients. They cannot, however, oppose clients in the name of the system because that would undermine the trust essential to the helping relationship. Both pulls must be acknowledged and dealt with.

The difficulty for the social worker is acute. It is very difficult for one human being to be many people, and many social workers yearn to become professionally one person. The search for integrity takes several forms.

1. *I am One with the client.* One way to deal with the conflict is to assert the dominance of one solidarity to the exclusion of others. To make an ideology out of the choice, social workers identify clients as representative of underprivileged, power-deprived, societal figures. All other solidarity groups are condensed to form "Them," the power of privileged groups that make war on the client figures. An adversarial arrangement arises, practitioners signing on as members of one camp or the other.

2. *Everyone really agrees.* Another way to alleviate the stress of conflicting solidarities is to assert their irrelevance. One makes the assumption of basic values that unite all human beings—compassion, the wish to relieve pain, the belief in self-betterment—and ignores the disagreements. Whereas the previous position simplified the set of conflicting solidarities by reducing them to two, this position wipes out conflict by asserting a transcendental solidarity. The position has some merit since one way in which political groups resolve conflicts is by an appeal to shared values. So, although this position may be ideologically limited, it has some

tactical strengths. It disposes of all the social worker's *internal* conflicts, since what he or she feels is right is what everyone would feel is right.

The basic weakness of this position is that it offers nothing to hang onto when reality denies it. Should an alcoholic be permitted to drink up his or her welfare check? Does his or her action represent a threat to others, or only to himself or herself? If a social worker affirms self-determination in this situation, he or she will be faced with the plain fact that everyone does not agree. Another idea is needed.

3. *I have a set of skills.* One can go one step further and simply bury the question of values altogether. Not only is there no conflict, multiple or dual, but value questions are out of the arena altogether.

This is, of course, exactly the position from which I began my discussion of the goals and purposes of social work. In fact, it is hard to sustain the fiction that social work is a value-free activity. Social workers concede that their practice is value committed. So this position, while appearing safe, inevitably leads to a kind of oscillation—forward to confrontation among solidarity groups, back to an aloof professionalism, and forward to confrontation again.

Power

The practice of social work involves the exercise of power, in a conventional sense of the term. Social workers tell people what to do and, if the people do not do it, then social workers may impose penalities such as (a) taking a person's child away (because of child neglect); (b) stopping or reducing the flow of money to the person (welfare); or (c) recommending that a person be sent to jail (for the protection of society). This very statement of what a social worker can do is offensive to social workers in the form in which it has just been stated. There are qualifications; social workers do not do anything unilaterally—they act in a system of checks and balances.

What social workers would like to feel is that they have professional authority based on knowledge rather than on status. The problems here go very deep. Near the turn of this century, when social work took part in the great wave of professionalization that came upon American society,[9] one essential feature of the movement was the conversion of authority relationships among people, as much as possible, to a legitimacy of knowledge. There was a great wave of interest in the "scientific management" of American business and political institutions—a wave that is still with us. Part of the impetus for this movement was a repugnance for older forms of authority based on coercive relationships. Free people could accept the authority of someone more knowledgeable than they, and such authority was not coercive.

Since social workers often work with people who are at the margins of the American power structure, and since social workers often strongly oppose the use of power and coercion for the settlement of human negotiations, their exercise of power-within-authority is especially troublesome to them. This is particularly true because their mask of knowledge—that which transforms power to authority—is so terribly thin.

The uncomfortable fact is that the power of social workers, without which they cannot function, depends on control over resources of several kinds. In effect, each of the solidarity groups of which the social worker is a member gives resources to the social worker in anticipation of future benefits. Some of these bargains are deeply buried in old legislation, and some are regularly horse-traded.

The executive and the legislature give the social worker money and access to municipal resources because they anticipate a more peaceful community and more votes in the next election. Clients give the social worker cooperation because they want access to these resources. The court gives the social worker a voice in sentencing because it wants a better decision. Citizens may give the social worker Community Chest funds because they want to buy insurance against possible disruption of the family, homeless children, and so on. The power of the social worker depends on access to scarce resources and legal sanctions.

Thus far I have discussed the fact that social workers use the power embodied in resource control and sanctions while at the same time denying it. They embrace skill and expertise as their true legitimation and the basis of their professional authority. In short, the social worker has use of the resources of a ward boss without significant power as an individual.

A society can best maintain an underclass of poor and desperate people without either the constant threat of disorder, revolution, or a troublesome degree of repression by the institutionalization of lifelines. Since poor people are at the mercy of whoever offers them a lifeline, a lot of normal politics works through the dispensation of such resources through political bargaining. This, however, plunders the public treasury and makes political decisions irrational and quixotic. What the social worker system does is to leach out of the political sector a great deal of lifeline power that might otherwise be used for this kind of disorderly power politics. Social workers dispense the substance of power, but a mighty commandment somewhere says that they must not regard it as power.

Myth

I use the term *myth* here to mean a special kind of story that organizes attention and legitimates action. It has these functions:

1. It connects the present moment with the past and the future. Because X happened in the past, then we have to do Y to achieve some desired end, Z, in the future.

2. It aligns rational action with normative ideals and historic commitments. We are doing this now because the world as we know it seeks C and suffers from D; our duly constituted forefathers committed themselves to K as the proper sphere of action.

3. It selects some familiar objects and events and imbues only them with rational and emotional meaning. Pay attention to E; be wary of I and J; ignore R.

4. It justifies rituals of practice and to some extent regulates them by stating the circumstances under which they may be altered. The myth asserts that these rituals work.

I am perfectly aware that positivistic views of science dominate professional practice today and condition the widespread view that myths are a form of witchcraft, to be sought out and dispelled. However, this positivistic view of professional practice is exactly a myth in the sense of points (1) to (4) above. It legitimates scientific action. In my view, the social sciences produce evidence that is embedded in stories that serve to bring meaning to human action in the way that stories always have in human societies. Stories that fit well are maintained and embellished; stories that get out of tune with experience get lost in history, and are replaced by new stories.

Social workers constantly tell each other stories about their profession, its mission, and its clientele. All this gossip and professional shoptalk has an instructive and value-forming function. The stories find pronouncements in practice, and are tested against the pronouncements of dogma. They justify. They communicate information that may sooner or later be encompassed in the corrigible mythic system—anomalies, critical incidents, exemplary anecdotes.

There are at least three classes of stories: stories about institutions, about people, and about professional practice. An institutionalized story is politically or sociologically oriented, and it tells how people got to be in the situation they are in. One current story says that with the coming of industrialization and urbanization, people have moved into cities and have been forced to exist in isolation, without ties to a nourishing community. The role of the social worker, in the light of this story, is to act in ways that will restore to people their sense of community. A variant story today explains the problems of blacks in American society by recalling that great numbers of them have only recently come up from a rural existence in the South into a rootless existence in Northern cities. (I am not here denying the credibility of these statements as stories; I am simply pointing out that they are, first and foremost, mythic stories.) Institutional stories generally place present-day clients in a situation of specified need that is the outcome of a historical process of institutional change. On the basis of these stories, clients may variously be pictured as victims of alienation, the decline of the family, inflation, the changing nature of the labor market, economic fluctuations, or shifting ethnic politics.

A contrasting kind of mythic story grounds practice in a story about people, how they change over time, how they get into trouble and out of it, where they are going, and what they ought to be. Consider the clients of a social work agency. What characterizes all categories of service users seems to be the fact that they seem to have gone to the edge of their resources. They need strength. Institutional myths generally take the position that the restoration of individuals to strength will occur only if they are reestablished in an appropriate social network. People myths, on the other hand, take a kind of redemptionist position: if one can restore the individuals' natural, latent strengths, they will make their own way in the social system.

Myths grounded in empiricism serve a prominent place in practice, but their existence and role have been neglected because of the prevailing positivistic emphasis. Bronislaw Malinowski suggests that all societies (and, I should add, all systems of social action) rest on a judicious combination of science, magic, and myth.[10] I call upon science to provide me with instrumental knowledge, to tell me what buttons to push in order to achieve desired action. There are things that we do in which this is always possible. I call upon magic when I am in situations where I have to act, where the stakes are high, but I am uncertain about what to do because I have no science to guide me. Practitioners cannot always say that they are uncertain, even to themselves. They have responsibility, social and moral, for acting on the problems that fall within their sphere. Finally, I call upon religion and myth to give me a vision of the goals and value structure of the system within which I act. Social work always thinks of itself as a profession committed to values, but the argument is more general. Humans need teleology. They need purposes for striving; they need faith to sustain commitment to those purposes. Myth and religion, in the end, provide us with dogma that anchors our activities in values.

What is the essential role of social scientists vis-à-vis human practice? Social scientists both create stories that bid for the guidance of practice and live under the positivistic myth that they are neutral and value-free contributors of facts to the practitioner. Denying myths, the social scientist deals in myths. Asserting the value of disinterested fact-gathering, social scientists search in vain for the influence of facts on practice and policy. They can accept the legitimacy of their role in destroying myths, but are much less comfortable in the role of creator of myths.

Professional practice stories, in the effort to create myth, picture the history of social work as progressive, with a major growth process entailed in the transition to professionalism. The myth "explains" why there are social work schools in universities, why social workers should worry about what social scientists have to say to them, why it is bad to practice social work without training, and why clients, sometimes against their will, should cooperate with social workers. In its simple form the commonly accepted myth addresses social work as one profession and speaks of the gradual acquisition of commonly grounded skills, with casework as the nuclear method. From this narrow base the profession achieves a posture that is, on the one hand, maximally legitimized by psychological theorizing and, on the other hand, minimally confrontational with the social order.

Roy Lubove epitomizes the trend in this way:

> The persistent efforts of caseworkers to establish a scientific knowledge base and methodology, to limit the area of intuition, moralism, and empirical insight, however much they fell short in practice, showed the extent to which the goal of rationality permeated the subculture ... Even before the 1920s, the nineteenth century distinction between the "worthy" and "unworthy" poor had been discredited; and the influence of psychiatry and mental hygiene persuaded some social workers that they were therapists whose skills were applicable to all cases of maladjustment ... Antisocial behavior became a challenge to the worker's professional skill, instead of a cause for moral indignation and condemnation.[11]

However, unhappily, this neat attempt at normative mythification did not survive the onslaught of the 1960s, with its major challenge to the social agency concept of rendering service through professional practitioners. There emerged a growing awareness that the vast majority of incoming cases close within several months after opening and that many of the same cases repeatedly reappear within the same agency or circulate in small networks of community agencies.

The Framework of Practice

I have developed at some length an argument about the structure of practice in social work. The essential feature of the argument is that practice takes place in an institutional setting. Not only do social workers exercise a set of skills: they work within an organized group structure that (1) maintains shared purposes, (2) receives legitimated power from the society at large and uses it, and (3) rationalizes itself through a set of stories about people, institutions, and the profession.

When things are going well and there is stability in the profession, there is an emphasis on skill and an implicit agreement that purposes are known and not problematic, that power relationships among clients, sponsors, and professionals are accepted, and that myths reaffirm consensual values.

Skill is the overt, discussable part of the profession; purpose, myth, and power are the latent. But when a practice transcends normal function, such as when government actions force unintended, unforeseen, and undesigned-for clients into the professional sphere, then a kind of crisis of consciousness ensues. The latent rises to consciousness, and the profession becomes concerned with "philosophy," purpose, myth, and power. These are discussed, amid a general feeling of uneasiness and impending disaster.

When we ask how knowledge contributes to practice, we generally assimilate that question instantly to the science-to-technology framework that has dominated our discussions of the social sciences and social practice in this century. Where does knowledge come from? It comes from scholars and scientists. Where does knowledge go? Why, of course, it goes into skills. I am here arguing that the knowledge necessary for practice must come from practice itself to a great extent, and I suspect that this already happens. Furthermore, I suspect that the importation of sophistication and "outside" knowledge into the context of practice depends on mechanisms other than traditional research and development. What is needed is changed knowledge-building structures to facilitate the growth of this kind of knowledge, which must address the institutional setting. Knowledge, adequate and satisfying knowledge of the world, is just as vital in legitimizing and rationalizing practice as it is in implementing the skills of the profession.

PRACTICE IN A CONTEXT OF FAITH AND DOUBT

In 1976, a meeting was held at Madison, Wisconsin, that took as its model the Milford Conference of 1929.[12] The meeting addressed the question "Is there a common conceptual framework for the social work profession?" Reporting on the meeting, Scott Briar states:

Based on this admittedly limited experience, the seemingly inescapable conclusion is that at this time in the history of social work there is not a widespread consensus about the profession's mission and purpose. One participant expressed the frustration of many by suggesting, "Maybe social work has no mission!"[13]

Briar goes on to state that "large areas of agreement were apparent if not always articulated . . . ," but perhaps this quotation is sufficient to suggest that the adherence of all social workers to a common conviction about their purposes, power, and myths is not unmarked by doubt.

I should like to suggest that the problem alluded to by Briar is not simply a matter of confusion or incoherence about the mission of social work. Social workers have negative feelings about the profession arising out of beliefs that (a) the skills they possess do not work, that they are not, in any real sense, skills; (b) those skills, even if they do work, are irrelevant to the vast majority of activities in everyday social work; and (c) the benign myth of professional skill masks, sugarcoats, the fundamental functions of the profession, which are political and unattractive. Political activity, in its more neutral role, consists of "cooling out" the victims of social injustice;[14] at its more negative pole, it involves the exercise of the political power of the social worker to inflict undemocratic, unjust infringements on the liberty of clients.

Coexisting with these negative feelings, living with them in contradiction, are strong positive feelings about the profession. These arise from the visibility of the human needs that pass before social workers every day and from the fact that there are clearly times when the client says sincerely that the social worker has been of help and when the social worker can clearly believe the client.

So the community of social workers, as I have here characterized it, is marked by strong doubts mingled with positive affirmations. This mixture of faith and doubt is enervating for the profession. It leads to what a good many today would characterize as a *malaise* among social workers. We feel that beginning attempts at resolution of the malaise would involve recognition that the positive and negative feelings arise at different loci of the institutional setting of social work.

Causes of Doubt

If we look at the causes of doubt in social work, we find several sources. First, there are, as noted earlier, a basic incoherence and uncertainty that afflicts all of the extant stories about the coherence of the work. The various stories about institutions, the profession, and people that should nourish professional solidarity do not form an integral mythic structure, but seem to be fragments of different sagas. Some stories align social work with the theme of personal redemption through reconstruction with the community; some align it with essentially religious themes of succor to the afflicted and needy; still others align it with something like a demonology, picturing social workers as the agents of capitalist repression. How can a social worker sustain faith when the testaments of the profession lead in so many directions?

Second, beyond the experience of incoherence is the fact that the social sciences, assumed to be thc friend and ally of the professional social worker, have turned to a posture of mixed friendship. Once positivist social science looked like a rock upon which the profession could build. Gordon Hamilton told the National Conference on Social Work, in 1941, that "The base of social work is potentially scientific; . . . the social sciences must increasingly throw light on social needs and social improvement . . ."[15] However, evaluations of projects and programs have yielded a growing body of scientific testimony that social work does not produce results and, indeed, that "professional" social work might just as well be carried out by nonprofessionals.

Not only are there no benefits but there may well be no needs. Studies at the Hoover Institute, an admittedly conservative bastion of social scientific analysis, have recently been used to support an argument that there is really no poverty in the United States (when in-kind government benefits are assigned a monetary value and added to the income of the poor). So social science has arisen to assail the most fundamental arguments for need and efficacy in social work. Positivist social science can be found that goes in the other direction, of course, but a debate among scientific polemicists cannot, by any stretch of the imagination, be considered an objective basis for the constitution of social work professionalism. The last straw, ultimately, is the genre of modern revisionist social science that argues that the use of positivist science as a basis for practice amounts to the impositions of a technocratic attack on human liberty. As Alan Keith-Lucas says:

> Once a positivist science becomes the rule of law, or once a group in our society arrogates to itself the right to judge or to treat another by the findings of such a science, no end to the process is in sight. What happens depends entirely on the good will of the self-appointed "social physician."[16]

A third source of contemporary doubt rests on the common discovery of the social worker that the system all around—the bureaucracy, the profession— frequently acts to subvert its own ends. The most obvious phenomenon is "slotting" clients into predetermined categories that reflect the needs of the agency rather than the needs of the client. The kind of service a claimant receives from an agency depends to a great extent on the kinds of service the agency is prepared to dispense. There is an abundance of documented cases in which clients have wandered through the social agencies of a city, changing labels and services in chameleon-like fashion as one agency after another sought to assimilate the client within its own organizational mandate. Frequent occurrences of this kind are demoralizing to the social worker.

A fourth and final cause of contemporary doubt seems to arise from the fact that some traditionally constituted justifications for professional social work seem to have eroded over time. One important device for the assertion of a professional core of knowledge was the appeal to psychoanalytic kinds of theorizing as the potential nucleus for a comprehensive professionalization of casework. It was felt that therapeutic techniques embodied in such casework would potentially be recognized as the nucleus of effective social work in all of its contemporary settings—

the hospitals, the schools, the prisons, the welfare departments, the charitable agencies—and the source of the definitive superiority of the paid worker, trained in a professional school, over volunteers and amateurs. Generic casework rested for its justification on psychoanalytically oriented casework.[17] The hoped-for assimilation of all sorts of social work to one generic methodology still remains only a hope some fifty years later, asserted, but in a rather diffuse and convictionless way, in the contemporary textbooks of the discipline.

Living with Doubt

One question that has to be faced is how a person manages to operate in a field of faith mixed with doubt. How do social workers contend with their own doubts? They deal with them, generally, in the way most people do when acting under uncertain convictions. I offer now a list of personal strategies by which social workers and others maintain their conventional patterns of action.

1. *Don't think. Act!* Much of the day-to-day work of social work is, happily, unproblematic. A large body of meaningful small pieces of business confronts the social worker each day. One common approach to social work is to concentrate on the business of the day and leave the rationalizations to others.

2. *Smile on the outside. Keep the crying on the inside.* One can accept thought but at the same time avoid contradiction by adopting a kind of "double vision" strategy. When events fall within conventional accounts of the field, reaffirm the positive stories. When events fall without, express doubts. But keep the two visions of the field separate and maintain, in effect, coexisting stories that the work is all right and not all right.

3. *Fight for more.* A classic way of maintaining faith in the myths of the profession while acknowledging their unreality is to argue that further resources or organizational efforts will make the myth real. Doubt is redefined as frustration. Festinger's classic study *When Prophecy Fails* offers a social psychological account of the way a fringe religious group redoubled its affirmation of a guiding myth when prophecy (a predicted day of doom for the Earth) failed to be confirmed by events.[18]

4. *Join a new club.* When doubt grows in a social group, there is a tendency to find a proliferation of small, variant subgroups that continue to offer a kind of organized faith in the future. These subgroups actually may be the seedlings of positive social change for the system as a whole. Psychotherapeutic practice today, within and without social work, is marked by a rather astonishing proliferation of diverse schools of therapy that moderate traditional practices and goals through developments such as co-counseling, family therapy, behavior modification, encounter groups, and the return to Jungian practice. Sometimes the club one joins is part of a broader social movement, such as the women's movement, the civil rights movement, or the Union of Black Social Workers. Often the same action is redefined as consistent with the new ideals, as what was once professional social work practice now becomes action in the service of blacks, women, or other disadvantaged groups.

5. *Limit your sights*. Some of the doubts that afflict social workers embody the argument that social work is arrogant and imperialistic and that it may do harm to people under the flag of doing good. One track the individual can take is to deliberately limit his or her own practice and scope for acting. "Do what you can" becomes an intuitively guided program for acts not articulated or detailed. The social worker can decide that rehabilitation and prevention are unworkable ideals and that practice should be restricted to the provision of care and the rendering of concrete services. The overall myths of the profession are denied, and the more problematic aspects of practice are curtailed.

6. *Focus on trivia*. One way to deal with doubts is through a kind of denial embodied in busywork. The social worker may choose to become an aficionado of process recording, self-awareness, licensing, professional committees—any of the hundred-odd details of professional practice and its organizational setting. Carried to extremes, such activities can serve as an effective escape from practice in a context of doubt.

7. *Search for a technological fix*. When social workers suffer from depression, they sometimes meet it by going off to get an advanced degree. They hope to acquire new analytic, conceptual, or methodological skills. At the very least, they will advance their professional status and buy an opportunity to switch jobs.

8. *"Reculer pour mieux sauter."* Social workers may go off to a university in a somewhat different spirit—"retreat in order to leap forward better." Michael Lipsky has sensitively observed, "Traditionally universities have provided strategic sanctuary for some of the most important dissenters from contemporary practice . . . .[19] In this case the social worker does not approach the university as a source of skills, but as a retreat and a center for intellectual search and debate. The precise issue to be faced is not the augmentation of personal skills so that one can, somehow, live more effectively in the skill-oriented myth of the present: it is that of a critical attack on the mythic system itself.

If we look at the field of action, we find patterns that do not really sort out. Different social workers, embracing different personal mixtures of faith and doubt, use different combinations of strategies to maintain their practice. The strategies are best understood, however, as a way action without full conviction is maintained. In short, in the field of social work, meaning and action are split. What social workers can act on, given their institutional setting, resources, skills, and time, does not always generate its own conviction.

If a man goes to the hospital and reads to children every Saturday morning, causing visible delight, this action, according to simple, human, emotional definitions of what is good, generates its own affirmation. But suppose someone comes to the man in the hospital on a Saturday morning and says, "What are you doing here? Why don't you spend the time being Big Brother to a poor kid who really needs you?", or "Do you realize that children are prolonging their stay in the hospital in order to hear your stories?" Then the simple value inherent in the man's action is thrown into an arena of contending values. It is obvious that the action now needs a higher meaning, a rationalization. Economists would suggest that what is being debated are the "opportunity costs" of the man's act, and they would hold that the man can, or should, cost-benefit himself out of the dilemma.

The economists' stratagem does not work convincingly, however; neither does any other stratagem anyone has yet invented. The social worker continues to live amidst dilemmas, with action divorced from meaning.

This tension between meaning and action, faith and doubt,[20] demythification and remythification, practice and rationalization is not simply a condition of the practice of social work: it is, in one way or another, a condition of any form of human rationalized social practice. The same issues of doubt afflict medicine, in which studies in recent years have suggested that (1) half the patients visiting doctors' offices are not really sick; (2) most diseases are self-limiting, that is, people get better by themselves, without care; (3) many surgical interventions are unnecesary, the ideals of service often being subordinated to profit; (4) human improvements in life span and health have much more to do with sanitation and public health measures than with the supply of medical care.

Note the peculiar role of the social sciences as revealed by these kinds of studies. Classically organized around the argument that they are basic sources for the skills of practice, their function in these and many other kinds of studies is to stir up debate about the meaning of practice.

KNOWLEDGE AND PRACTICE IN CONTEXT

Let me summarize the major themes of my discussion up to this point:

1. The dominant view for some time has been that knowledge, produced in universities, will benefit the practice of social work. This knowledge has been assumed to be objective and context free, created by scholars and scientists who are not in practice. It is then adapted or worked up into a practical form. Critics have expressed skepticism about the meaningfulness, or even the existence, of context-free knowledge about humans.

2. This dominant view is essentially one of social work as an embodiment of a set of skills based on knowledge. The professionalization of social work is achieved when people come to universities to acquire the defining skills of the discipline.

3. Social workers have always acknowledged that their skills are in the service of a set of shared values that derive from a humanitarian ethic. We have argued that social workers share a commitment not only to a set of skills but also to a set of purposes, power relationships, and myths.

4. The definition of a profession as embodying pure skills is based on the assumptions that (*a*) a professional is much like a mechanic and must be dealt with in similar terms; (*b*) skills are "know-how"—that is, instrumental or operational abilities; (*c*) professional skills are added on to people through training.

5. I have maintained that the exercise of professional skills, a set of operating abilities, is effectively limited by institutional settings. One major element of the institutional settings of social work is a set of shared purposes that professional dogma has held to be context free and consensual: universalism, humanitarianism,

and faith in the development of individuals. Of course, social workers never meet consensual values, but live instead amid the pull of competing and conflicting solidarities. They construct various individual attitudes and styles to manage tensions between abstract values and reality, and among conflicting solidarities.

6. Social workers share an important form of power in American society in the sense that they function in governmental and bureaucratic systems with discretion over resources that are lifelines for poor people: money, food, child care, treatment, community service. These vestiges of power are embarrassing to social workers, so they appeal to the skills myth and to the authority vested in them by their special knowledge and view themselves as essentially powerless.

7. Social workers use mythic stories to bring the disparate acts and facts of social work practice into rationalized unity. These myths provide meaning for the practice and align the practice with the specific institutional contexts in which work is carried out. Social scientists are an important source of such myths, although they are by no means the only source.

8. After reviewing the broad structure of social work practice, I have argued that the profession as a whole is characterized by a contemporary malaise, caused, fundamentally, by the strain of coping with mixed doubt and faith. Social workers cope with the problem of meaning through various strategies.

I now address the problem of meaning and doubt and the relationship of the social sciences to that problem. It is possible that the malaise that afflicts social work (and, generally, all the "minor professions" today)[21] may arise from the fact that basic human arrangements for creating meaning for the profession—the myth-making system—are now misdirected, and fall short of their creative potential. We are particularly concerned with the agency of the institutionalized part of the myth-making system, the social sciences, which bring "knowledge" to the profession.

Let us, at this point, return to the reservations of Dewey, Mishler, and Argyris, cited earlier, and consider their basic point in a little more detail. The apparatus of the social sciences and the professionalized social services was built largely by borrowings from the physical sciences, with their idealization of objective, decontextualized knowledge. Let us think the unthinkable for a few moments. What if (*a*) the role of the social sciences is to make *contextual* knowledge—knowledge about events that is not timeless, spaceless, and personless—unfold the possibilities of human action in specific settings of human action and (*b*) social work, together with other social practices, used such context-appropriate knowledge to bring meaning to the events occurring within the context?

Social work in this century has been embodied in relatively routinized and traditional kinds of practices that have, episodically, been confronted with issues and events that challenged those customary practices. Some of these short-lived challenges have led to permanent changes in social work; others have disturbed its equilibrium for a while and then departed without leaving much of a lasting trace.

Any new issue is a challenge to social work practice and to its knowledge. I think that a major use of knowledge-gathering by social work is episodic, in the sense that it is addressed to issues that are limited in time, and that it is context specific in that it addresses part, but not all, of the larger institutional setting in which social work operates. The entire body of social work practice that I have been discussing—skills, purposes, power, and myths—becomes the target of inquiry. The process of knowledge-gathering focuses on identifying the social context and construing it in mythic form. It is directed toward finding purposes for the profession and locating and rationalizing the power that the social worker can bring to bear on the issue.

If all this is true, the knowledge that social work seeks cannot be produced solely in universities, but must be developed in living situations relevant to contemporary problems. This calls for practitioner-scientists who can seek knowledge relevant to social work practice in the agency setting. Scott Briar observes:

> By far the most important trend for the future of the practice-research relationship is already under way and that is the reduction of the separation between research and practice activities . . . The concept of the practitioner-scientist symbolizes that trend . . . the concept makes possible an empirically-based model of practice, a possibility that was unthinkable only a few years ago.[22]

If the social scientist serves social work along these new lines, it is possible that the "applied" segments of the behavioral and social sciences, now generally regarded as secondary and peripheral aspects of the disciplines, may in fact be the leading edges of knowledge development in the social sciences.

NOTES AND REFERENCES

1. John Dewey, "Psychology and Social Practice." In Joseph Ratner, ed., *John Dewey: Philosophy, Psychology and Social Practice.* New York: Capricorn Books, 1965. Pp. 309–310.
2. Elliot Mishler, "Meaning in Context: Is There Any Other Kind?" *Harvard Educational Review*, 1978, *49* (February), 1–19.
3. Chris Argyris, "Some Unintended Consequences of Rigorous Research." *Psychological Bulletin,* 1968, *70*(3), 185–96; see also Chris Argyris, *Inner Contradictions of Rigorous Research.* New York: Academic Press, 1980.
4. See *Fundamental Research and the Process of Education.* Report prepared for the Committee on Fundamental Research Relevant to Education. Washington, D.C.: Assembly of Behavioral and Social Sciences, National Research Council, May 1977. Chap. 2, p. 20.
5. Dewey, Op. cit.
6. Charles Gilbert, "Public Assistance." Unpublished manuscript, Swarthmore College, 1970 (mimeographed). P. 8.
7. Helen Harris Perlman, "Social Casework." In Neil Gilbert and Harry Specht, eds., *Handbook of the Social Services.* Englewood Cliffs, N.J.: Prentice-Hall, 1981. Chap. 20.

8. In some situations, "clients hold considerable leverage in determining whether such work [e.g., abortion counseling] can be experienced by counselors as morally suspect or heroic." Carole Joffe, "What Abortion Counselors Want from Their Clients." *Social Problems*, 1978, *26* (October), 112–21.
9. Burton J. Bledstein, *The Culture of Professionalism: The Middle Class and the Development of Higher Education in America.* New York: Norton, 1976.
10. Bronislaw Malinowski, *Magic, Science and Religion.* Boston: Beacon Press, 1948.
11. Roy Lubove, *The Professional Altruist.* Cambridge, Mass.: Harvard University Press, 1965. P. 121.
12. The Milford Conference provided the basis for the assertion that social casework was unified by a generic method and was not based merely on the institutional settings in which social workers were employed.
13. Scott Briar, "In Summary." *Social Work*, 1977, *22*(1) (special issue on Conceptual Frameworks), 145.
14. Typical of this criticism is the argument advanced by Jeffrey Galper, who writes: "It is not enough, then, to look only at the fact that social work has had concern for social reform . . . It is necessary to look more closely at . . . the political purposes which have been served. When we do so, it becomes more clear that social work has represented a conservatized version of social reform. Much of that success . . . has not advanced the pursuit of a more fundamentally just society." Jeffrey H. Galper, *The Politics of Social Services.* Englewood Cliffs, N.J.: Prentice-Hall, 1975. P. 110.
15. Cited in Alan Keith-Lucas, "The Political Theory Implicit in Social Case Work Theory." *American Political Science Review*, 1953, XLVII, 1086.
16. Ibid. P. 1091.
17. See, for example, Florence Hollis, "Development of a Casework Treatment Typology." NIMH grant MH-00513, December 1966 (mimeographed). The typology she proposes derives from the "main theoretical concerns of the field. The listing is informative not so much for the items that are included, but for the items which are excluded. The theoretical concerns include: a warm, supportive accepting relationship, the degree of directiveness . . . The extent to which the promotion of self-understanding should be the caseworker's concern . . . The context or the form of reflective communications and explanatory ventilative communications." P. 86.
18. Leon Festinger, H. W. Rietan, and S. Schachter, *When Prophecy Fails.* Minneapolis, Minn.: University of Minnesota Press, 1956.
19. Michael Lipsky, *The Street-Level Bureaucrat.* New York: Russell Sage Foundation, 1980. Chap. 14.
20. See Peter Marris's lecture entitled "Meaning and Action," presented at a seminar in the Sociology Colloquium at Harvard University in December 1977. We are indebted to Marris's insightful analysis of how meaning and action can be split in professional practice. He takes his examples from the Community Development Program in Britain, where, over time, the program suffered from a severe split between its interpretation of the meaning of the problem and the action that could be taken from this analysis. What planners could do was not

meaningful; what was meaningful they could not do.
21. The conflict between scholars and the practitioner in the schools of social work is thoughtfully discussed by Nathan Glazer, "The Schools of the Minor Professions." *Minerva*, 1974, xii(3), 346–64.
22. Scott Briar, "Toward the Integration of Practice and Research." Paper prepared for the National Conference on the Future of Social Work Research, San Antonio, Texas, October 1978. P. 10.

Chapter 11

Policy Research: Belief and Doubt

Support for policy analysis—and, more broadly, policy research—has grown impressively in the last decade and a half; but all along there has been a chronic sense of frustration, shared broadly by those who carry out, and by those who sponsor, the work. This twin theme of acceptance and disappointment can be illustrated by a number of examples drawn from recent American experience.

Perhaps the most obvious way to document the acceptance of policy research is to examine trends in the level of expenditure for its product. How has government spending in this area changed in the last decade? Since no one really has an exact definition of the bounds of policy research, the answer requires some estimation.

Faced with congressional pressures to learn about research expenditures, the General Accounting Office (GAO) in 1974 conducted a telephone survey on behalf of the Joint Committee on Congressional Operations, but the survey covered only program evaluations. This, clearly, is the narrow definition of policy research, for it excludes studies designed not to evaluate a concrete program, but to understand the scope and trends of some condition of concern or to explore many sorts of planning activities. Nevertheless, despite this limitation and despite the GAO's failure to define an evaluation, the results are informative. They suggest that, in fiscal year 1974, expenditures on nondefense program evaluations amounted to approximately $146 million—a 500 percent increase since 1969.[1] About 60 percent of the 1974 outlays, or close to $88 million, were for contract research, half going to profit-making organizations, 30 percent to nonprofit organizations, and 20 percent to universities. If we add to that $88 million some modest estimate of what is being spent on policy-relevant research that cannot be narrowly defined as evaluation, it is not unreasonable to suggest that, aside from the in-house programs that government itself maintains, we are dealing with a $100 million a year research industry.

As for the in-house studies, the GAO and the Office of Management and Budget (OMB) have expanded considerably their evaluative functions for the Executive and Congress. The GAO, for example, estimates that about 30 percent of its professional staff over the past 5 years have been conducting evaluations of federal programs under the authority granted the agency by the Legislative Reorganization Act of 1970. This act has given the GAO considerable leeway both to initiate evaluations and to respond to congressional requests.

Governmental acceptance of evaluative research is further evidenced by the increasing tendency to write evaluation requirements into new social legislation. The GAO uncovered 40 legislative acts—directed at health, education, transportation, law enforcement, housing, the environment, economic opportunity, and agriculture—that include varying stipulations for evaluation. Six call for the specific authorization of funds, mandating that a fixed percentage of the funding of the program be set aside for evaluation. Another eight acts specify methods of data collection.[2]

If Congress insists that social programs be evaluated, it is argued, then it must also come to terms with the problem of specifying evaluable objectives. To assist Congress in this task, the GAO has developed a model statute intended to illustrate how specific and detailed program objectives can be developed in future legislation. One can question whether Congress can, will, or should meet these kinds of demands, but certainly the demands are logical: the Congress is simply being asked to be consistent with itself.[3]

This kind of argument is symptomatic of a third type of evidence of the growing belief in policy research in government. There are now centers for policy planning, management, and evaluation in all the large domestic agencies, some small and some big, some influential and some not, some tied closely to budgetary planning and some more tenuously linked. The resources these centers command make their thinking and their needs a force in bureaucratic politics. And this kind of influence, in the context of institutions and institutional learning, provides us with virtually an operational definition of "belief" translated into action. So, according to a number of reasonable criteria—allocation of resources, allocation of management capability, and the assignment of place and power to specialized facilities—the support for research in the policy community appears to be growing.

Since policy research is so clearly a growth industry, we might expect all the parties involved in it to show, if not a gentle and self-righteous glow, then at least some satisfaction with what has already been achieved. But what we see instead is disappointment. Some administrators responsible for program planning and evaluation have been surprisingly outspoken: "We might as well be candid: federal program evaluations so far have been largely ineffective.[4]   OMB officials, somewhat less directly, also report that evaluations have largely been neither timely, relevant, accurate, nor accessible.[5]

It is easy to find other examples of disenchantment, but it is difficult to determine whether they mean that research findings are in fact being ignored. There has been little systematic investigation of the extent to which research enters the policy process. Nathan Caplan and his colleagues at the Institute for Social Research at the University of Michigan have broken ground with an empirical study of the issue.[6] Their approach was simply to ask decision makers whether and how they made use of social science findings. Between October 1973 and March 1974, they interviewed, for an hour and a half each, 204 persons high in the executive branch of government. Whatever may be the limitations of self-reported accounts of utilization, Caplan's report contains a great deal of interesting information. The refrains of belief and doubt run contrapuntally through the report; and indeed, Caplan himself appears to be ambivalent about the thrust of the findings, largely because of ambiguities surrounding the meaning of the term *use*.

The respondents clearly register their faith, showing a "very positive attitude . . . toward the social sciences in general, and more specifically, to the use of social science knowledge in the formation of policy."[7] Only those who intend to make government administration their career are more skeptical about research and less likely to use it.

At times, Caplan also registers faith: "Knowledge is used at the top levels of government decision making and probably to a greater extent than most experts in the area of utilization would expect . . . . The most pervasive effects of social science information on policy making occur in the context of soft information use."[8]

But he also conveys his concern about underutilization: if policymakers are really so eager to apply social science information, he asks, and if the level of information input is high, why, then, are their level of utilization and the quality of the information they use not higher?[9]

To answer this question, Caplan defines use in what may well be described as an instrumental-decisional framework, in which empirical studies are assumed to be the means for reaching a specific decision by a decision maker. By this standard, only 13 percent of the respondents could cite 5 to 10 instances of use with good supporting evidence. And even more strikingly, 44 percent reported instances in which they purposely disregarded or rejected relevant social science information in reaching policy decisions. In order to reach a utilization rate of 13 percent, the decisional aspect of the definition of utilization had to be considerably relaxed. Originally the term was intended to refer to cases in which knowledge was applied only to a specific policy decision. Caplan found, however, that "rarely is policy formulation determined by a concrete, point-by-point reliance on empirically grounded data."[10]

Caplan's distinction between the nature of the information and the way it is useful to those responsible for developing policy helps to account for these conflicting conclusions. Information can be data-based (hard) or nonempirical (soft), and use can be conceptual (a way of thinking about issues) or decisional (directed toward reaching a specific decision); Caplan concluded that there were 350 examples of the conceptual use of soft information. In all, 575 self-reported examples of utilization were identified. With conceptual use it is difficult to determine how the information actually influenced the policymaker. The respondent integrated the information with his own values and experiences. The two "merge to form a frame of reference or perspective within which the social implications of alternative policies . . . are evaluated."[11]

Having documented that research findings were both sought and not used, in the narrow definition of the interface between knowledge and policy, Caplan attempts to identify the major factors contributing to use. Each respondent is given a utilization score. He translates the major theories about why studies are not used for public policy into a series of open-ended questions and, by a multivariate analysis, tries to identify which theories best explain the utilization score differences. The best results, which account for 14 percent of the variance of use, are achieved by what he calls the "two-communities theories" that depict social scientists and policymakers as living in different worlds characterized by conflicting values, rewards, and language. Caplan concludes that lack of contact and lack of trust are the major explanations for variations in utilization.

PROPOSALS FOR REFORM

Accepting a decisionistic-instrumental view of policy research, members of the research and policy communities have repeatedly asked how we might improve the transmissions between research and policy.[12] It is worthwhile to discuss certain recurring conceptions of how the policy/research alliance should be reformed from this perspective. To sharpen the issue, I restrict my discussion to four strategies by which one can make evaluation research more useful. Two of these imperatives are directed at the researcher (Be good in what you do, and recognize that not every program can be evaluated), and two at the policymaker (Be clear about your purposes, and organize government so that decisions can be taken).

1. *Improve the rigor of the research according to accepted canons of scientific quality.* Ilene Bernstein and Howard Freeman have evaluated all the evaluation studies that received support from the federal government in 1970 and that had a research budget of over $10,000.[13] Their primary purpose was to obtain a measure of the quality of these studies, and they defined quality in methodological terms: adequacy of the sampling procedure, of the data analysis, of the statistical procedures, of the study design itself, and so forth. Their main finding was that less than 20 percent of the evaluation studies followed the canons of acceptable scientific investigation with respect to design, data collection, and data analysis. Having attained a measure of quality, Bernstein and Freeman then tried to examine the characteristics accounting for variation in quality. Briefly, their major conclusions

tend to show that academic research yields work of high quality, whereas entrepreneurial research does not. The characteristics of academic research are that the funds are obtained for a relatively long period of time, are in the form of a grant, and are awarded to university-based academicians who design the research in consultation with the staff administering the program being studied. If we wish to improve the quality of research, we must first find ways of making sure that evaluations funded in the future have these properties.

What is remarkable about this evaluation of evaluations—and, indeed, about most critiques of evaluation research from within the research community—is that quality is defined only on technical grounds, without regard to relevance. But surely a good study must be not only methodologically sophisticated but also relevant to the purposes and special activities of the program being analyzed. It seems unlikely that the wholesale statistical and methodological purification of evaluation research would answer all the questions posed by policy consumers. Like the OMB officials I quoted earlier, policymakers complain not only about the soundness of the research but about its lack of relevance. Furthermore, the creation of conditions necessary to upgrade the research methodologically would probably exacerbate another frequent complaint about evaluation, namely, that it rarely arrives in time for a decision. Finally, there is a third problem that is somewhat out of the hands of the research group: some programs are difficult to evaluate either because their objectives are not well specified or because it is difficult to translate their stipulated objectives into measurable outputs. Other proposals for reform try to tackle these residual questions.

2. *Restrict evaluations to those selected cases that provide the conditions necessary for effective research.* This proposal is based on the recognition that political practicalities sometimes preclude the establishment of a good research design. It is not always possible to create control groups through random assignment. It is not always possible to construct a sound study within the time, resources, and managerial capability available. And it is not always possible to devise indices that are reasonably representative of the issues at stake for the program. One way to increase the credibility of research would be to conduct evaluations only in those situations that allow for a good research design. This would render a significant number of federal programs unsuitable for analysis, for, as Joseph Wholey and his colleagues point out,

> the typical federal program cannot be managed to achieve its stated objectives (as implied for example in the authorizing legislation) because: a) the program lacks specific, measurable objectives related to program goals, or b) the program lacks plausible, testable assumptions linking program activities to the achievement of program objectives, or c) managers lack the motivation, ability, or authority to manage.[14]

It might be sensible, then, as a precondition for study, to set up a procedure by which programs are screened for their manageability and evaluability. A side benefit of such screening might be institutional learning, promoting the redesign of programs so that they can be both managed and evaluated.

But suppose one were actually to restrict policy research to cases satisfying specified boundary conditions, which appears to be the reform that Wholey and his colleagues go on to propose? One question is whether this selective procedure would yield a sufficiently large or useful universe for study. The most overwhelming problem in conducting evaluations is the mismatch between stated program objectives and researchable indices. This problem can be traced to both (1) the policymaker, who fails to specify program objectives in terms that are clear and potentially measurable; and (2) the researcher, whose armamentarium of measurement techniques is simply not developed to the point where he can empirically examine the issues at stake for policy. Wherever the problem lies, it is severe. Consider, for example, the extended examination by Sheldon White and co-workers of the indices available or potentially available for evaluating federal programs for young children in the areas of preschool and primary-school education, day care, several kinds of family intervention, health care, income, and housing.[15] It seems reasonably clear that virtually no program in these areas is evaluable—at least not in the sense in which policymakers use the term *evaluation* and legislate for it. Interesting indices of *aspects* of program performance exist. But indices definitive and credible enough to define the total value of programs do not seem to be available.

So one problem with the proposal for selectivity is that it is likely to lead to a null set of evaluation studies. Even if a handful of cases were to prove favorable for study, one might question whether such a small number would be useful and whether the pressure for evaluation could be confined to so few.

3. *Require policymakers to spell out their objectives in researchable terms.* I noted earlier that the GAO has drafted a model statute suggesting to Congress how goals can be defined in reasonably objective terms. This is the essence of the third proposal, that the political process be modified to make more evaluations possible. This is, in a sense, fair, since it is the political process itself that is increasingly responsible for the pressure for evaluation. But a host of questions and potential ripple effects attend this modest proposal, and the questions extend far beyond the values associated with research and its utilization. I can raise only some of the questions here. Does legislation arise generally, or even occasionally, out of a conception of one objective or purpose? Head Start, for example, appears to have been created out of a confluence of very different purposes: (1) to stimulate the development of poor children; (2) to provide a stimulant for community action; (3) to provide a basis for coordinating services to poor children and their families; and (4) to provide a seedbed for ventures in school reform. Is it politically expedient or possible to hierarchize the multiple purposes involved in program creation? Is the vagueness of the goals in legislation symptomatic of fuzzy-mindedness on the part of politicians, or is it, rather, an attempt to find a generalized formula for action on which all parties will agree? Does the political process always lead to a *direct* statement of the intended goal? For example, the Elementary and Secondary Education Act had as its stated goal the improvement of the school achievement of disadvan-

taged children—and it is in terms of that goal, using school achievement tests, that the program has repeatedly been evaluated. But many regard that legislation as a device for bringing in a federal subsidy to education. If that was in fact the predominant goal, then the transfer of funds is self-evaluating.

The questions raised by the third proposal seem to be of special importance, because this proposal strikes at the heart of the political process: by arguing that we should "clean up" the matter of vaguely stated agreements to specific courses of action, it attacks what in fact gives that process its utility. We have a political process precisely because people have multiple goals that must somehow be reconciled into a single course of governmental action. One can call this resultant course of action a "policy," but that term is misleading, because it carries with it the assumption that the one action betokens one mind, one will, and one theory. To try to force that mind to speak, to spell out once and for all what on earth it wants, is to reach blindly behind the fantasy and to try to strangle the life of the system. Legislation requires ambiguity in its statement about goals so that coalitions in support of legislation can be formed, each group viewing the legislation as serving its special purposes. Charles L. Schultze explains, "The first rule of a successful political process is, 'don't force a specification of goals or ends.'. . . necessary agreement on particular policies can often be secured among individuals or groups who hold 'quite divergent ends.' "[16] The insistence that government's purposes be clear may reduce the scope for legislation and thus limit the government's involvement in social programs.

4. *Make decision making more centralized.* Finally, I note the occasional charge that the decision-making process in government is too decentralized and too "noisy" to allow for the effective utilization of policy research. The criticism is directed not so much at the multiple purposes present in legislative activity as at the multiple administrative and decision-making responsibilities distributed across the bureaucracy. A related problem concerns the stability of decision makers. This arises when those who commission studies are no longer in government to accept the product they requested or, put the other way around, when those empowered to act have formed a new agenda and are uninterested in using the findings of studies they did not request.

This fourth kind of proposal, then, rests on the assumption that there are some efficacy and utility in the transmission from research to policy but that, at the last stage of the transmission, lack of continuity, lack of commitment, and the dispersal of authority inhibit the capacity to act. The research findings have been brought in; they reach the ear of some in the bureaucratic network, but by now interest has waned. Perhaps some find the evidence persuasive, but their influence in the network is limited. So, for all practical purposes, the research message is not heard.

To this proposal I respond with much the same questions and much the same doubts as to the preceding one. Again, the proposal calls for a change in the political process to accommodate policy research—in this case, a change in the bureaucracy toward centralization of authority. That would be a rather heroic treatment for what may be only a modest problem.

Together, these four proposals for reform indicate nicely a kind of ideal conception of what the policy/research alliance should be. Some of the proposals have been put forth rather steadily over the last ten years, ever since policy research began to be a going enterprise, yet there is little detectable movement of the system toward serious implementation of any of them. Why? Perhaps the kinds of objections I have suggested have stalemated movement, committing us to live with an imperfect system, with belief and doubt forever commingled in the steadfast and more modest execution of what is possible. On the other hand, perhaps there is no problem—or perhaps the problems are different from those assumed in the proposals outlined above.

The four proposals sketch out, in what artists would call "negative space," a dominant conception, or image, of the way research and policy should be brought together. Let us call it a *problem-solving image.*[17] Belief in policy research, according to this image, appears to rest on the conviction that policy expresses a theory of action that includes: (1) a definition of the problem; (2) a set of possible courses of action; and (3) a goal or goals one seeks to achieve. The role of policy research is to provide data that clarify the problem, conduct pilot projects or planned-variation studies to estimate whether the conceived courses of action approach the goals, evaluate implemented programs to determine if, and under what conditions, they are achieving their goals. The results of such research, transmitted to the policymaker, permit him or her to change or modify his or her target. Nathan Caplan has succinctly summarized this view. He explains that knowledge does not have to dictate policy for it to be of instrumental importance. The acts of retrieving it in response to a problem and attempting to relate it to a policy alternative or other discrete element in a decision situation constitute the instrumental nature of knowledge use.[18] All this is in the dominant image in which belief in policy research is usually cast. And it specifies legitimated grounds on which government pays for policy research.

But the belief in policy research also rests on grounds lying outside the scope of the image. That is, beyond the narrow instrumental terms described above, there are some other reasons why people in government support policy research. I now turn to an examination of these reasons.

NEGLECTED PATHWAYS BETWEEN RESEARCH AND POLICY

In this section I shall review four rather straightforward, but nevertheless neglected, paths between research and action. In each case I shall explore real-life examples to see whether they support the logic contending that the particular path exists. Part of the difficulty of this exploration of the politics of research is that a given example often illustrates several kinds of interplay at once. Therefore, at times I shall be guilty of oversimplifying the process by which research influences policy in order to picture one kind of influence.

The question of the influence and use of research is, by its very nature, extremely difficult to pin down. Consider the great American debate about educational effects. It is easy for people to say now that changes in education alone obviously will not bring about a change in the distribution of income in American society. After all, how can education, all by itself, have such a fundamental impact? But some of the very people who now insist on the utter obviousness of Christopher Jencks's findings[19] advocated educational interventions strenuously only a decade ago. They may indeed have changed their old views because of the research findings; yet, when asked whether empirical studies altered their perspective on the world, they answer no. It is more likely that they have not entirely shed their old beliefs, but maintain coexisting theories of intervention. One does not have to believe fully in order to act. When these people's action takes a new turn—when, say, they turn from an education to an income strategy—they may have some valid basis for claiming that they have believed "all along" in the new strategy.

Despite these difficulties, let us pursue the question of influence. What moves policy research? What usefulness does research have?

Policy Research as Containment

One function of policy research derives largely from the consequences of evaluative research in a political context of mixed commitment. At this point we need briefly to examine the nature of evaluative inquiries and their role in the political context in which recent social legislation developed in the United States. Again, I do not wish to equate evaluative research with the broader spectrum of policy research of which it is a part. Yet, in America, most federally sponsored policy research in recent years has been evaluative. It appears that analyses that measure the gap between programmatic purposes and outcomes are mainly what policy-makers are willing to fund.

We have now felt the influence of the first wave of evaluation studies, directed broadly at the spectrum of the poverty programs of the 1960s. These studies appear to have had a negative influence politically, even though many can, and do, argue that their having any influence at all is improper on both scientific and substantive grounds.

Consider, as an example, the 1968—69 Westinghouse evaluation of Head Start. That study has been widely discussed, and many have considered the issues of its design and political efficacy paradigmatic for generalized questions about evaluation and its utility. Was the study a definitive evaluation of the program? Did its largely negative findings have any political impact? A host of subsidiary considerations enter into the discussion of these questions; but our judgment is that, on balance, although the evaluation was neither scientifically nor substantively definitive, it did have a political impact on Head Start and served to contain the program in several ways.

From the reams that have been written about the quality of the Westinghouse study, there emerge three kinds of arguments that seem to have some force in discounting it as a conclusive evaluation.

The study was premature; it assessed the program before it had been firmly established as a program. Head Start was designed and implemented during an incredibly brief period between November 1964 and the summer of 1965. The Westinghouse evaluation, undertaken in 1968, included third-graders who had experienced the first summer's work, when start-up problems were severe. Thus, it is easy to discount the entire sample as unrepresentative of what a fully formed Head Start program might achieve.[20]

There were technical problems in the design of the study that made it inconclusive. Marshall S. Smith and Joan Bissell[21] have noted that the sampling of Head Start was imperfect, and Don Campbell and A. E. Erlebacher[22] have pointed out that regression artifacts may well have served to suppress evidence of Head Start's effectiveness. In answer to these criticisms, defenders of the study have claimed that such problems are necessarily encountered in applied research, and do not completely negate its value.[23] Nevertheless, the scientific compromises necessarily embedded in the Westinghouse study served to make it inconclusive—informative, certainly, but not sufficient for a definitive judgment of Head Start.

The study did not deal with some important goals of the program. In seeking to determine Head Start's effects on school achievement, the Westinghouse evaluation addressed a goal that was important to some of the program's proponents. However, as I have already suggested, during the writing of the guidelines it was clear that many of the involved bureaucrats were not persuaded that one could directly intervene in child development,[24] but thought that Head Start could have importance as a catalyst for such things as community action. The legislative intent with respect to the several kinds of goals was unclear, probably deliberately so. Hence, substantively as well as scientifically, the Westinghouse evaluation was inconclusive; it addressed only a subset of the program's goals.

In light of the uncertainties remaining in its wake, the Westinghouse evaluation should not have had such a negative effect on the program; and, in a sense, it did not. Head Start lives today. Nor was the evidence authoritative enough to alter significantly the management of the program. But if we examine the scope of Head Start subsequent to the study, we see signs that the evaluation did have an impact. It was an important element in a set of factors that has led to the program's containment. First, immediately after the Westinghouse evaluation, and in fairly explicit response to it, Head Start began and completed the phasing-out of its summer programs. The Westinghouse study had found no effect from the summer programs, but marginal effects from the full-year programs. Second, for some years after the evaluation, the budget allocated to Head Start stayed steady at about $350 million a year; and some high officials in the Department of Health, Education, and Welfare took to characterizing it as an "experimental" program. Undoubtedly, some of Head Start's staying power rests on its sentimental appeal for many and on the able defense voiced for it by a small but belligerent constituency. These sustained the program even during the latter part of the Nixon administration, when a serious effort was made to dismantle almost all the other poverty programs. But this kind of basic support normally enlarges rather than merely sustains a program; the Westinghouse evaluation was probably a factor in keeping program funding down to about the level it had reached at the time of the study. A third kind of containment effect was more indirect, but perhaps most important. The dramatic impact of the Westinghouse findings (coupled, it may be remembered, with the virtually simultaneous publication of Arthur Jensen's IQ piece[25]) was instrumental in advancing the "nothing works" refrain that, over the years, has led many in the policy community to disinvest in service programs ideologically and to put their faith instead in an income-redistribution strategy. The Westinghouse evaluation cast a shadow not simply on the program to which it was directed but on the problem concept of which that program was an expression.

Recall again that that concept was proposed on the most tentative and uncertain grounds. It did not reflect a national commitment, but only a cautious exploration. Thus, it would certainly be reasonable to assume that negative evaluations of programs such as Head Start would have a containing effect. (I suspect that evaluations may be used quite differently when political commitment is firm.) At the least, they would cement the disbelief of those who never thought that social programs were much good or who believed that such programs pursued the wrong goals. Their impact on the committed, however, is less clear. Naturally, supporters of the programs manufactured antitoxins to discount the evaluations' toxic effect, largely by attacking the studies on methodological grounds. If nothing else, the committed found that they could not count on research as an ally in overcoming the tentativeness of others.

We have taken the Westinghouse work as reasonably representative of the quality and net efficacy of current evaluation studies. Speaking of the cumulative effect of a whole variety of such studies, David K. Cohen and Michael S. Garret argue that they may, in fact, alter the context in which policy is shaped.

> ... taken together, the Coleman report, its progeny and the stream of negative Title I evaluations have gradually eroded the assumptions underlying compensatory policy. The changing climate of opinion has made it more difficult to maintain or expand compensatory projects and has weakened support for categorical educational programs.[26]

The precise magnitude of this containment effect is hard to calculate. But if Cohen and Garret's argument is right, recent research has had a serious influence on the system of ideas and commitments that is the basis of educational policy in the United States.

Research as an Instrument of Power and Political Positioning

The argument that knowledge is power is widely accepted. Present-day funding of research by government agencies appears to reflect a modification of the principle, the idea that the act of producing knowledge can be a device in the bid for power. A fairly clear case for this use of research occurred within the last few years when the question of a day-care bill was on the table. It was uncertain which of several day-care bills would ultimately be passed by Congress and how day care, when passed, would ultimately be managed by the administration. During the period before the passing of the first Mondale-Brademas bill, one found rival agencies—the Office of Economic Opportunity, the Office of Child Development, the Department of Labor, and the Office of Education—actively sponsoring research on day care. There were, of course, the usual substantive reasons for the commissioning of such research. Information was needed on the demand for day care, on the trade-offs between cost and quality, on day care's effects on child development, and so forth. But, at the same time, those dealing with the day-to-day management of contract research in Washington understood that each of the rival agencies was "establishing a position" on day care, trying to build up information, staff competencies, and visibility with regard to upcoming legislation.

Research is commissioned not only out of the need for information but in the service of political positioning. Individuals, research offices, and agencies periodically find it necessary to make visible commitments to significant issues and constituencies.

There are a variety of well-known techniques by which a symbolic gesture can substitute for the risks of a definite political action. Systematic research buys time for political leaders while maintaining the commitment to action. Commissions, national surveys, task forces, experiments, and demonstrations all provide concrete and symbolic benefits to interested parties. Commissioning research thus gives the politician a way of taking a position that risks little but offers some groups some hope. A politician can widen his or her political base and neutralize opposition by mixing judiciously his programmatic and research commitments.

Politicians are not the only ones who use research in this fashion: so do bureaucrats. Francine F. Rabinovitz cites some examples of the utility of research, drawing from recent studies of the police:

> The Police Foundation experiments contain a number of examples of ways in which the research is not used and yet the experiments are useful. For example, in Cincinnati, an experiment with neighborhood team policing is being conducted. The department adopted the neighborhood team concept widely, even as the experimental results, which were continuously fed into the process, began to show that while there was not much harm in the new idea, it didn't do terribly much. The experiment *was* useful because it reassured the department that it could adopt neighborhood team policing without anything horrible happening as a consequence, even if there were no measurable benefits. The chief knew there *were* benefits (public relations, the ability to sell the city council on acquiring a centralized information gathering system to support the experiment), but was mainly afraid of the costs. This has happened over and over in the police experiments, where departments are afraid to try new things for fear of the costs and don't really expect that the reforms will "work" immediately.[27]

It appears that one reason why research functions are institutionalized in government is that they allow agencies to make marginal commitments and gestures toward the competing constituencies and issues with which they must deal. They allow agencies to take options at relatively low cost. This political use of research for postponing decisions and winning political leverage does not necessarily betoken complete cynicism about the substantive value of the work: in the research-producing agencies, there are always at least a few people who are passionately committed to the value of general or specific research activities; and the majority appear quite willing to be receptive to substantive research conclusions if they prove useful. So an agency is able to approach research with a mixed commitment, viewing the activity both as a means to gain knowledge and as an end in itself.

Once research functions have been institutionalized in an agency, a second level of instrumental use appears. There are now individuals within the agency who are identified with research. They have a direct and personal interest in the extent and apparent value of the research work commissioned by the agency. It is in their interest to have a "portfolio" of grants and contracts that promise help with critical problems or groups. It is in their interest to enlarge budget and staff, to move research into a position of leverage in the agency—for example, vis-à-vis budget and planning functions. But, again, it is important not to take the instrumental use of research, this time for career advancement, as betokening complete and cold-blooded calculation. Indeed, many research managers have a more thoroughgoing faith in the value of research than do most pure scientists. They use their research activities for power and positioning because, in a sense, they have to. The rules of the game require it.

Research as Policing

Evaluative research now serves as a management device to ensure that agencies do what is expected of them. In this sense, evaluation has become linked increasingly to monitoring and auditing responsibilities at several levels of government. The most prominent expression of this, of course, is in the current demand for "accountability." The delivery of benefits intended by new legislation cannot be taken on faith or proved merely through the judgment and testimony of professionals and administrators. Ideally, a program's value should be expressed in hard, objective numbers. Pressures for accountability have been building over the years at all levels of government and without doubt are at the root of much of the recent congressional interest in writing evaluation provisions into social programs. Conservatives skeptical about such programs usually insist on such a provision, and liberals accept it, begrudgingly or happily. One is left with all the puzzles about what a cost-benefit analysis of housing or income redistribution or community action really means. In any case, because of the recent pressures for accountability, government now has more pieces of fragmentary information about the costs and benefits of the programs it manages than it has ever had before.

Furthermore, there are monitors and auditors outside government, and there are questions of accountability not covered by the cost-benefit formula. Guerrilla groups outside the federal establishment have used research as a policing device. Consider the Title I programs of the Elementary and Secondary Education Act of

1965. Title I funds are meant to ensure that the poor end up getting more of the resources available for education than the well-to-do. Theoretically, before local communities can be allocated Title I funds, they have to satisfy the condition of equal expenditure across income classes. In the early days of Title I, particularly, there was fairly widespread failure to satisfy this condition—and there were, as well, some cases of more serious misallocation of funding. A number of black militant groups brought legal suits against local Title I programs, using monitoring and evaluation information available under the program's statutory requirement.

Such outside policing has been actively stimulated by the frequent legislative requirement that parent or community advisory groups be associated with new social programs. The requirement may stipulate that information about local programs be made available to such groups in a timely and convenient form. The government has thus stimulated consumerism and, as a consequence, a demand for consumer-relevant information. To the extent that parent or community groups can influence professional and agency activities, they can and will demand the production of information relevant to their interests, thus giving rise to a different kind of demand for research in the interest of accountability. Because of the local, distributed, and often informal nature of advisor-manager interactions, it is difficult to know how large or significant this kind of influence is.

At times there is a close relationship between the formal and the grass-roots auditors. Bureaucrats may feel that the case for reform is stronger when outside pressure groups make it; and since they lack the power to translate information into action, they may leak the information to such groups. (Some observers suggest that this is what happened in the case of Title I.) Thus, internal auditors and external pressure constitute a unified system of action.

Evaluation as control also played a prominent part in the thinking of the social reformers of the early 1960s who helped expand the public role in social programs. These reformers hoped to win acceptance for the new idea that governments should become involved in comprehensive social planning, a domain preempted till then by private voluntary agencies. The reformers, highly critical of the way these private agencies were perverting their stated purposes, wanted to use evaluation as a way of assuring that funds would be used as intended rather than end up as subsidies to private organizations.

Research as Social Reform

Research is used as a weapon in efforts to reform government. In the early days of the Poverty Program, for example, the federal administration tried to use research and evaluation as a way of wresting control from the local voluntary agencies that had preempted social welfare activities. The history of education provides an interesting parallel.[28] In the late nineteenth and early twentieth centuries, there was a movement toward making educational management professional and scientific. American education, then largely controlled at the local level, had become quite diversified and pluralistic as ethnic and social movements led to greater differentiation among localities; now the variety of American styles of education was to be brought toward a "one best system." A coalition of the social elite and distinguished academics, working together to bring this about, took as the ostensible basis for the reform the desirability of making education and educational management more scientific. The survey movement was an example of research that brought in outside personnel to survey school districts as a means of turning the political structure upside down. Out of such initiative, the superintendency was to become a "learned profession." Schooling was to be taken out of the realm of politics and placed on the higher plane of scientific administration on the basis of the best research evidence at hand:

> Nicholas Murray Butler could confidently assert, to the applause of the Merchant's Club of Chicago, that he should "as soon think of talking about the democratization of the treatment of appendicitis" as to speak of "the democratization of the schools." "The fundamental confusion is this: Democracy is a principle of government; the schools belong to the administration; and a democracy is as much entitled as a monarchy to have its business well done." A common school run for the people but not by the people. . . .[29]

In large and in small ways, research and reform forged a coalition at the turn of the century. The reform movement tried to depart from a pluralistic system of local control, which we are now taking some pains to revive—the Democrats, under slogans like Community Action; the Republicans, under revenue sharing and slogans like New Federalism. It seems ironic that in our own day, as noted above, community groups are turning to research in counterrevolutions aimed at restoring pluralism.

Another example of research as reform comes from the bureaucratic history of the negative income tax idea.[30] The idea, remarkably, was first brought into government circles and most staunchly defended by the Office of Economic Opportunity (OEO), a federal agency whose legislative mandate embraced the idea of "opportunity" but rejected the principle of transfers. In the following account, Joseph Kershaw, the first director of OEO's Office of Research, Plans, Programs, and Evaluation (RPPE) and later assistant director of OEO, lucidly describes the rationale underlying the agency's activities (and also illustrates the political use of social theory):

> The Economic Opportunity Act was seen by its supporters . . . as being new and different in two significant ways. First, it was thought to be aimed at the correction of the causes of poverty rather than at the alleviation of symptoms. "Opportunity is our middle name" the poverty warriors were fond of saying. "We don't give handouts," Director Sargent Shriver said on many occasions. . . . Training programs, the teaching of adult literacy, family planning and most things OEO does or did are directed at making it possible for people to pull themselves out of poverty, whereas most welfare expenditures can only be regarded as relief in one form or another. . . .[31]

How, then, did support for income maintenance take so firm a hold in the OEO? In principle, OEO was hostile to the idea of unproductive welfare relief and deeply committed to what President Johnson described as the goal of making "tax eaters" into "tax payers." Its ostensible aim was not merely to remove the poor from poverty but to divest them of the poverty of skill and of will. That the idea of income maintenance intruded is due in large measure to the staff of economists who worked in the RPPE office. This group acted at least to some extent as bureaucratic insurgents struggling against the rationale of the agency that employed them. As economists, they accepted as self-evident that the poor needed money as well as jobs, services, and community power. Many believed not only that a mix of programs was desirable but that cash transfers in the form of a negative income tax—which preserved work incentives and expanded personal choice—would be one of the decisive strategies in any war against poverty. They were determined to promote the negative income tax idea and to keep it alive as an issue not only in the OEO but also in the Department of Health, Education, and Welfare, the agency officially responsible for welfare policy. An informal type of "club" developed that sought to pursue the idea in and out of government until the moment of opportunity for reform was ripe. In this sense, the story of the OEO suggests that it is often social scientists acting as reformers, rather than social science per se, who contribute to the development of policy.

So far I have discussed, all too briefly, three functions that research seems to serve in the policy community. These functions—of containment, of achieving power and political positioning, and of policing—are not absolutely distinct from one another. They are aspects of an integral part of the structure of the political process in which a multiplicity of individuals contend for the assertion of ideology and the mobilization of power. Research, as some would say, inevitably "becomes politicized." This politicization is not, I should contend, a subversion of research. It is among the principal sources of its utility. What we lack is a concept of utility that would allow us to recognize the political role of scientific inquiry.

TOWARD A LARGER CONCEPTION OF THE
INTERPLAY BETWEEN POLICY AND RESEARCH

If policy formation were problem solving, it would not logically entail the three functions discussed above. One could attempt to set aside such functions by arguing that the term *policy* refers to the ideas or concepts that guide political action, whereas *politics* refers to efforts to influence the structures of social action and management—and that the two, somehow, are separate. But all the examples I have given refer to a kind of traffic in ideas and concepts that goes on in and around government activity and that seems designed to influence both thought and action simultaneously. Policy develops out of a politics of ideas; and unless one wants somehow to set up a sociological equivalent of the mind–body problem, this politics of ideas is not freestanding, separate, or distinct: it is a facet of normal, everyday, political action.

In my view, policy formation involves: (1) problem setting as a step toward issue setting; (2) mobilization of the fine structure of governmental action; and (3) achievement of settlements in the face of dilemmas and trade-offs among values. The research of the social sciences enters into all stages of policy formation. But, first, the influence of this research on policy is never sufficient; and, second, some deep differences between the games of research and the games of politics seem to assure that, as an individual becomes more legitimated for one set of games, he or she becomes de-legitimated for the other. These imperfections of the research/ policy alliance are quite painful to all participants—painful to researchers for one reason, and painful to the policy people for quite another. And so a long-standing image of policy formation as problem solving tends to be sustained as a soothing fantasy, denying large parts of the reality of the interplay between research and government but, on the positive side, emphasizing certain ideals and values that, other things being equal, both sides hope to maximize in the relationship. In short, the problem-solving image is a myth, with the positive and the negative properties of most myths.

Problem Setting

The problem-solving image holds that the work of policy begins with articulated and self-evident problems. Supposedly, policy begins when recognizable problems appear, problems about which one can hypothesize possible courses of action and in relation to which one can articulate goals. But is that really the beginning of the policy-forming process? It seems more realistic to posit a precursor period, often quite extended, during which various indications of stress emerge in the system. It is not clear problems, but diffuse worries, that appear. Political pressure groups become unusually active, or their activities become more telling; formal and in-formal social indicators give signs of unfavorable trends, or of trends that may be interpreted as unfavorable. There are signals, then, of a problem; but no one knows yet what the problem is. So, in the development of most government activities, there is an important period of incoherence during which troublesome elements must be interpreted in order to arrive at a statement of the problem. In other words, the situation is such that the definition of the problem itself is problematic. Policy analysis contains processes for finding and construing problems; it involves problem setting in order to interpret inchoate signs of stress in the system.

The process of problem setting is a species of pattern recognition and involves finding in events, or imposing on them, an order or structure. It is an integral part of the work of the scientist, perhaps the most crucial part; but it has traditionally been the part least well codified in the canons of methodology and "normal science."[32] There is, in fact, no orderly or prescribed way to do it. In politics, problem setting is no less fundamental and crucial, and the processes are no more orderly. Different interest groups vie with one another in imposing a pattern on events. Labor takes selected social indicators to indicate a crisis in worker satisfaction; business takes other indicators to proclaim a crisis in worker productivity. As rival claimants seek to impose meaning on events, they implicitly bid for a mandate for structures of action. The search for "an issue" is the lifeblood of politics. Issues are a pattern of events with significance for human values. Increasingly, it is the social scientist who locates and reports events, who probes for patterns, and who uses instruments of inference to try to confirm or deny those patterns asserted by others. So, in a very fundamental way, the social scientist is a participant in that business of defining and challenging issues that is basic to American politics. He or she is not the only participant, but undoubtedly has the special credentials and the competence to cope with the demands of problem setting.

In short, the researcher is not only in the business of finding or sorting among Answers: he or she is inevitably involved in finding or sorting among Questions as well. His or her special competence for the second enterprise lies in being uniquely conversant with that anonymous beast who is of little interest in everyday life, but of central concern in public policy: the generalized, average, model, human being. No one— no social worker, teacher, physician, or politician—has ever met an average child, a median unemployed factory worker in the Northeast, a model big-city superintendent of schools. Ordinarily one projects toward the normative and the average from a limited series of personal encounters. The value of this approach should not be underestimated: much can be done by projecting from a few particulars to the general case; and, in politics, much *is* done. But there are times when one needs aggregate estimates that go beyond the precision and detail given by private and casual encounters. Then one calls into play the armamentarium of the social scientist—those capabilities of sampling, of statistics, and of methodology that make it possible to infer in some detail what the average child knows at the end of the first grade, what the ethnic distribution of disease is in the Southwest, what the recidivism rate is for juvenile reformatories, what the average voter thinks about fluoridation, and so on. Because public policy ministers to the generalized human being, the social scientist must be involved if the policymaker is to look before he leaps.

The role of the social scientist in problem setting is significant and, in and of itself, not problematic. The only real difficulty in defining this role is technical. Scientists are curiously awkward in articulating the processes of finding questions, in either the scientific or the policy arena. But in the political arena, of course, problem setting is only one facet of the broader process of issue setting. And issue setting is problematic. Contending political groups vie with one another in construing the problematic situation, but not in the spirit of rival scientific theorists. Each seeks to mobilize belief in an issue with implications for action, and the fundamental goal of the effort is the mobilization of the fine structure of governmental action—the creation of an effective coalition on either the legislative or the administrative plane.

Organization of the Fine Structure of Action

The problem-solving image embodies the assumption that a policy issue, either before or after its formulation, is simultaneously and automatically installed in the beliefs and actions of all members of the policy community. The image also appears to anthropomorphize the government, assuming that many individuals often and easily think as one, and it sets aside important questions of the sociology of knowledge and action. But governments do not think. Nor do individuals wired together in a table of organization think in unison. Consider the public bureaucracy, a community of individuals whose actions are to some extent interorganized by a bureaucratic system that provides for division of labor, lines of responsibility, and the ultimate integration of each person's differentiated efforts. This bureaucratic harmonization of the actions of dispersed individuals is at best loose. Cooperative action is grossly structured; but as is well known, there is much room for individuals to work at cross-purposes and to nullify one another's actions. Each actor faces his or her own unique decision matrix defined by the position occupied in the institutional structure. He or she chooses among courses of action, but with a set of possible actions different from that of any other actor. Policy research can almost never dictate in so many words just what decision each person will make, but it can contribute to a kind of fine structure of action, superimposed on the broad structure of action given by the bureaucratic table of organization.

Policy research can lead individuals within the bureaucratic web to hold to the same conception of the problem at hand, thus ensuring that each emphasizes similar purposes in addressing his or her unique decision matrix. Patterns imposed on data can lead, ultimately, to evocative slogans—for example, the Need for a Sense of Community, the Need to Avoid Weakening the Family, Equality of Educational Opportunity, Advocacy, the Need for Income Redistribution. Such slogans and the metaphors that underlie them can provide a basis for harmonized action. Individuals influenced by a given conception emphasize it within their discretionary powers—here favoring a service or research project that seems in line with the conception, there adopting the conception as a criterion of quality for personnel selection, elsewhere allowing it to influence budget allocations. Thus, without an overt plan of cooperation, individuals distributed through the bureaucracy nevertheless make a particular conception of the problem a force in the system's pattern of action. Individual adherences are reinforced by more formal but secondary organizations of action: committees, interagency task forces, societies coordinating newsletters. It is these individual adjustments of emphasis, together with the secondary institutional organization, that I refer to as the fine structure of action.

The use of ideology to create coalitions is, of course, "old hat" in politics. As things go nowadays, it is *de rigueur* for assertions of ideology to rest on patterns of asserted facts about the state of the social situation. But these facts, although predicated on the authority of social scientists who are experts at looking at large things like a society, seem at times to be selected, exaggerated, and distorted in such a way that the social scientist must feel that their use exceeds and even jeopardizes his authority. Indeed, contending political claimants may use social scientists pretty much as contending court claimants often use psychiatrists. Each side marshals experts to speak for it, providing a seemingly paradoxical situation. Scientific, objective evidence is mustered to assert different, and at times radically opposed, courses of political action. Science speaks out of both sides of its mouth about the course that policy should take. Or perhaps the polarities of political action are such that political choices can be articulated (but never resolved) only by the provision of scientific information.

The Management of Dilemmas and Trade-offs

A third shortcoming of the problem-solving image of policy formation overlooks the essential presence of dilemmas and trade-offs. Charles de Gaulle is reported to have said, "I have lived a long life and I have never seen a single problem solved." Larger policy questions rest on dilemmas and trade-offs in a virtually definitional manner. That is, if a problem is clear, uncontested, and univalued, it ordinarily does not emerge at high levels of political debate. It is a technical problem. Its solution will ordinarily be debated and resolved through technical and bureaucratic institutions outside the central policymaking arenas of government.

Dilemmas of social policy arise, for example, in the effort to preserve work incentives and to provide adequate income support for those unable to be gainfully employed. Or they arise in manifold ways in efforts to design a program so that it will not reach those for whom it is not intended: administrative screening devices that focus on weeding out ineligibles also reduce the likelihood of reaching eligibles. Dilemmas also arise in education when, on the one hand, one strives for the kind of parity of input or output envisaged in the notion of equality of educational opportunity while, on the other hand, one tries to provide the disparities envisaged by the notions of pluralism and cultural democracy. Or they arise in the recurrent efforts to set forth federal day-care standards that both aid the mother and benefit the child: minimal standards and low expenditures for day care are essential if the program is to reduce welfare costs by helping women enter work, but much professional testimony indicates that day care demands high standards if it is to be beneficial for children.

Dilemmas such as these pose a conflict of values, two ideals pointing toward action in diametrically opposite directions. In practice, one can act only along a continuum of shifting trade-offs, where more of one ideal is purchased at the expense of less of the other. The manifold dilemmas that exist in the political arena all constitute "problems," in the general sense of the word *problem*; but these are not the kinds of problems that are envisaged in the problem-solving image and that are resolvable in its terms. What research can do is articulate and clarify the field of practical choices and elucidate in concrete terms the practical consequences of a choice. But research cannot arbitrate the underlying value choices and thus solve these problems.

Research, if it is to be legitimate, is, or is supposed to be, value free and value neutral. Yet the research work brought into policy determination is used as an ally in negotiating for the supremacy of some value positions. The researcher can be chagrined by this use of his or her work, stoutly asserting the irrelevance of the work for policy; or he or she can cooperate in the political exploitation of the findings, running a real risk that he or she or the work will be discounted by the scientific community that is the fundamental basis of its credibility.

The games of science are, in one sense, always value neutral but, in another sense, never so. Scientists who participate in a research collectivity for trading information and reaching consensus operate in a social proof structure in which there are socially approved rules. This social system, by its very nature, stresses rule observance and will not transmit values or adjudicate among the diverse values of the collectivity. In the execution of the work of the group, members engage in common routines of action: they record those patterns of experience that the scientific group agrees are "events"; they trade reports of observed patterns of events and engage in procedures for separating the factual from the artifactual; they come to agreements about the locations of factual patterns of events in frames of time, space, person, and contingency.[33] The basic analytic operations on which this social proof structure rests—pattern recognition, induction, inference—strive to be value neutral; or, at least, it is hoped that individual values get fairly well washed out in the trading back and forth that goes on in the scientific collectivity. But the collectivity is made up of individuals, and the individual's work is always an expression of personal values. The individual expresses values not only by choice of area and problem but by the way he or she imposes patterns on phenomena and assigns meaning to relationships. Part of the work of the social proof structure is to guard against this, to keep the individual "honest" by insisting that the findings offered with one bias be confirmed by the observations of individuals with other biases. This is not a description of practice, but a statement of how ideally value-neutral knowledge is produced out of the work of the collectivity.

Since politics depends on the articulation and expression of contending values, the basic intent of political action is not to wash out values, but to arrive at courses of action that are as satisfactory as possible to contending interests. And, as noted above, proposals for the reform of the research/policy alliance offered under the problem-solving image generally have the effect either of taking research further away from policy relevance or of changing the basic nature of political processes.

THE PROBLEM-SOLVING IMAGE AS MYTH

If the above arguments are compelling, then we may be able to address the paradox of belief and doubt in policy research in a different light. Research is receiving increasing support, in resources and in institutionalization, because it has genuine value for American political debate. But the policy/research alliance is an uneasy marriage, posing deep dilemmas that threaten continually to erode the responsibility and credibility of each partner in the match, the researcher and the policymaker alike. As is characteristic of all political dilemmas, the fundamental problem probably cannot be resolved. The marriage will always be a little painful. To soothe the pain, and to direct both parties as much as possible toward a safe union, the problem-solving image is upheld and cherished as a norming myth. The myth is inadequate as a model of reality, but it has genuine value in both a psychological and a sociological sense. As policy research grows in extent, more and more people make contact with the activity and with the norming myth that covers it. Doubt grows as there is dawning awareness of all those aspects of reality not covered by the myth.

The painfulness of the alliance arises out of the fundamental incompatibility of the games of science and the games of politics. The games of science seek to establish patterns of experience that all may share. They are value neutral in the sense that they are deliberately designed to filter out the values of the participants so as to arrive at the "unbiased truth." Best play in such games leads to assertions of findings that must be accepted by individuals whether they find them palatable or not. The proper posture for a gamesman of science must be one of restraint, dispassion, conservatism, the willingness to suspend belief pending more evidence. The games of politics are quite different. They are designed to find one purpose or course of action acceptable to individuals who have begun the play by espousing diverse purposes, values, and actions. They are value expressive, and the facts enter in only as subordinated to and sustaining values, only as contributing to the delineation of an issue. Best play in such games leads toward the maximum possible satisfaction of one's purposes in the group action. The proper posture for a gamesman of politics is one of boldness, persistence, opportunism; the good gamesman is able to mobilize and sustain belief and commitment.

It is extremely difficult for a person to maintain credibility across the two kinds of games. Generally, the scientific gamesman who is too action-oriented loses credibility, and, in pretty much the same way, the political gamesman who is too theory-oriented loses credibility. But the basic problem is the incompatibility of the two games. One trades in facts, and the other, in values.

The problem-solving image is the kind of long-standing fantasy in which the games and the roles of science and politics are not in conflict. On the scientific side, it expresses the hope that participation in political activities is, or can be made to be, a matter of value-neutral decision making. But the work of the researcher is always dragged into political debate, because (1) the valid functions of problem setter are perceived, through the political lens, as functions of advocating and legitimizing issues; and (2) the valid functions of problem solver, in the narrow sense of the problem-solving image, are perceived as applicable to the "problems" posed by the dilemmas and trade-offs of policy. By holding to the myth, the scientist does not consent to "see" these utilizations. (He or she sees them, but considering them illegitimate and deplorable, resists them as much as possible.)

On the political side, the fantasy expresses the hope that contributory science can retain its authority while remaining employable for the settlement of political value questions. Political games settle disputes through a limited number of devices: through the use of parity (one man, one vote), through an appeal to common values, and through an appeal to common knowledge. In the case of researchers, political activity regularly defers the settlement of value questions to scientific refereeing, somehow hoping or expecting that such questions can be settled definitively by scientific authority. Scientists will resolve the problem by finding common knowledge that can serve as a basis of resolution. The clearest and best case of this can be seen in the most popular current species of policy-relevant research, the evaluation study.

Policy analysts are now regularly asked to evaluate any and all species of program—in education, housing, law enforcement, community development, and so on. They are never told concretely what values or what value-derived goals to inquire about (because, virtually by definition, the political body presenting these programs cannot make up its mind about a consensual goal, much less specify it with precision).[34] So the researcher proceeding to execute his supposedly technical function must decide what constitutes good child development, good education, good housing, a good family, a good community. In a very real way, the political community has handed over to the scientific community part of the problem of arriving at consensual social purposes and values. But this delegation transfers to the researcher a problem that exceeds his or her professional competence, and it divests the policymaker of some of his or her genuine political responsibility. It is, strictly speaking, improper.

By holding to the problem-solving myth, the policymakers have been unable to "see" their delegation of value decisions. The consequence is that political issues regularly bubble up out of research projects that are conceived in innocence. Evaluations, originally seen as technical assistance, coalesce to form a potent "nothing works" theory. The National Science Foundation commissions the creation of a curriculum to improve the teaching of social studies in the schools. That curriculum—*Man: A Course of Study*—produces serious political perturbation because it can be viewed as an attack on the separation of church and state. There arises the image of the researcher as someone at the fringes of power endeavoring to intrude values of social planning, liberalism, and secular humanism into government. But, in fact, requests for research by government regularly require the researcher to interpolate value decisions into work if it is ever to be completed. Whose values will be used?

In sum, the coexistence of belief and doubt in policy research seems to be an outcome of one of the many disparities between myth and reality that exist in any society. Can this disparity be resolved? We might try to make reality conform more fully to the myth. This is, in fact, the gist of the GAO reform proposal discussed above. The Congress could require itself to articulate more fully its goals and objectives in legislation. Conceivably, then, the games of research and politics would not clash. But it does not seem likely that drastic political reorganization will be undertaken to resolve an issue that is, after all, relatively small as political issues go. Can we try to find a myth that conforms more fully to the reality of the research/policy alliance? Perhaps. But let it be noted that the myth given by the problem-solving image has some useful properties in its present imperfect form. It delineates the safe ground between research and policy, discourages but does not forbid interaction on other ground, and so tends to steer interactions between researchers and policymakers toward the kinds of issues least likely to disrupt the politics of consensus building.

NOTES AND REFERENCES

1. Genevieve J. Kelezo, "Program Evaluation: Emerging Issues of Possible Legislative Concern Relating to the Conduct and Use of Evaluation in the Congress and the Executive Branch." Washington, D.C.: Congressional Research Service, Library of Congress, November 1974. This report provides a useful review of government documents and of the academic literature on the weaknesses of evaluation together with proposals for its reform.
2. For a summary of the 40 acts requiring evaluation, see U.S. General Accounting Office, *Program Evaluation: Legislative Language and a User's Guide to Selected Sources.* Washington, D.C.: U.S. Government Printing Office, 1973.
3. For an example of a model statutory evaluation requirement, see Marvin Keith and James J. Hendrick, "GAO Helps Congress Evaluate Programs." *Public Administration Review,* July-August 1974, p. 331.
4. This statement was made by Robert G. Bruce, assistant administrator for program planning and evaluation in the Department of Health, Education, and Welfare, in "What Goes Wrong with Evaluations and How to Prevent It." *Human Needs* (HEW publication), 1972, *1*(1).
5. Frank L. Lewis and Frank G. Zarb, "Federal Program Evaluation from the OMB Perspective." *Public Administration Review,* July-August 1974, p. 314. This paper is cast in terms of recommendations. I have assumed that they are based on experience with evaluations that have failed to be timely, relevant, and so forth. Of course, the problem and the solution may not be identical, but discussion with the director of evaluation suggests that my interpretation is not misleading.
6. Nathan Caplan et al., *The Use of Social Science Knowledge in Policy Decisions at the National Level.* Ann Arbor, Mich.: University of Michigan, Institute for Social Research, 1975.
7. Ibid. P. 48.
8. Ibid. P. 47.
9. Ibid. P. 26.
10. Ibid. P. 47.
11. Ibid. P. 19.
12. Caplan has argued, as we have just seen, that lack of contact and lack of trust account for variations in use. If one follows this view, one might provide for more utilization through bridge building and through procedures that would develop, say, consumerism on the policy side and quality control on the research side.
13. Ilene Nagel Bernstein and Howard E. Freeman, *Academic and Entrepreneurial Research: The Consequences of Diversity in Federal Evaluation Studies.* New York: Russell Sage Foundation, 1975.

14. Joseph Wholey et al., "If You Don't Care Where You Get To, Then It Doesn't Matter Which Way You Go." In Gene M. Lyons, ed., *Social Research and Public Policies* (The Dartmouth/OECD Conference). Hanover, N.H.: University Press of New England, 1975. Pp. 175–76.

15. Sheldon H. White et al., *Federal Programs for Young Children: Review and Recommmendations.* Washington, D.C.: U. S. Government Printing Office, 1973.

16. Charles L. Schultze, *The Politics and Economics of Public Spending.* Washington, D. C.: Brookings Institution, 1968. Pp. 47–49.

17. For a formal exposition of the problem-solving approach in terms of objective functions, constraining variables, and problem-space, see Herbert A. Simon, *The Sciences of the Artificial.* Cambridge, Mass.: MIT Press, 1969.

18. Caplan et al., Op. cit. P. 18.

19. See Christopher Jencks et al., *Inequality: A Reassessment of the Effects of Family and Schooling in America.* New York: Basic Books, 1972. It is ironic and unusual that the judgments stimulated by this volume may now be challenged by the authors of the work itself. Jencks, in a report yet to be published, reestimated the relationship among family background, education, and income on the basis of new data and somewhat different assumptions about the reliability of self-reported educational achievement. There is new evidence, depending on the data source used, that there is much more determinancy (less "luck") in accounting for variations in income, and that the role of education is larger than earlier estimates showed.

20. Sheldon H. White, "The National Impact Study of Head Start." In Jerome Hellmuth, ed., *Disadvantaged Child.* Vol. 3, *Compensatory Education: A National Debate.* New York: Brunner/Mazel, 1970.

21. Marshall S. Smith and Joan Bissell, "Report Analysis: The Impact of Head Start." *Harvard Educational Review,* 1970, *40,* 51–104.

22. Don T. Campbell and A. E. Erlebacher, "How Regression Effects in Quasi-experimental Evaluations Can Mistakenly Make Compensatory Education Look Harmful." In Jerome Hellmuth, ed., Op. cit.

23. Victor G. Cicirelli, John W. Evans, and J. S. Schiller, "The Impact of Head Start: A Reply to the Report Analysis." *Harvard Educational Review,* 1970, *40,* 120–26. See also Victor G. Cicirelli, "The Relevance of the Regression Artifact Problem to the Westinghouse–Ohio Evaluation of Head Start: A Reply to Campbell and Erlebacher." In Jerome Hellmuth, ed., Op. cit.; and John W. Evans and J. S. Schiller, "How Preoccupation with Possible Regression Artifacts Can Lead to a Faculty Strategy for the Evaluation of Social Action Programs: A Reply to Campbell." Ibid.

24. For a discussion of the problem of developing guidelines, see Chapter 7 in the present volume.

25. Arthur R. Jensen, "How Much Can We Boost IQ and Scholastic Achievement?" *Harvard Educational Review,* 1969, *39,* 1–123.

26. David K. Cohen and Michael S. Garret, "Reforming Educational Policy with Applied Research." *Harvard Educational Review,* 1975, *45,* 23.

27. Personal communication, 20 October 1975.

28. David B. Tyack, *The One Best System: A History of American Urban Experience.* Cambridge, Mass: Harvard University Press, 1974.

29. Ibid. P. 77.
30. For a full account of this case, see Martin Rein and Hugh Heclo, "Social Sciences and the Negative Income Tax." In *The Utilization of the Social Sciences in Policy Making in the United States*. Paris. Organization for Economic Co-operation and Development, 1980. Pp. 29–66.
31. Joseph Kershaw, *Government against Poverty*. Washington, D.C.: Brookings Institution, 1970. P. 22.
32. See Michel Foucault, *The Archaeology of Knowledge and the Discourse on Language* (New York: Pantheon Books, 1972), for an important and stimulating development of this topic. Foucault argues that "there is no knowledge without a particular discursive practice; any discursive practice may be defined by the knowledge that it forms" (P. 183). This idea, that knowledge is specified by a discourse, closely parallels Thomas S. Kuhn's theory that shared paradigms that form a research consensus are prerequisites for normal science. However, Foucault's analysis of discursive practice is explicitly about inquiry in social science and is therefore particularly relevant for policy analysts. He defines discursive practice in terms of "a body of anonymous historical rules always determined in the time and space that have defined a given period, and for a given social, economic, geographical, or linguistic area." For a stimulating, searching review of Foucault's work, see Edward Said, "An Ethics of Functional Language." *Diacritics*, Summer 1974, pp. 28–37.
33. For analyses of social proof structures in psychology, see Sheldon H. White, "Social Proof Structures: The Dialectic of Method and Theory in the Work of Psychology." In N. Datan and H. W. Reese, eds., *Life-span Developmental Psychology: Dialectical Perspectives on Experimental Research*. New York: Academic Press, 1977.
34. For an excellent discussion of these issues, see Richard A. Beck and Peter H. Rossi, "Doing Good or Worse: Evaluation Research Politically Reexamined." *Social Problems*, 1976, *23*(3), 337–49.

Chapter 12

Action Frames and Problem Setting

It is believed that the simple prescription that we ought to take thought before we take action provides the foundation on which much policy analysis rests. As we have seen in the previous chapter, ideally at least, there should be an orderly progression from empirically grounded description to analytic understanding to the prescription of a strategy for change. Some see values entering this process at the level of prescription; others, as involved at the level of description or of problem selection. But the process is in general one of moving from problem description to problem remedy.

I do not believe that this is either an adequate description of the policy process as it actually exists or an ideal toward which we should strive. In reality, I think, both analysis and prescription start from action.

Both the categories of description and the lines of investigation we pursue are shaped by our experience of trying to act on the world, and are limited by the sorts of action we see as possible. For instance, when we look into the problem of poverty, our analysis of causality is constrained and focused by plausible remedial activities. Analysis outside these boundaries appears utopian, outrageous, or silly. Consider one example: when eugenics was a politically discussable topic, the possibility of relationships among poverty, mental ability, and birthrate could be investigated; now the very idea seems not only repugnant but odd. The problem of households that are poor because they have no employable members could conceivably suggest an investigation of forms of social organization that would disperse the members of such households as dependents on more economically viable ones—as, indeed, occurred to some extent in past ages —or of ways in which child labor could be reestablished; but such possibilities, too, are unthinkable for us, and so research in this vein seems to make no sense. "Poverty research" hardly deals with the underlying societal mechanisms generating a given pattern of income distribution, because our political system seems to offer no way to deal with the issue directly.

The major large-scale social experiments of the 1970s in education, health, housing, and welfare all started with an action position. In the educational voucher experiment the view was that competition among schools might improve the quality of education. Health experiments were based on the belief that government could save money if patients participated in paying for the cost of their medical care (co-pay) and if producers had an incentive to save (prepay). In housing, we find a conservative government's preference for subsidies to individuals rather than subsidies to production. In welfare, the negative income tax experiment assumed that if income guarantees were a sound public policy to pursue, they would not lead to labor force withdrawal or break up families.

Thus, I think that the categories of description arise from institutions and programs of action. I also think that prescription arises from the realm of action, because our ideas of the desirable come from our experiences of the real and the possible. I do not believe that the situation should be more like that of the positivist ideal; to define a problem as independent of the actions addressing it is to propose unattainable utopias and to treat research as though it possessed some sort of timeless validity separate from the world of becoming, to which it should properly belong. The center of both fact and value is the world of action.

Accordingly, we start with an answer, a solution, a way of acting; and this, in turn, shapes the nature of policy analysis we shall undertake. If we begin with action, or solutions, why, then, do we undertake policy analysis? We do so in a search for validation and meaning.

One reason is to legitimate the action we have undertaken on other grounds. Robert Park made this observation many years ago when he wrote:

> As a matter of fact and natural history, the problems which attract public attention are usually problems of administration. When emergencies arise, we meet them with some novel administrative measures. But later on we formulate a policy to justify the innovation; we do this by interpreting our legislative and administrative experiments... on the whole, theory follows practice and serves to generalize, justify, and rationalize it.[1]

In the course of doing this, we interpret our actions and give them meaning.

In an altogether different context, Hannah Arendt observed that "the need for reason is inspired not by the quest for truth but by the quest for meaning. And truth and meaning are not same. The basic fallacy . . . is to interpret meaning on the model of truth . . . questions of meaning . . . are all unanswerable by common sense and the refinement of it we call science."[2]

But we also use research to improve the world of action. By reflecting on the world of action, we identify both the desirable and the undesirable, and then generalize them into values grounded in experience. We also refine our understanding of the circumstances in which values can be attained. Policy research can thus be seen not as preceding or above the world of action, but as a part of it.

When we look at the world of action from which our thinking arises and with which it preserves its connection, we see that this world of action is not simply the world of politics and programs: there is also an organized world of thinking, researching, and advice-giving centered in universities, which is itself a domain of action. The way in which these activities are organized—administrative structure, division of labor, reward system—forms the basis of what we call the disciplinary interest in research. Thus, research arises out of two spheres of action: the disciplinary and the programmatic.

The things we think about and the ways we think about them, as well as the ways we act, are shaped by the institutional arrangements of the society in which we live. Since both spheres of action are shaped by a single set of institutions, there is a congruence in their underlying assumptions. Both programmatic institutions and disciplinary ideas in policy research seem implicitly to divide reality into three different realms: the political, the economic, and the social. Political science investigates the political realm, which is thought of in the programmatic sphere as the institutions of government. The discipline of economics deals mainly with the institutions identified as business firms, and the markets in which they operate. In the programmatic realm this is the "private sector." The social realm deals with the lives of people, and the primary institution in which they organize their lives is the family. No one discipline dominates the study of individuals and their families; but when these units are thought about in a societal context, that is called a "sociological approach." In the programmatic area, these units are defined as recipients of services.

A programmatic interest, in market-dominated societies, interprets the three realms in much the same way as the disciplines do—that is to say, it accepts the unity of the realms, treats them separately, and agonizes about the unintended effects of treating wholes as parts. The critical practical assumption that a programmatic perspective accepts is that two of the realms are regarded as natural—the family and the economy—and that the political realm is where there is scope for intervention.

Given the institutional arrangements that implicitly embody the conception of these three realms as unified but separate and the assumption that intervention arises in the political realm and enters the social and economic realms only when their proper or natural arrangements break down, how are problems set?

This general issue of problem setting may be seen as raising a number of more particular questions.

1. What are the appropriate channels of action or the problem-setting traditions?
2. What action should be taken within a problem-setting tradition?
3. How do various problem-setting traditions relate to each other?
4. What is the relationship of the traditions in one realm to the other two realms?
5. What do the academic disciplines contribute to the proposed traditions of action?

6. How do changes in the family, the economy, and the political realm influence both the scope for action and ideas in the disciplines?

It is at this point that it is necessary to narrow the scope of our inquiry and examine a more restricted domain in policy research. We cannot discuss problem setting without focusing on a specific problem area. We shall look at the problem of poverty, giving special attention to how academic interests relate to programmatic interests. Naturally, if we were considering a different substantive area, such as energy or the environment, we would encounter different problem-setting traditions.

PROBLEM-SETTING TRADITIONS

Within poverty research there are two problem-setting traditions. One, concerned with the creation of a "secondary income distribution," is designed to provide transfers, or cash income. Transfers are social programs for distributing income and goods, such as food and housing, outside the market. The second tradition defines the occupational structure as the strategic point for intervention, since it is through jobs that the original or primary distribution of resources begins. This approach is directed to intervention in labor markets.

Unemployment is an example of a problem that is treated both in the direct distribution tradition and in the work tradition. When the consequences of unemployment are seen as a problem of the loss of earnings, the remedy sought is a strategy of earning replacement. This strategy provides the intellectual rationale that underlies most social security programs. However, unemployment can also be viewed as a problem of job loss or as, in the cases of youth and housewives, a problem of job entry. The latter requires a manpower-training strategy rather than earning replacement.

CHOICE WITHIN A TRADITION

Within each of these problem-setting traditions there are further choices to be made. In the direct distribution tradition, the critical question is: On what principles should the secondary income distribution system be organized? More specifically, should transfers be distributed on the basis of need or on the basis of past contributions? In the work tradition, we are concerned with how to intervene in labor markets. This can be done (1) by increasing individual human capital, so as to better enable individuals to enter the market; (2) from a more strategic perspective, by removing barriers to access to labor submarkets, when market imperfections create politically unacceptable forms of discrimination; and (3) by actively creating public jobs, as a last resort, so that people will depend for their economic well-being on the primary rather than the secondary system of income distribution.

These interventions would start with different premises. On the one hand, programs can start with the individual and try to alter his or her motivation, information, skills, and competence to hold and perform jobs. On the other hand, programs can see the institutional arrangements of hiring, promotion, compensation, working conditions, and the availability of jobs as related more to the structure of the occupation and industry in labor markets than as properties of individuals.

CONFLICTING TRADITIONS

The task of relating different traditions with respect to poverty may be undertaken by examining the difficulties encountered, in recent attempts at welfare reform, in combining transfer and work programs. The two traditions conflict with the economic realm in different ways. A jobs-related program that is consistent with the requirements in the economic realm proceeds from the assumption that employment should be based on ability: those who can do the job best should get work. By contrast, intervention in secondary income distribution is based on the assumption that transfers should help those who are the worst off. Thus, within a framework of poverty, the transfer and work traditions clash to some extent.

TRADITION AND THE INSTITUTIONAL REALMS

In the transfer tradition, the realm of programmatic intervention is viewed as separate from, although related to, the other two realms; intervention is not seen as altering the operations of the economic and political realms, but as correcting for their undesired effects. The economic and societal realms are treated as natural or given, and the programmatic realm must accommodate to them or explicitly try to alter them. The obvious example of accommodation is that income transfer programs must not disrupt the organization of family life in the societal realm. Witness the consternation and dismay that follow when welfare is alleged to break up families. On the other hand, income transfers may be judged to have a positive effect, as in the example of efforts to increase the generosity of children's allowances in order to increase the birthrate. Programs are expected to be at least neutral with respect to family life. They may fall short of the positive ideal of doing good, but they should not damage valued societal institutions. Since the economic realm is assumed to generate all the resources to be distributed, its continued integrity has a special position. Above all, efforts to improve the distribution of income must not damage the incentive to work. Ideally, income reshuffling efforts should be neutral or positive with respect to work incentives.

In the work tradition, the programmatic realm is prepared to alter economic processes in order to maintain the norms of the societal realm. What is at issue is how deeply to intervene in the structure of capitalist society; there is a search for points of intervention that will have minimal consequences for the general functioning of both economic and societal realms. The justification for intervening in the natural economic realm is that the economy is not functioning properly. Ideally, the intervention should be temporary, until the breakdown in the natural realm is remedied.

Public employment jobs are viewed as a temporary expedient until individuals can be absorbed into the private sector, where the "real" jobs are presumed to reside.

Intervention in the world of work (by training, by affirmative action, by public employment) is, paradoxically, both more controversial and more acceptable. The controversy violates the assumption of the natural realms and threatens the axioms that organize our disciplinary understanding of the realms and our programmatic commitments. At the same time, intervention at work is more acceptable because it reinforces the view about the primacy of the economic realm as a source of economic well-being. (In this discussion I omit indirect ways of stimulating the economy through macroeconomic policy and restrict my comments to direct interventions in the area of work.) In both the work and the transfer traditions, ideally interventions should be positive, as a handmaiden to the economy by stimulating economic growth and development; and, as discussed above, they should be neutral in that they do not disrupt family solidarity or erode family members' incentive to participate in the economy.

TRADITIONS AND DISCIPLINARY INTEREST

What, then, is the contribution of knowledge from the disciplinary inquiries about the social and economic realms for programmatic problem-setting? The answer is complicated by the fact that academic research is also influenced by practice in the social and economic realms, not just by the conceptual and methodological paradigms of their disciplines. This societal influence is most strongly felt at the margin of the discipline, and it is typically the academicians at the margin who try to influence the programmatic realms. If one's point of reference is the discipline, then the professional payoff is to address the central puzzle of the discipline. But if one is marginal to the central scholarly concerns of the discipline, then one tries to get leverage by being useful to the outer world; one gives up trying to be central to the discipline.

Academic researchers interested in income distribution and dual labor markets provide an example. In this process it is not so much the research findings that are critical as the cast of mind of the researchers. They grasp from their discipline an essential insight, which is converted into a programmatic format. In the case of scholars interested in income distribution, it is the comprehensive means-tested negative income tax (NIT), ideally administered through the tax system, that serves as the prototype. Whatever may be its origins in the academic discipline, the NIT is now a reform in the programmatic realm, and poverty research is inspired by an effort to work out the design problems presented by the conception with the economists' tools of analysis. Advice to policymakers then centers on these design issues rather than the study of the other realms. After a decade of experimentation and research, a sense of malaise is now being felt, which is leading to doubt about the assumptions of selectivity on which the NIT rests and also, more generally, to doubt about the desirability of further expansion of direct distribution as a remedy for poverty. Those who are disillusioned are searching in the occupational tradition for a better answer.

The apparent need, in program design, to choose between a direct distribution approach and an occupational approach reveals a split that hardly seems to appear in study of the economic and societal realms within the academic tradition. Here we find an implicit assumption of a unity between study of the production system and study of the system of well-being, because it is assumed that a considerable degree of congruence exists between rewards and occupational position, on the one hand, and rewards and well-being, on the other. The performance of markets in industrial societies binds together the two systems of occupation and reward. Approaching the problem from one perspective or the other is regarded as not particularly important, because each puzzle can lead to the other, if pursued far enough. Since relational and distributional issues are both aspects of the same question, it does not appear necessary, or even useful, to make a clear distinction between the study of structure or the aspects of class having to do with the individual's relation to the means of production and the study of the distributional dimensions of stratification.[3]

In the distinction between poverty and inequality it is sometimes believed that issues of structure are addressed through study of distribution; the framework of inequality is seen as providing a vocabulary for describing the arrangement of society. Studies of economic inequality as measured by the size distribution of income usually divided income into arbitrary units such as deciles, quintiles, etc., these measures serving as summary indicators of the outcome of structure and process. This approach can be assimilated into a programmatic framework when looking at the impact of benefits and taxes on what is sometimes seen as the "original" distribution, an approach that, though useful as an indicator of the impact of programmatic intervention, does not itself yield leverage for intervention. The same argument applies with respect to the distribution of wealth.

Theorists identified with the dual labor market would go further in seeing "labor market imperfections" not only as phenomena of central interest but also as phenomena central to the functioning of the system as a whole. The intervention issues have to deal not so much with barriers to individual access as with the differences between "dirty jobs" and "good jobs." For this group, job security as well as earnings are central to analysts. Such interventions as job training and job creation, and the research associated with these intervention strategies, are criticized by dual labor market theorists as superficial and unrealistic in light of the underlying characteristics of economic structure.

Much of the work of this group stands as a criticism of the character of industrial society itself rather than as a contribution to remediation. The "dirty jobs" are seen as making up a "secondary labor market" that enables industrial societies to deal with economic fluctuations. Since, it is argued, the economic fluctuations are an inevitable feature of such societies, it seems to follow that to do something about one set of "dirty jobs" would be merely to pass on the uncertainty to another group too weak to protect itself. Hence, any improvement for one group is counterbalanced by increased uncertainty for another group. However, the dual labor market theorists have also attempted to derive from their analysis general recommendations for intervention, for example: reduce the proportion of "dirty" jobs; clean up the work settings and remuneration of the "dirty" jobs that remain essential; and promote circulation between "dirty" and "good" jobs so that the dirty ones do not become the definers of entrenched status and economic differences.

Dualistic studies of the economic realm lead to a radical diagnosis because they hold that both the fluctuations in the economy and the unequal apportionment of the costs of these fluctuations are inherent features of an industrial (or perhaps of capitalist industrial) society. Such an assessment has contributed little to programmatic design in the occupational tradition, because the very nature of the diagnosis asserts that no fundamental reform within the system is possible.

DISCIPLINARY INTENT AND CHANGES IN THE REALMS

How, then, is poverty research that derives from programmatic interventions related to the economic and societal realms? Research is shaped by the prevailing practices in those realms that serve as the context or climate within which problems are set and remedies are accepted. When the context changes and new practices evolve in response, new research issues arise in the programmatic realm.

Social movements, such as the civil rights and the women's movements, send out ripples signaling a change in the context, stimulating thought and action, and creating a diffuse sense that there is a need for a new programmatic agenda for research. In this process the implicit assumptions that organized current programs and research are made visible. For example, the direct distributional tradition is organized around the assumption of pooled resources. Study and programmatic action are devoted to unraveling the intellectual and political puzzles posed by pooling, but the women's movement has created a climate in which individuals are able to challenge the assumptions of pooling. What is particularly interesting is that this challenge seems to be taking place almost simultaneously in many industrial societies. A new principle of distribution is being sought that takes an individual, rather than some pooled unit (such as kin, household, nuclear family), as the focus. This new challenge assaults the conventional treatment of economic dependency that is the foundation on which the welfare state rests.[4]

Since, I believe, intervention pushes research rather than the other way around, there is a tendency to explore areas about which one conceivably could do something and to neglect areas that appear intractable to intervention. This explains why, at the program level, the focus is on the individual and the occupational group and, at the macro level, on money transfers rather than on institutional structures. In this distribution of programmatic elements, sociology concerns itself with individuals and small groups; economics tends to dominate the large-scale income redistribution programs.

* * *

At this point, it may be useful to summarize my argument. First, I identify three realms, the programmatic or political, the economic, and the social, and argue that poverty research springs primarily from the puzzles presented in the programmatic realm. These puzzles are of a special kind because, in this realm most clearly of all three, it is the remedies or answers that shape the theory and questions rather than the other way around. If one accepts as a remedy a selectivist welfare program, a universalist family allowance, or a contributory social insurance, the research questions that need to be addressed arise in each case from the proposed solution; one does not examine the question of whether the intervention is the best remedy for poverty.

Second, I argue that within the programmatic frame of reference there are two main sets of answers, which I have labeled the direct distributional and the occupational distributional traditions. If one works within one of these traditions, the ambiguities and doubtful underlying assumptions of the tradition are almost never subject to critical review. If questions are raised, they usually come from challenges arising in other traditions. For example, some scholars grounded in the occupational tradition are currently trying to uncover weaknesses in the direct distributional tradition by showing that such programs tend to break up families. In this way, social practice helps to define programmatic research.

Third, research is carried out within a problem-setting tradition, not across traditions. Interests of disciplines and programs reinforce the pattern.

We need next to examine the conceptualization of intervention itself. We should recognize that there is an implicit map that dominates policy research for both the direct distribution and the work traditions. The realm of programmatic intervention is thought about quite differently from the other two realms—the economic and the societal. The societal and economic realms are thought of as "natural" realms of ongoing processes; these natural processes, however, generate the problems that are addressed by action in the political realm of intervention. Intervention relates to them by altering their arrangement, or by taking account of their arrangement so as to adapt intervention to leave them unaltered. (Although from this perspective societal and economic processes have a sort of prior status as natural and ongoing, the fact that intervention can at times be framed to change them indicates that the design of intervention to leave them as they are also represents a positive choice, not neutrality.)

If one thinks about this map as a whole, one may be struck by the peculiarity of a manner of thinking that treats the societal and the economic realms as natural social processes, but intervention as a framework of rational activity. Furthermore, this map not only separates natural and artificial but is hierarchical in structure: there are actors and those acted upon. The language seems to imply a group of benefactors. Indeed, the history of interventions starts with charity, and the vocabulary of benefits and benefactors is derived from that background. One might think of modern poverty research as an effort to rise conceptually above this way of viewing the world. The concepts of entitlement and universalism are ways of trying to rise above it in the area of practice.

This leads to a view of intervention that places it outside politics and outside history, that construes it as a process by which those who have or control give to those who do not. The benefit is thought of as flowing through the actions of those who "initiate" programs, rather than through some complex process in which groups accommodate to each other through a struggle in which even those at the bottom—the "beneficiaries"—have a role.

When private and religious charity became transformed into modern social policy, programs carried out on behalf of the poor were regarded as the product of a societal expression of compassion and humanity, not as serving the interest of any particular group. In somewhat the same way, the research associated with poverty issues bears similar assumptions of neutrality. In fact, of course, it is the established groups in society whose perspectives dominate the framing of problems; nevertheless, these problem frames and fields of interest are seen as self-evident and therefore are not themselves subject to question.

"Poverty research" can be thought of as a component in this process. It is not merely that ideas guide intervention: ideas are also a reflection of interventions or, to put the matter more sharply, a weapon for proposed interventions. It is not that research is dishonest or that the rules of evidence are improperly applied; more precisely, it is an issue of what subjects are to be investigated and how problems are framed. We note further that value-critical, nonprogrammatic research is also important to the basic conceptual structure that guides both research and intervention. Programmatic research can draw on ideas and evidence that arise from an intellectual process more directly responsive to the drive for cognitive orientation than to the wish to act.

But to look at poverty research in this way is also to look at intervention in a different light. It is to see the realm of intervention itself as "natural process" in the same sense as the societal and the economic appear to us now. I believe that a more realistic approach joins the realms of the economic and the social with that of intervention in a common framework.

CLAIMING AS A REFRAMING OF ACTION

I have found it useful to substitute for the form of thought implied by benefits and welfare system one centering on the concept of claims and claims structures. The theory is sketched out in Chapter 2. Here I shall review how the argument is relevant for the analysis of action.

A claim is a distributional rule. Claims express what people receive in society. The distributional rules we call claims have an element of established right or entitlement; but in addition there is a fringe, which is less clear, which is open to bargaining, benefaction, pressure, and demand. We assume, moreover, that elements which now appear as entitlements may have been less well established in the past, and are themselves the outcome of some historic process of claiming and claims definition.

The utility of this way of thinking is that it integrates the three realms of the societal, the economic, and intervention into a single framework. Each of these realms may be thought of as one within which distributional rules arise. The realms are, however, not independent, so that the processes by which distributional rules arise and become established are claiming processes involving all three realms. This way of thinking about distributional rules permits us to join the structural and the distributional patterns in society by social conventions rather than by a set of laws in which the economic and societal realms are separated and that of intervention is not only separate from the other two but is also outside the sphere of lawlike regularities that govern the first two realms.

The debate about claims is formulated in terms of normative argument, in which "policy research" plays a major role; the establishment of claims is a process of pressure, leverage, bargaining. Thus, in taking a claims framework, we view the output of the realm of interventions not as benefits, but as claims derived from an interactive process of claiming and granting.

Another consequence of this perspective is the focus on the relationships between the claims that arise in the realm of programmed intervention and those that arise in the societal and economic realms. As I explained in Chapter 2, we see the main claim-managing institution in the economic sphere as being firms and property. Each of these spheres has its own vocabulary to describe the process of claiming and the rules of distribution that are acceptable. In the economic realm the main distribution rules concern compensation for work and compensation for use of capital. In the societal realm, mediated through the family as an institution, kinship solidarity is the organizing rule of distribution. In the political realm we find that government is both an employer, subject to the rules of compensation for work, and a provider, in which it is governed by at least three distributional rules—based on need, on contribution, and on citizenship. Underlying and legitimizing government intervention for all three rules is a conception of common membership in a solidarity unit.

We are witnessing a growth of claims against government, which we call the "welfare state." At the same time we are also experiencing the growth of political claims against business corporations, leading to more job security for some, improved quality of the work environment, and fringe benefits, from pensions to medical care to educational grants. (See Chapter 1.) We do not have a consensual basis for judgment of changes with respect either to the kinds of institutions within which and against which claiming takes place or to the content and amount of the claims themselves. Shall we interpret these trends as a sign of success or a cause of failure? Do these claims erode or nourish productivity? Do they lead to less worker alienation, more collective identification, and hence to larger output, or do they lead to undermining incentives? If production and growth affect the structure of claims, then is it true that in time the claims arising from the growth of society will erode the structure that made that growth possible?

The claims perspective I have developed here also suggests that more than content and methodology must be addressed if we are to understand the problem-setting process. Since its inception, social science has yearned for an adjudication role by means of which research could rise above particular claiming perspectives and become the instrument of discovering some general interest within which competing claims could be assimilated. I think this is illusory. Believing this leads to questions concerning the social organization of research. Who frames the problems? To whom are the findings useful? What is the sponsorship of research? What new, alternative bases for research are possible? And what problem formulations would they employ?

Institutions of poverty research have their social sponsorship in the federal government and its interest in the administration of the welfare system in the context of political issues surrounding public expenditure. Academic scholars share this framework as being not only reasonable but obvious and hence requiring no inquiry as to its appropriateness. Through this process, an intellectual and political hegemony is formed. If this interpretation is correct, it seems unlikely that policy research can address other issues in a substantial way without a constituent group or groups to support such a programmatic agenda.

One could imagine poverty research arising from the initiative of social movements such as civil rights, the women's movement, environmental concerns, and new political conservatism such as that represented by the American Enterprise Institute. In the past decade poverty researchers have advanced their own programmatic agenda (the negative income tax reform, the extension of welfare to the working poor, the integration of the tax and benefits systems, etc.). In the future, they may be called upon to adjudicate the reform agendas created by the new movements on the political horizon, some of which seek to expand the welfare state and others to constrict it. The new context of a debate about overload will shape the research agenda in ways that are not obvious at the moment. It is possible that at any time one of these movements or a coalition of several of them might call into question the existing hegemonic structure of problem definition. This seems plausible when we consider how traditions established in the past, such as comprehensive planning, have been successfully undermined. Only when such an assault is launched is it likely that the social organization of poverty research can be critically examined and alternatives explored.

Finally, we need to elaborate on the implications for action of a different interpretation of the three realms. Briefly, I see the policy implications of this interpretation as follows:

1. It leads to much more willingness to intervene directly in the economic realm.

2. It rejects the view of "an original" or a natural distribution of income on which policy acts. Instead, it recognizes that there is a continual process of accommodation and that there is no "original" or "natural" income distribution that can be unambiguously separated from policy.

3. Instead of treating programmatic intervention as a handmaiden of the econ-

omy and as neutral with regard to the family, a claiming perspective is more concerned with *processes* by which claims against one realm are passed on to those in another realm. The study of process is almost completely neglected in public policy studies. (See Chapter 9.)

4. It suggests a new way of thinking about program evaluation. The growth of program evaluation can be appreciated as an inquiry into the legitimacy of claims not by the claimers and not by the claim distributors, but by those against whom the claims are made, in particular, Congress and the Executive. It is for this reason that most evaluations are concerned with oversight and accountability to the government that finances the activity. We are dominated by oversight evaluation rather than managerial or client evaluation.

* * *

I have argued here that knowledge of fact and commitment to values both arise from the realm of action. It follows from this perspective that policy research must start from a commitment to action and to actors.

Policy research always regards itself as scientific and neutral, dispassionately assessing the pros and cons of various policies or inferring advice from disinterested empirical inquiry. In practice conventional analysis is analysis adapted to a hierarchical top-down view of policymaking in which government is viewed as the provider of largesse. The vocabulary of benefits and benefactors and the public interest provides the intellectual foundation on which the research rests. As Gunnar Myrdal has said, "To escape facing political issues by 'objectifying' concepts and theories is an old tradition of economics and the social sciences generally."[5]

This chapter is an attempt to provide an intellectual basis on which an alternative practice of policy research might be built.

NOTES AND REFERENCES

1. Robert E. Park, "Sociology and the War." *American Journal of Sociology*, 1907, *23* (July 27), 65.
2. Hannah Arendt, "Thinking." *The New Yorker*, November 21, 1977. P. 74.
3. John Goldthorpe argues, "In liberal interpretations of stratification in Western industrial societies two distinctive features may be noted. First, there is an emphasis on the *distributive* rather than the *relational* aspects of social class; that is, on differences in economic resources, prestige, education, etc., considered as attributes of individuals and groups, rather than on the ways in which differential power and advantage actually operate in social interaction between individuals and groups, and thus shape the social structure. . . . Secondly there is the assumption . . . that processes inherent in the development of industrialism . . . are working to bring about an automatic secular decline in inequalities of condition and opportunity alike." John Goldthorpe, "Class,

Status, and Power in Modern Britain: Some Recent Interpretations, Marxist and Marxisant." *The European Archives of Sociology,* 1972, *13*(2), 344.

4. The equal treatment of one-earner versus two-earner families is at issue, because a two-earner family gets the same retirement benefits as a family in which there is only one wage-earner.

5. Gunnar Myrdal, *Asian Drama.* New York: Pantheon, 1968. Vol 3, p. 2061.

Chapter 13

Social Science
and Social Policy

Study of the interplay of science and policy has grown enormously in recent years, in part because of the dramatic increase in expenditures for social science, the congressional mandate for evaluation of new social legislation as implemented in programs, and the possible development of "sunset" legislation, which requires periodic reassessment of a large portion of national legislation. Even if expenditures decline as projected in President Reagan's budget, we anticipate that concern for utilization of social science will continue, in order to assure effective use of the resources that are spent on social science. A similar interest in the contribution of social science to policymaking is evident in the reports of international organizations such as the Organization for Economic Cooperation and Development (OECD) and UNESCO.

I have chosen the term *interplay* to describe the relationship between social science and policy rather than the more customary word *use* because the concept of utilization and the empirical attempts to study it are so heterogeneous that we need a more general term. Moreover, because the term *use* implies a one-way process, it is not appropriate for interpreting an essentially interactive process. *Interplay* is a neutral term that can encompass the many ways social science and social policy influence each other; it allows for competition as well as cooperation.

Although it is not my purpose here to explore substantively the many different theories about the conceptualization of the research/policy interplay, a brief review of some of them will set the stage for a discussion of methods.

Jerka Roos's study of welfare and social policy[1] provides a subtle analysis of the substantive issues involved in the nature of the research/policy alliance. His work essentially criticizes a narrow concept of policymaking that, he believes, runs the risk of undermining the democratic model of decision making as a political process by focusing exclusively on a single decision maker as the user of social science knowledge.

Roos is concerned with the decision-maker bias in studies of utilization, and we should note that there is a strong empirical bias in much of the writing on the subject. A great many analyses of underutilization have implicitly been concerned with social science research. One of these is an influential book edited by Carol Weiss, *Using Social Research in Public Policy Making.*[2] This emphasis on empirical inquiry, i.e., research, rather than on the more general subject "social science" obscures the question of the critical role of theory in gathering and analyzing the world of facts. Modern science now recognizes that there are no facts independent of the theory that organizes them. Hence, to talk about research one must also, even if only implicitly, presume a theoretical concept that organizes the study. Theory provides a screen for the observer, making some events important and others trivial; it supplies an intellectual framework for the interpretation of evidence and the discovery of meaning in fact.

Another analytical approach addresses the implicit assumption of a unilateral direction in which knowledge essentially is thought to influence action, but action is not believed to influence thought. To correct the weakness of this position, a number of writers, such as David Donnison and Carol Weiss, have tried to suggest either interactive models of mutual influence or a model that highlights the way policy shapes the research agenda.

Yet another line of theorizing is directed at the hidden normative assumption involved in the concept of use. There are often unspecified standards by which research utilization is judged, and these standards imply the concept of "good" and "bad" use. For example, the political use of information to postpone action or the use of knowledge to justify positions that have been reached on other grounds is regarded as misuse of social science "knowledge," which should contribute to political decision-making. In fact, any disinterested review of the alliance between social science and policymaking would discover many obvious political uses of knowledge. Some of these uses are regarded as disreputable because they violate the norms of science rather than the norms of politics.

This brief review of the biases in how research is used in decision making clearly shows that a substantive analysis of the science/policy alliance raises fundamental issues about the nature of policy and the nature of social science. These deeply philosophical and sociological questions are about the nature of knowing and acting. They question the forum in which various social groups try to establish their legitimacy, because knowing is a form of acting. This latter point needs to be emphasized. Knowing and acting are linked when people's livelihood and social position depend on the social importance of theory. The idea that theory precedes and should influence action assigns a privileged role to socially defined groups and, in this sense, reflects class interest: ideas are considered the "stock in trade" of various occupational groups, including both academics and policymakers.

The papers of Robert Redfield contain a clear statement of the values grounded in the academic tradition. Redfield argues that scientific knowledge requires a commitment to "objectivity, honesty, accuracy and humility before the facts."[3] But these values reflect the interests of a certain position in society, namely, the position of the institutionally supported scholar who does not need, at a particular point in time, to gain support from any other specific interest group. Hence, the scholar is privileged to be able to think in an individual way. Of course, when the scholar turns to mission-oriented agencies and to contract research for financial support, he or she then becomes entrapped in a conflict between autonomy and responsiveness.

Any discussion of methods for the study of the science/policy alliance encounters unresolved conceptual issues, because the analytic conception of the phenomenon, the interplay between knowledge and action, and the methods of studying it cannot be separated. I shall start, then, by reviewing the assumptions under which we study the knowledge/action alliance.

1. The first assumption is that knowledge in the social sciences exists independently of policy. It carries a secondary assumption that politics in action is not a form of knowing, but only of doing. Thus, the process of thinking and acting is split. From this there follows the second assumption.

2. Knowing and acting are different activities, usually carried out by different people.

3. One of the corollaries of this separation and the idealization of science as a way of knowing is that, ideally, knowledge should precede action—that is, we should think before we act.

4. Optimistically, many believe that there is more organizational "knowledge" available than is now used for policy and practice and that this "underuse" of knowledge is largely a result of the arcane nature of knowledge and the rigidity of politics.

5. Therefore, a program of interpreting and simplifying social science is essential, and intermediaries are needed to interpret knowledge for the politician. Hence, a process designed to "educate" the politician can increase the utilization of knowledge.

It is these assumptions that inform many studies of social science/research utilization and constitute the methods for studying the interplay between knowledge and action. At the end of this chapter I shall reexamine these assumptions and propose an alternative approach. We need now to review three of the most interesting methodological approaches to the study of the research/policy interplay—usability, use, and diffusion.

STUDYING USABILITY

Usability studies are an attempt to answer questions about the usefulness of particular types of information for the policy process. Usability studies deal either with information that actors in the policymaking process believe to be inherently or potentially useful or with information that analysts consider potentially useful, depending on their interpretation of the nature of the policy process. The two approaches call for somewhat different methodologies.

An essay by Carol Weiss illustrates the study of usability from the actors' perspective. It is an attempt to define which characteristics of social research can be most useful for decision making. Weiss explains why she and her colleagues avoided the concept of "use":

> We decided to finesse the collection of data on actual use of social research for a variety of reasons. First, it is exceedingly unclear what constitutes use. Is "use" the adaptation of research recommendations intact, the nudging of a decision in the direction suggested by research findings, the reinforcement of a likely decision by research, the consideration of research findings (even if these are overwhelmed by other considerations in the situation), rethinking the nature of the policy issue, redefining informational needs? What kind of use is "real" use?[4]

In order to avoid these difficulties, Weiss attempts a study of usability, which she defines as research that makes a substantive contribution and/or is likely to be considered by policy actors. She and her colleagues selected 50 empirical studies as a basis for reviewing usability defined by these criteria. The research reports were on mental health, alcoholism, and drug abuse and, of course, varied in research quality, conformity to user expectations, action orientation, and challenge to the *status quo*. Weiss and her associates conducted a series of 250 intensive interviews of policymakers who occupied five different positions in the administrative hierarchy in mental health. Abstracts of the major findings of the 50 studies were given to these policymakers, who were asked to comment on their intrinsic merit and potential usefulness in their work.

The study explores how usable knowledge reinforces already established beliefs. According to the authors a further distinction should be drawn between personal beliefs and the beliefs underlying professional practices carried out in agencies. Research that challenges personal belief systems, they say, is interpreted as counterintuitive and is rejected, but research that challenges agency practices is seen as usable. It may be surprising that studies challenging agency practices are just as likely to conform to user expectations as they are to conflict with them, and that decision makers appear so willing to question existing agency practices.

A quite different approach to the study of usability is found in the work of Charles Lindblom and David Cohen.[5] Their approach is more synthetic. Instead of interviewing policymakers, they reviewed the literature on the subject and, drawing on their personal experiences, proposed a critical framework for examining the issue as they understood it. Their approach to usability rests on a number of assumptions. Most important is that there are many ways of knowing: ordinary knowledge, social learning and interactive problem-solving, and knowledge derived from science. Second, there is a mistaken pursuit of authoritativeness in social science. Human beings have only a limited cognitive capacity to grasp the complexity inherent in the social world, and social science research is inherently inconclusive. Third, social science is most usable when it serves as a supplement to other ways of knowing. Fourth, the search for authoritative and definitive knowledge is illusory, and most positivist social scientists work within a framework that overestimates the contribution of their work to policy.

The Lindblom and Cohen approach to usability is based essentially on an attempt to grasp the nature of the research/policy interplay as a whole and to deduce from that conception a set of propositions about potential usability. Theirs is a critical study of usability that tries to challenge the axioms on which policy studies rest. They feel that to interview policymakers and to accept their definition of usability would be a mistake, because policymakers share a common assumption about the authoritativeness of social science knowledge.

THE DIRECT STUDY OF USE

There are several different approaches to direct, empirical study of use. First is the case-study method. Robert Rich's study of unemployment insurance provides a good example.[6] Rich identified a single policy arena, and within it he selected a single, substantive, policy issue—the duration of benefits.

Rich defines bureaucrats as experts whose behavior depends on the acquisition, processing, and utilization of knowledge. He sees a latent conflict between the social scientist's imperative to maximize organizational interest and his technical imperative as an expert to acquire scientific knowledge. The effort to resolve this dilemma informs this particular study of use and dictates the types of issues examined. Briefly, Rich studied in depth the following issues: the channels used to communicate information to officials, the level of use of information, the extent to which information is shared and/or kept secret by officials working in a common problem area, the extent to which officials within the same department communicate with each other and/or share information, and the extent to which officials from different departments communicate with each other and work on the particular issue of the duration of benefits.

The study is based on direct interviews with 28 federal officials who were responsible for decision making or who devoted at least 10 percent of their working time to dealing with the problem of the duration of benefits in unemployment insurance. Such an in-depth case study rests on the assumption that the issue and the arena in which the issue is worked out significantly influence the findings. However, a comparative analysis of use across arenas and issues is premature, because we still lack a clear conceptual framework of what the units of comparison are and where use is most or least likely to occur.

In contrast to the case-study method, the survey research approach takes a random sample of decision makers and asks them directly to cite instances in which research has influenced decisions they have taken. Karen Knorr's study of policymakers in Vienna and Nathan Caplan's study of federal decision-making in the United States are examples of this method.[7] These studies permit the investigators to examine the stage of the policy processing at which research enters, the kind of information used, and the quality of the study cited. A major conclusion is that knowledge is used in a variety of ways—instrumentally, as a means toward solving a problem, or, more broadly, as a source of insight for understanding or interpreting problems. Thus, these studies help clarify the interpretive and instrumental uses of knowledge.

A third type of study examines research utilization as only incidental to a broader case study of the development of policy. The National Academy of Science, for example, carried out a study of the policy-formation process.[8] The Academy identified five components in the policy-formation process: contextual conditions (socioeconomic, political, and cultural conditions in society), principles and ideas as they are represented or promoted by various individual leaders, politics (including legislative, bureaucratic, and interest-group politics), research and analysis, and the media as they represent public information and understanding. This kind of study permits the exploration of the relative importance of research and analysis as a component of a broader decision-making process; it also allows comparisons of the ways in which knowledge is used for decision making by assuming that pragmatic considerations shape the policy process.

A fourth approach to the direct empirical study of use identifies different types of knowledge and examines their individual contributions in a field of action. This approach attempts to examine knowledge in a decision-making context, but the critical variable is neither the decision maker, the policy process, nor the comparison across arenas, but the nature of the knowledge itself. A two-year collaborative research program between the Massachusetts Institute of Technology (MIT) and the Centre National des Recherches Scientifiques (CNRS) in Paris on science and decision making provides an example of this approach.[9] This case study, carried out in the field of health, focused on the problem of tobacco smoking, its effects on health, and the issues surrounding the introduction of policies designed to alter the behavior of smokers and the toxicity of tobacco by the tobacco industry. The research examined three types of information: medical evidence, economic evidence, and anthropological or sociological evidence. Medical evidence came from retrospective etiological studies of smokers compared with control groups of non-smokers to determine the link between cancer and smoking. Economic evidence came from information on the costs of smoking to society and to the individuals in terms of sickness and mortality. The economic analysis had to address the question of the balance between the cost of sickness and death and the benefits of the income generated by the manufacture and sale of tobacco. The sociological evidence addressed the question of why people smoke, on the assumption that understanding the causes of behavior can contribute to the development of effective policies for changing it.

This kind of study permits a much more subtle answer to the question of the role of social science knowledge, because the different types of knowledge raised different questions about the authoritativeness of the knowledge and an ethical issue surrounding the control of individual behavior. The MIT-CNRS tobacco case study revealed that the medical evidence was least open to controversy, that the economic data were inconclusive, and that the sociological and cultural evidence was ultimately decisive, but presented ethical and morally agonizing questions. Because the ethical issues are so important, it is worth quoting Edmund Lisle's analysis of the policy issue posed by sociological research:

> The ultimate effectiveness of policy will turn on the public's response and whether or not deeply ingrained social or cultural behavior patterns and the pleasures associated with them will alter significantly once the risks attached thereto are made much more fully perceived. But this in turn rests on individuals' attitudes to life and death, hedonism or pleasure versus asceticism, and more prosaically to their "time preference," to their relative appreciation of the future (their life expectancy) as against the present, an appreciation which itself tends to change with age but which is nevertheless largely the product of the education received at home and at school and thus reinforces the ethical values embodied in the educational process.[10]

Another case-study approach tries to differentiate types of knowledge and stages of the policy-development process. A study of the negative income tax in the United States, carried out by Martin Rein and Hugh Heclo, examines three types of knowledge—economic, administrative, and sociological—and tries to show how different types of knowledge entered at different stages of policymaking.[11] Thus, economic knowledge dominated the initiation phase of policy, but administrative and sociological knowledge entered at the legislative stage. The different types of knowledge, however, by entering at different stages in the policymaking process, created paralysis and inaction, because each type of knowledge addressed different questions and had different insights into the nature of the process under review. Like the MIT-CNRS study of tobacco, the study of the negative income tax showed how different types of knowledge must be differentiated because each makes a somewhat different contribution to the policy-formation process.

THE DIFFUSION OF KNOWLEDGE

Studies of knowledge diffusion are similar to the other studies of the use of knowledge, but they tend to use a very different time frame in examining the research/policy interplay. Diffusion studies are historical studies of the evolution and the transmission of knowledge over time and across space. This broad time frame permits an assessment of a much more subtle understanding of the process of dissemination.

Two studies of diffusion can be cited: the attempt of M. T. Manning and Robert Rappoport to perform a retrospective analysis of the diffusion of knowledge about

242 Fm Policy to Pmctice

milieu therapy in mental health, and Robert Cole's study of the diffusion of knowledge about worker participation in business enterprise.[12]

M. T. Manning and Robert Rappoport examined the processes affecting the utilization and reception of new ideas in mental health by tracing, over a 25-year period, the reception of a book they had written entitled *Community as Doctor: New Perspectives on a Therapeutic Community*. Their study of diffusion examines the development of the initial research project in its social context up to the time of publication of the book, the initial reactions of the community to the book, and the broader reaction of the academic and professional community at a later point. Their main conclusion is that the reception of ideas depends on a process in which ideas are first rejected before they are ultimately accepted.

Robert Cole's study of innovative work structures at the plant level examines the processes of the diffusion of social science knowledge across space and time. Methodologically he presents a rich and detailed descriptive account of actors, events, and processes. He does not operate within a hypothetical-deductive framework. Instead, his task is interpretive: how to make sense of the detailed evidence he has accumulated. The story he tells can be summarized as follows: Drawing on the literature, Cole frames his narrative as a stage in the process of diffusion, moving from motivation, to search, to discovery, to transmission, to decision, to implementation. Of course, since events unfold simultaneously as well as sequentially, a staging story poses awkward analytic problems because it assumes that events follow each other over time. Nevertheless, the framework provides insights about the processes of rejection or incorporation, which are often missed in cross-sectional survey studies of use and usability. Cole's analysis of the diffusion of ideas concerning employee participation in workplace decisions aimed at reducing alienation and increasing job satisfaction shows that the American model of diffusion moved through three stages: experimentation, detailed scientific measurement, and dissemination.

> A striking characteristic of the American effort to build an institution infrastructure is the concentration on measurement of results. A great deal of resources are being invested in developing systematic scientific and complex evaluations of ongoing evaluations in new work structures.
> ... the implicit assumption of American evaluation efforts seems to be that management will only adopt work restructuring initiatives if they are successfully proven to be effective.

The results were dismal. Virtually none of the innovations was accepted. By contrast, in Sweden and Japan interest focused on "purging academic theories from their more radical connotations to make them more compatible with existing management orientation." Once the innovations had been "sanitized," the focus was on getting things done, only minor interest being shown in formal evaluation and measurement.[13] The importation of "outside" knowledge into the context of the practical depends on mechanisms that translate or transform (sanitize and purge) that knowledge into the currency of the practical setting. Attention to science without practice leads to inaction.

Cole's analysis poses troublesome questions about the reputable and disreputable uses of social science theory. Does sanitization, a means of transforming ideas so that they are administratively acceptable in the new setting in which they are to develop, violate the integrity of the research?

In Cole's study the use of social science ideas also depended on a high measure of consensus about the direction policy should take. In Japan, a managerial consensus, and in Sweden, a broad national consensus, emerged that accepted worker participation in some aspects of decision making at the plant level as an acceptable remedy for such problems as absenteeism and turnover. The decision makers proceeded to create an institutional infrastructure that could promote these innovative ideas.

By contrast, no consensus prevailed in the United States. Only a modest and unstable infrastructure developed; and research was carried out by outsiders, with a strong emphasis on objectivism and measurement. For every dollar spent on the innovation, three dollars were spent on evaluation. But the search for a disinterested or truthful answer to the question of whether the innovations worked or failed seemed only to threaten the very consensus it hoped to inspire. Paradoxically, this attention to science in quest of truth was accompanied by proprietary knowledge used by consultants entrepreneurally to promote "the sale" of the innovation for profit.

By calling attention to the way theory is purged and redefined and by focusing on consensus as a precondition of diffusion and on measurement as a threat to consensus, Cole provides us with a subtle, reflective analysis of the interplay between inquiry and action.

These two diffusion studies differ both methodologically and in the insights they offer. The Manning and Rappoport study relies largely on the reception of ideas as they appear in academic journals and as experienced by the authors. The Cole study relies on detailed, in-depth interviews, which are informed by a historical and cross-national perspective.

A CHALLENGE TO THE STUDY OF UTILIZATION

All the various studies of usability, use, and diffusion share the assumptions outlined at the beginning of this chapter, which in varying degrees accept a dichotomy between the knowing and the acting person and take as a premise that knowledge should inform action. Now I shall review a study of the interplay between research and policy that proceeds under a very different assumption about the nature of the interplay between knowing and acting. The critical assumption in this approach is that concepts, ideas, and knowledge have no meaning independent of their use. Hence, the task of research is to uncover the uses and interests that are served by knowledge, rather than the other way around. This approach can be studied methodologically from two perspectives: the overt uses of knowledge and action and their latent uses.

Gunnar Myrdal is perhaps the most articulate spokesman for the general argument I am developing here. In a detailed review of the concept of the utilization of labor he demonstrates the close connection between ideas and their practical implication. Myrdal argues that ". . . the study of the functional relationship between policies and the utilization of the labor force . . . cannot be assisted by the use of the concept of 'underemployment' in general, allowed to be 'objectively' established in relation merely to the facts, and perhaps even measured, in advance of any consideration of policy."[14]

Myrdal's awkwardly worded statement is essentially an argument that one cannot study the facts of underemployment without having a clear understanding of the policy implications to which the concept leads. In other words, there are no facts about underemployment that are independent of the policy considerations that inform them. Hence, all studies that use these analytical concepts and attempt empirically to measure the extent to which they take place have an implicit policy reference because the meaning of the concept is derived from the practical policy significance. In other words, the analytic concepts are themselves policy concepts and are derived from a coherent conception of the policies behind them.

One example of Myrdal's point is Joan Robinson's classic essay, written in 1936, on "Disguised Unemployment."[15] She argued that many workers who lost their jobs were forced to accept inferior employment. These workers were pushed down to less productive and less remunerative jobs in order to acquire income so that they could avoid making a claim against their family and kin, against the dole, or against their limited reserve of assets and personal savings. This mismatch between the level of skill and the occupational position of workers during the Depression she defined as "disguised unemployment." Thus, disguised unemployment, when combined with the more obvious measure of actual unemployment, provided a better understanding and measure of the malperformance of the economy.

Robinson saw a close link between personal economic hardship and the performance of the economy. She argued that if the economy were functioning so that it could make use of all its resources, including human resources, then personal economic hardship would become a residual problem. The key to improving the performance of the economy was the stimulation of aggregate demand. The way to rescue skilled labor from its inferior position was to create a full-employment economy that could make efficient use of all available talents. Keynesian economics provided a programmatic course of action for governments to follow to remedy the unproductivity of the economy and at the same time relieve personal hardship.

There is an alternative interpretation of the nature of underutilization that asserts that the economy is of such a nature that even when it is functioning efficiently, many people will suffer personal hardship, because the economy always produces low wages and unstable jobs. According to this viewpoint, low earnings and short hours are related to the structure of the labor market. Marginal jobs arise because capital investment, technological advances, and high-paying and stable jobs are concentrated in one sector while in the other sectors the opposite processes occur. The two processes are linked by a backwash, or negative effect. It is this structure of the labor market, sometimes called the secondary labor market or informal employment, that generates inadequate hours of work and inadequate wages. The Keynesian legacy does not apply to this interpretation of the dynamics of the labor market.

Such an interpretation of the underlying processes is deeply disturbing. Most important of all, if we accept this view of the world, *we no longer can interpret misery as inefficiency.* In the earlier interpretation, the problem of personal economic hardship and human misery could be addressed by making the economy more efficient since it was the inefficiency of the economy that produced injustice and personal misery. But this newer interpretation sees the problem of personal hardship as more intractable because it is attributable to the problematic structure of the labor market, not merely to its inefficiency. Robinson's image of workers being pushed down a rung on the employment ladder is misleading. Not everyone goes down a notch on the employment ladder: some workers stay at the same level, and others are pushed down several notches. This happens largely because the metaphor of a single job ladder is false. In fact, there are many job ladders; and workers get jostled on some of these ladders more than they do on others. Moreover, efforts to solve the problem by trying to pull marginal labor into the modern sector of the economy by strategies of human capital and economic development seem to have failed. The secondary, or informal, labor market appears to thrive, and even grow, alongside a vigorous and well-functioning capital-intensive sector.

This approach to study of the research/policy interplay requires an altogether different methodology, because it proceeds from a different starting assumption than the earlier studies. The studies I have reviewed focus primarily on the gathering of empirical evidence for the later utilization by policy. This is, of course, consistent with the first proposition that positive knowledge is grounded in empirical evidence about the world of facts. A now generally accepted proposition is that factual knowledge is based on definitions, rules of logic, and theory. Thus, the analytic and the theoretical cannot be divorced from the empirical.[16] The methodology for the study of use I am proposing is based on the position that theory itself cannot be divorced from practice or policy and is simply another expression of it. The study of utilization seeks to elucidate the interplay of theory and policy because they provide the framework in which facts are gathered. The challenge is not linking research to policy, but uncovering the latent policies that organize the empirical research carried out by social science—or, to put the matter in other terms, we need to discover a method for the "doing of understanding." This may require not only translation of theory into practice but also study of the implicit theory governing the action of practitioners.

NOTES AND REFERENCES

1. Jerka Pekka Roos, "Welfare State and Social Policy: A Study in Policy Science." In *Commentationes Scientiarum Socialium.* Helsinki: The Finnish Scientific Society, 1973. Pp. 212–25.

2. Carol H. Weiss, ed., *Using Social Research in Public Policy Making*. Lexington, Mass.: Lexington Books, 1977.

3. Robert Redfield, *The Social Uses of Social Science: The Papers of Robert Redfield*, edited by M. P. Redfield. Chicago: University of Chicago Press, 1963. Vol. 2, p. 193.

4. Carol Weiss, "The Challenge of Social Research to Decision Making." In Carol Weiss, ed., Op. cit. P. 213.

5. Charles A. Lindblom and David K. Cohen, *Usable Knowledge: Social Science and Social Problem Solving*. New Haven: Yale University Press, 1979.

6. Robert S. Rich, "Can Evaluation Be Used for Policy Action?" In R. A. Levine et al., eds., *Evaluation Research and Practice: Comparative and International Perspectives*. Beverly Hills, Calif.: Sage Publications, 1981. Pp. 178–91.

7. Karen D. Knorr, "Policymakers' Use of Social Science Knowledge: Symbolic or Instrumental." In Carol H. Weiss, ed., Op. cit.; and Nathan Caplan, A. Morrison, and R. J. Stambugh, *The Use of Social Science Knowledge in Policy Decisions at the National Level*. Ann Arbor, Mich.: University of Michigan, Institute for Social Research, 1975.

8. *Evaluating Federal Support for Policy Research: The Committee on Evaluation of Policy Research, Assembly of Behavioral and Social Science, National Research Council*. Washington, D. C.: National Academy of Sciences, 1979.

9. Edmund Lisle, "Politics, Science and Science Policy: The Case of the Social Sciences." Lecture given at the London School of Economics and Political Science, February 1979 (mimeographed).

10. Ibid.

11. Martin Rein and Hugh Heclo, "Social Science and Negative Income Taxation." In *The Utilization of the Social Sciences in Policy Making in the United States*. Paris: OECD, 1980.

12. M. T. Manning and Robert Rappoport, "Rejection and Reincorporation: Case Study in Social Research Utilization." *Social Science and Medicine*, 1976, *10*, 459–68; Robert Cole, "The Diffusion of New Work Structures in Japan, Sweden and the United States." Ann Arbor, Mich.: University of Michigan, 1979 (mimeographed).

13. Cole, Ibid. Pp. 22, 29.

14. Gunnar Myrdal, *Asian Drama*. New York: Pantheon, 1968. Vol. 3, p. 2060.

15. Joan Robinson, "Disguised Unemployment." *Economic Journal*, 1936, *46*, 225–37.

16. Recognition of this link has given rise to what has been described as the theory/fact dilemma: Choice among competing theories must depend on fact, but facts derive their meaning from the prior choice of a theory that organizes and selects facts.

Index

248   *Index*

Change
costs in, 70-71
and incentives, 70-71
Charity Organization Society (COS), 51, 52, 92
Chartists, 31
Cheshire Central Consultive Committee, 62
Child Benefits, British, 88
Child Development Office, U.S., 206
Children
child-care programs, 60
and consumption, 27
foster care of, 144
and housing, 85
nutrition of, 167-68
and income, 83
rights to education of, 46
and service comprehensiveness, 63
and service coordination, 59-61
and technology of social services, 63-65
China, claims in, 36
Chrysler Corporation, 10
Circularity, principle of, 128-31
Civil rights movement, 188, 228
Claims, xv, 23-38
conceptual language in, 25-27
and culture, 30
and economic process, 33-36
establishment of, 31-33
group representation, 32
phases of, 31-32
forms of, 27
and income, 30, 33
and language, 25-27
and life cycle, 30
and life style, 27
and occupational mobility, 30
packages of, 29-31
and productivity, 28
rationales for, 32-33, 37
as reframing of action, 230-33
for security and stability, 27, 28
and seniority, 31
structures of, conflict among, 36-38
systems of, 27-29
capital, 28-29
family, 27
government, 28
work, 27-28
and taxation, 28-29
of women, 36
Classification of cases, 177
Class structure and schools, 169-70
Coalition

legislative, 120
in research, 212-14
Co-counseling, 188
Cohen, David K., 205, 238, 239
Cold knowledge
and hot knowledge, 142-43
paradox in, 142-43
Cole, Robert, 242, 243
Coleman, Alan, 65
Collective bargaining and fringe benefits, 11
Community Action Program, 48, 209
Community as Doctor: New Perspectives on a Therapeutic Community (Manning and Rappoport), 242
Community Chest movement, 92, 182
Community Coordinated Child Care, 60
Community Development Program, British, 193
Compliance and democratic theory, 114
Comprehensive Education and Training Act (CETA), 164
Computerization, 110
Conference Board, 15
Congressional Appropriations Committee, 97
Congressional Budget Office, 160
Construals, 142-43
Consumption subsidies, 16-17
Context-stripping in experimental design, 175
Coordination of services, 51-56, 59-76
for children, 59-61
sources of pleas for, 60-67
see also Social services, coordination of
Corbit, John D., 156
Core issues, 50
Corporatism, 35
Cost of Living Council, 120
Crisis, professional, 152-53
Cuba, claims in, 35, 36
Culture and claims, 30
Cunningham, Mary, 168-69

Davis, Kenneth, 120
Decentralization and service delivery, 48-51, 59
Declarative moments, 141-42
De Gaulle, Charles, 214
Delinquency, 52, 54, 166
Democratic theory
and compliance, 114
and implementation, 114-18
Denmark, 86
fringe benefits in, 11, 12

income-tested programs in, 84, 85
welfare expenditures in, 7
Departments of U.S. Government, *see specific departments, e.g.,* Health, Education, and Welfare Department, U.S.
Dependency on state, 44-46, 52
Design of social services, 40-56
and implementation, xiii
of in-kind benefits, 78-92
and policy and practice, xi-xiii
value tensions in, 96-111
see also In-kind benefits, design of
Dewey, John, 175-77, 191
Dicey, Albert Venn, 42
Donnison, David, 236
Downs, Anthony, 116
Dunlop, John, 116

Early and Periodic Screening, Diagnosis, and Treatment Program (EPSDT), 70
Economic and institutional analysis, 23, 25
Economic Development Act (EDA), 120, 121, 134
Economic Opportunity Act, 209
Economic Opportunity Office (OEO), 54, 61, 206, 209, 210
Office of Research, Plans, Programs, and Evaluation (RPPE), 209, 210
Economic Stabilization Act, 120
Economy of scale, 74
Edelman, Murray, 67
Education
rights to, 46
subsidies for, 81-83
Education Office, 206
EEC (European Economic Community), 6, 7, 11, 98
Effectiveness, 71
Efficiency, 71, 148, 153
Ehrlichman, John, 124
Elementary and Secondary Education Act, 121, 200-1, 207-8
Encounter groups, 188
England, *see* Great Britain
Entitlement to benefits, 18
and need, 78
in family, 27
and inclusion and exclusion dilemma, 98
and rights, 26
universal, 4
see also Claims
Environmental Protection Agency (EPA), 122

EPSDT (Early and Periodic Screening, Diagnosis, and Treatment), 70
Equality, models of, 82-83
Equity and income testing, 80
Erlebacher, A. E., 204
Esping-Andersen, Gösta, 85
European Economic Community (EEC), 6, 7, 11, 98
Evaluation, *see* Program evaluation
Exceptional Circumstances Additions, British, 106
Exhaustion of professionals, 152
Exit strategies, 50-51

Family
as claim system, 27
entitlements and obligations in, 27
instability of and state assistance, 171
and solidarity, 27
structure of and values, 98-99
Family Assistance Plan (FAP), 81, 105
Family Income Supplement, British, 87, 105, 106
Family Service Association, 52
Family therapy, 188
FAP (Family Assistance Plan), 81, 105
Federal Bureau of Elementary and Secondary Education, 121, 134
Federal Register, 123, 128
Feedback, administrative, 134
Festinger, Leon, 188
Finance Committee, Senate, 125
"Finding Out How Programs Are Working: Suggestions for Congressional Oversight" (GAO), 158-59, 164
Firm, social policy of, xii, 3-20
and welfare state perspective, 6-8
First-order decisions, 101
Flexitime, 14, 22
Foltz, Anne-Marie, 70
Food stamps, 30, 53, 90
student application for, 98
Forest Service, U.S., 134
Foucault, Michael, 220
Frames of action, *see* Action frames and problem setting
France
fringe benefits in, 11, 12
public employment in, 21
welfare expenditures in, 7
Freeman, Howard, 198-99
Fried, Mark, 50
Fringe benefits, 4, 35

supporting in, 10
Statsföretag, 10
Steffens, Lincoln, 152
Stigma and benefits, 103
Sunset legislation, 235
Supplementary Benefits program, British,
87, 88
Supplemental Security Information (SSI),
104, 109
Surrey, Stanley, 120
Sweden, 10, 86
action orientation in, 242, 243
fringe benefits in, 11, 12
housing programs of, 94
income-tested programs in, 84-87
mandating in, 9
public employment in, 21
sick leave in, 16
welfare expenditures in, 7
Switzerland, welfare expenditures in, 7
Syson, L., 43

Tawney, R. H., 35, 37
Taxation, 79, 89, 93, 94, 120, 133
and circularity, 128
and claims, 28-29
and discounting, 89-91
exemption of benefits, 13-14
homeowner exemption, 84-86
indirect, 5
international comparison of, 6
negative income, 167, 226-27, 232, 241
reduction of as incentive, 9-10
Technological context, 109-10
Third-order effects, 102
Thurow, Lester C., 4, 20
Tiebout, Charles, 48, 49, 51
Titmuss, Richard, 5, 21, 164
Townsend, Peter, 18
Transportation Department (DOT), 129

Unemployment, 8, 155, 224
compensation, 8, 27
and budget, 163
disguised, 244
UNESCO, 235
Union of Black Social Workers, 188
Unions, labor
bargaining of, 11
claims of, 38
Universalism of social worker, 179, 180,
190

Universalist-formalist service philosophy,
42-47, 55-56, 78
Universities as professional sanctuaries, 189
University of Michigan Institute for Social
Research, 197
University of Wisconsin, 90
Upper-case social services, 41
Urban Institute, 167-68
Usability, 237-41
Using Social Research in Public Policy Making (Weiss), 236
Utilization, 239-40, 243-45
second-order decision of, 101
variations of, 197-98

Vacation benefits, 15-16
Values
of capitalism, 37
and need, 100, 103
in practices, 174-92, 235-45
and program design, 96-111
elements in and context, 108-10
elements in and objectives, 97-102
and income-support program, 102-8
and normative options, 104-5
and research, 151, 217
value-committed approach, x
value-critical approach, ix-xi
Vinter, Robert, 45
Vocational Rehabilitation Administration
(VRA), 55
Voice (demand) strategies, 49-51
Voltaire, 147
Voucher systems, 49, 55

Wages
definition of, 3
freeze and control of, 14
and fringe benefits, 4, 5
gender differences in, 4
for housework, 32
and productivity, 4, 33-34
and salaries, 4, 16
and well-being, 37-38
Wealth of Nations, The (Smith), 24
Webb, Adrian, 72, 73
Weidenbaum, Murray, 162
Weisbrod, Burton, 48, 82, 93
Weiss, Carol, 236, 238
Weiss, Janet, 55
Welfare, 4, 30
and dependency, 45